Washington

Contributions by Daniel Jack Chasan, Matthew Chasan,
and John Doerper

Photography by Bruce Hands

COMPASS AMERICAN GUIDES
An Imprint of Fodor's Travel Publications, Inc.

Washington

Copyright © 1995 Fodor's Travel Publications, Inc.
Maps Copyright © 1995 Fodor's Travel Publications, Inc.

Library of Congress Cataloging-In-Publication Data
Chasan, Daniel Jack
    Washington/Daniel Jack Chasan; photography by Bruce Hands
    p. cm. —(Compass American Guides)
    Includes bibliographical references and index
    ISBN 1-878867-58-X (paper) $17.95
    1. Washington—Guidebooks.   2. Washington—Pictorial works
I. Title. II. Series: Compass American Guides
F889.3.C48   1995
94-42462
917.5504'43—dc20   CIP

Editors: Kit Duane, Barry Parr,
    Debi Dunn, Julia Dillon
Managing Editor: Kit Duane
Photo Editor: Christopher Burt

Designers: Christopher Burt,
    Candace Compton-Pappas
Map Design: Mark Stroud of Moon Street
    Cartography

Production House: Twin Age Ltd., Hong Kong Printed in China
Compass American Guides, Inc., 6051 Margarido Drive, Oakland, CA 94618

10 9 8 7 6 5 4 3 2 1

Cover: Mount Shuksan

The Publisher gratefully acknowledges the following institutions and individuals for the use of their photographs and/or illustrations on the following pages: Ed Cooper, pp. 114-115; Rocky Kolberg, pp. 196-197; Russell Johnson and Dale Chihuly, p. 68; Kelly Duane, p. 231; Microsoft, p. 45; Sisters of Providence Archives, p. 203; Margaret Burt, p. 252; Boeing Company Archives, pp. 42-43; Puget Sound Maritime Historical Society, p. 52; Underwood Photo Archives, San Francisco, pp. 14, 41, 191, 243, 250, 256, 280; Washington State Historical Society, Tacoma, pp. 22, 27, 67, 78, 86, 102, 179, 186, 200; University of Washington Libraries, Special Collections, pp. 29, 61, 113, 138, 176, 177, 194, 210, 220, 221, 236, 239, 244, 247, 251; Museum of History and Industry, Seattle, pp. 32, 35, 37, 38, 58, 64, 83, 104, 143, 145, 173, 174, 178, 234, 268-269. We would also like to thank Joan Hutchinson at the Elliott Bay Book Company for carefully reviewing the text and making many cogent suggestions; Julia Dillon for the piece on Seattle nightlife on pp. 74-75. We also wish to thank the following individuals for their contributions to this book: Judy Jewell, author of Compass's *Oregon* title, for editorial comment, Ellen Klages for proofreading, and Pati Belichick for typography.

The Washington Territory is interesting to tourists and pleasure seekers for its splendid prairies covered with groves, laid out by the greatest of landscape gardeners—Nature. These groves rival in beauty the finest of the natural parks, and the latter sink in significance in comparison of extent.

—*Tourists' guide, 1872*

C O N T E N T S

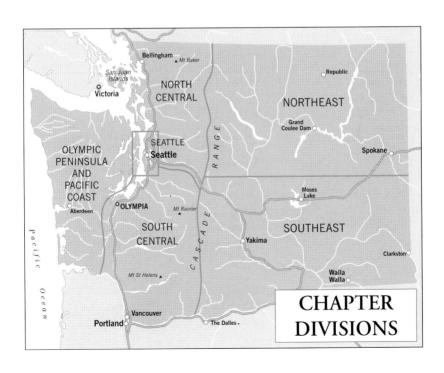

Timelines and Topical Essays

Literary Extracts

Maps

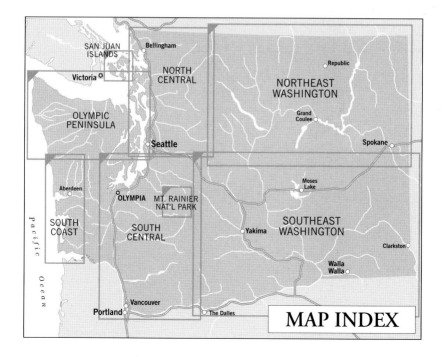

MAP INDEX

Facts About Washington

The Evergreen State

CAPITAL: Olympia
STATE FLOWER: Western rhododendron
STATE BIRD: Willow goldfinch
STATE TREE: Western hemlock
ENTERED UNION: Nov. 11, 1889

Willow goldfinch

FIVE LARGEST CITIES:	
Seattle	516,260
Spokane	177,200
Tacoma	176,660
Bellevue	86, 870
Everett	69,960

POPULATION (1991): 5,017,724 (16th largest)

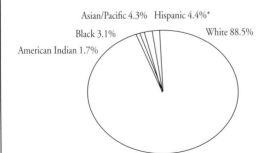

Asian/Pacific 4.3%   Hispanic 4.4%*
Black 3.1%   White 88.5%
American Indian 1.7%

*Population of Hispanic origin
is an ethnic grouping and not
additive to the population
racial groupings*

*W*estern hemlock

ECONOMY:

Principal industries:
   Aerospace, forest products, primary metals, agriculture

Principal manufactured goods:
   aircraft, pulp and paper, aluminum

Chief agricultural products:
   hops, spearmint and peppermint oil, apples, cherries, pears, asparagus, potatoes, raspberries

Per capita income: (1991)
   $19,442 (16th highest)

GEOGRAPHY:

Size:	71,303 sq miles, 18th largest
Highest point:	14,410 feet, Mt. Rainier
Lowest point:	Sea level at the Pacific Ocean

CLIMATE:

Wettest Place	**Driest Place**	**Lowest Temp.**	**Highest Temp.**
Quinault	Hanford	Mazama and Winthrop	Ice Harbor Dam
Grays Harbor County	Benton County	-48° F (-42° C)	118° F (47° C)
129" annual rainfall	5" annual rainfall	Dec. 30, 1968	Aug. 5, 1961

FAMOUS WASHINGTONIANS:

Bing Crosby ❖ William O. Douglas ❖ Jimi Hendrix ❖ Henry M. Jackson
Gary Larson ❖ Mary McCarthy ❖ Edward R. Murrow
Theodore Roethke ❖ Marcus Whitman ❖ Minoru Yamasaki

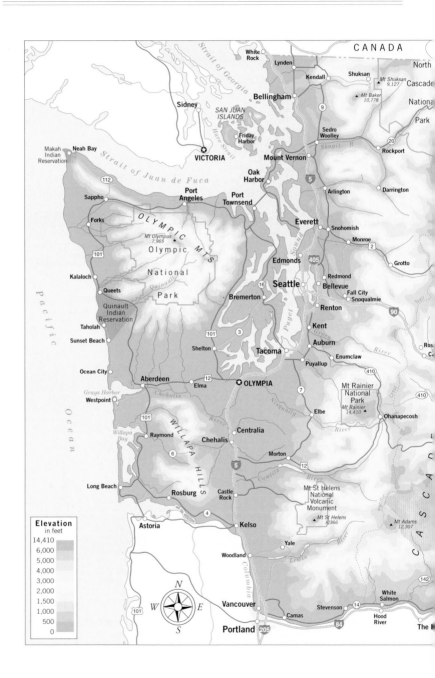

Elevation
in feet

14,410
6,000
5,000
4,000
3,000
2,000
1,500
1,000
500
0

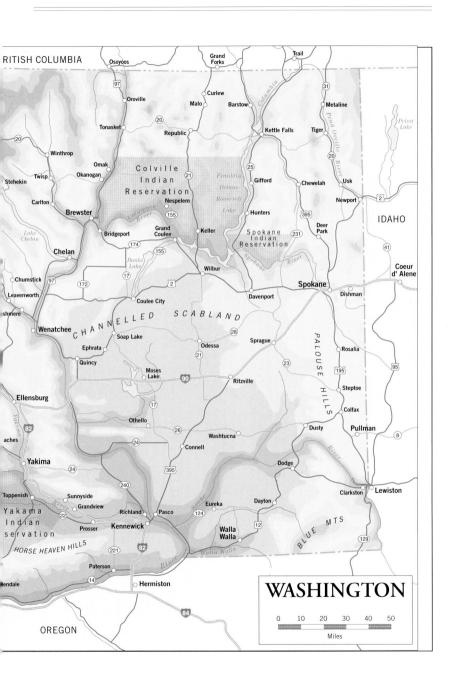

WASHINGTON

BRITISH COLUMBIA

Osoyoos
Grand Forks
Trail
97
31
Oroville
Curlew
Metaline
Malo
Barstow
Priest Lake
Tonasket
20
Kettle Falls
Tiger
20
Republic
Winthrop
Omak
Colville
Indian
Reservation
Franklin
Delano
Roosevelt
Lake
Gifford
Chewelah
Usk
Newport
2
Twisp
Okanogan
21
25
Stehekin
Carlton
Nespelem
155
Hunters
395
Deer Park
IDAHO
Brewster
Bridgeport
Grand Coulee
Keller
Spokane
Indian
Reservation
231
Lake Chelan
Chelan
174
155
Wilbur
Spokane River
41
Chumstick
97
172
Banks Lake
17
2
Davenport
Spokane
Dishman
Coeur d' Alene
Leavenworth
Coulee City
shmere
Wenatchee
CHANNELLED SCABLAND
Soap Lake
28
PALOUSE HILLS
Rosalia
195
95
Ephrata
Odessa
Sprague
23
Quincy
21
Moses Lake
90
Ritzville
Steptoe
Ellensburg
17
Colfax
82
Othello
26
Washtucna
Dusty
Pullman
8
aches
24
Connell
Yakima
24
Dodge
Snake River
Toppenish
240
Clarkston
Lewiston
Sunnyside
395
Eureka
Dayton
Yakima
Indian
Grandview
Richland
Pasco
124
12
22
Prosser
Kennewick
Walla Walla
servation
HORSE HEAVEN HILLS
221
82
BLUE MTS
129
Paterson
Walla Walla River
endale
14
Hermiston
84
OREGON

0   10   20   30   40   50
Miles

FINDING THE PERFECT SPOT

by John Doerper

A Washington enthusiast describes the unfolding pleasures of getting to know the state he loves best.

Salmon swimming up a *road* near the lumber town of Shelton! That's what the television news report said—and backed it up with a video of chum salmon, backs exposed, mistaking flooded tarmac for the gravelly shallows of a stream. The wonder of it took me back more than 20 years, to the first time I visited Washington State.

It all began in the summer of 1975, when one of my paintings was accepted in a competitive art show in Seattle, and my wife and I decided this was as good an excuse for a vacation as we'd ever come up with. Seattle was a delight—we took in the sights, rode the monorail from the Seattle Center downtown, and explored the Pike Place Market before heading out of town to find a campground. We soon discovered the perfect spot, a small county park on the Stillaguamish River, surrounded by woods that looked like scenery from Grimm's Fairy Tales, with a jagged, snowcapped peak for a backdrop. The next day, we drove north to Mount Baker. Even now, 20 years later, there's a spot on the Mount Baker Highway where I involuntarily take my foot off the gas pedal as the road rounds a turn: the woods open up and Mount Shuksan, a steep-cliffed, glacier-covered peak rises from a cleft. It's an incredible sight, especially on a bright day, when the sun strikes the glaciers and the ice of the crevasses radiates an unearthly blue light. At the end of the road, we found alpine lakes, and ate our fill of blueberries as we hiked into the backcountry. We were in love.

By the time we explored Bellingham the next day, we had made up our minds. This is where we wanted to live. Twenty years later, I have explored most of the state, but feel I hardly know it—there's too much to see, to explore, to enjoy.

After I moved to Washington State, I felt overwhelmed by the complexity of its scenery and history. To me, its map looked like a giant puzzle, with key pieces missing. Slowly, over the years, I've been filling in the pieces—in what has been a most delightful learning process.

A lily bed in Paradise Valley in the shadow of Mount Rainier makes the "perfect spot" for these modern dancers of the 1920s. (Underwood Archives, San Francisco)

My initial explorations took me to Whidbey Island, settled by Yankee ship captains in the 1850s. The captains came to Puget Sound for lumber, liked what they saw, and stayed.

Whidbey Island has a unique landscape for western Washington, since even in prehistoric times it had little forest, but many wide open prairies covered with wildflowers in spring. (Eighteenth-century British explorer George Vancouver compared it to the parks of British country estates.) Here grow the blue iris and other wildflowers rare elsewhere in western Washington. The village of Coupeville, on the waterfront of Penn Cove, an inlet that almost cuts the island in half, has some of the oldest houses in the state. It is off the beaten path and has changed little in the last hundred years, as you'll note when you negotiate the narrow main street (it has stood in for New England villages in several movies).

We explored the San Juan Islands with friends who had boats and took us to secluded beaches and quiet coves. Here we have fished for salmon, set pots for Dungeness crab, and just come to relax. The San Juans, like Whidbey Island, lie in the rain shadow of the Olympic Mountains and are thus drier and get more sun than other areas of western Washington. That translates into more wildflowers and birds, making the islands a naturalist's paradise. (Many of the smaller islets are bird sanctuaries.) Best of all, you don't need a boat of your own to explore them, as you can take a ferry to all of the larger ones. I sometimes take the ferry just to get away from things. It's a perfect writer's haven: I snag a window seat, take out the old lap-top computer and hack away, while islands, boats, seals, and an occasional bald eagle drift by.

It took me longer to start exploring eastern Washington—there was simply too much to see in the west. But I still remember my first drive to Spokane. I took backroads instead of the Interstate, crossing the Cascades on Stevens Pass, dropping down past the Wenatchee apple orchards—which were in fragrant bloom—crossing the Columbia, climbing the switchbacks to the wheat fields of the Waterville Plateau, and driving for what seemed like endless miles through fields of pale green wheat, until pine-studded grasslands began to dominate the

(previous pages) Rolling hills of the Palouse region in southeast Washington.

landscape near Spokane. I returned by way of the Methow Valley and the North Cascade Highway.

There were several firsts on this trip: The first time I saw the whitewater canyon of the Wenatchee with its steep sides of glacier-cut rock. The first time I saw the upper canyon of the Columbia River, which is as spectacular as the more famous gorge separating Oregon and Washington. Seeing it veiled in morning haze painted golden and pink by the rising sun is an other-earthly experience. So are the coulees: dry, flat-bottomed Moses Coulee, dotted with wildflowers of the season, and the Grand Coulee, a chasm of awesome proportions with straight-sided walls cut not by the slow, abrasive action of glaciers but by the waters of one horrid flood pouring down from the valleys of Montana. Dry Falls, a basalt ledge several miles wide, still marks the spot where the flood waters tore a gash through the rocks of the plateau before losing their strength and fanning out into a maze of smaller channels. (I took the trail to the base of the cliff and, in a small moist cave, found several swallows resting on a moist rock, perhaps to escape the heat of the sunbaked canyon walls. They were within easy touching distance, but did not stir. Rarely have I met wild birds so unafraid of man.) The swallows nest on the steep walls of the canyons and feed on the myriad insects spawned by the lakes dotting the floors of the coulees. All over this land you can see the basalt ledges left behind after the waters cut away the softer rock. They stand like walls built by men; some look like the broken castles of giants, remnants of the heroic age of geology.

On my way home, I drove across the vast granite shield of the Okanogan Highlands, with its park-like groves of quaking aspen, and watched hawks soar in the sky.

On other trips I lost myself among the gnarled rocks and dense woods of the northeastern mountains—the only place in Washington visited by caribou and moose. I cruised the gentle hills of the Palouse, a magic landscape in late spring and early summer when the green culms of wheat change to a silky gold, and when every gentle breeze blowing up the valley ruffles the leaves, making it look like the soft fur of a vast, gentle animal.

From the Palouse, I have driven south into the precipitous canyons of the Blue Mountains and crossed the dramatic dryness of the lower Snake River Valley to

the arid canyons of the northern bank, where the Palouse River falls over a basalt ledge in a tall roaring waterfall.

The state has many waterfalls, some of them tall and well-known, like the Nooksack or Snoqualmie. Countless smaller ones are all but unknown, sparkling jewels surprising the hiker.

Most importantly, I learned that Washington is not as wet as I thought: it has a dry season and a wet one—summer is mostly dry, sunny, and pleasantly warm. Yet what makes Washington truly unique is the state's complexity: the "wet" side is not all soggy rain forests and the "dry" side is no arid desert. Small prairies alternate with forests in the lowlands and islands of the west. Because they are protected from heavy coastal rains by the tall Olympic and Vancouver Island ranges, these have a climate much like that of central California—with wildflowers to match. East of the Cascades, dry grasslands lead into moist valleys of tall cedars, dense hemlock, and lacy vine maple where cold brooks burble in beds of mossy boulders. This kaleidoscopic variety of mountains and valleys, forests and prairies, sunshine and rain, truly makes Washington a state for all seasons. It's also the reason why I will continue to explore the state: I always find something new.

BEAUTY UNSURPASSED

*T*o add to the beauty, a cluster of crystalline lakes, upon which the sunbeams dance and glisten, meets the vision in several places. A ride or a drive through these natural parks, is a feast of scenery to be found nowhere else in the world. In the first place there is the enjoyment of having a beautiful turf road, which cannot be excelled, beneath you; before you spread miles of flower beds, which perfume the air, their brilliant hues being contrasted and made more striking by the quiet shades of evergreen groves or dark green of the oaks, while the towering snow-clad peaks, with their cool, refreshing appearance, make up a grand background and complete a tableaux which would be difficult to surpass.

—Tourists' guide, circa 1872

Llama trekking along the Pacific Crest Trail in the Mount Adams Wilderness Area.

H   I   S   T   O   R   Y

WHERE DO YOU START? With the time, long before the Cascade Mountains rose, when the current Selkirk Mountains marked the western edge of North America? With the slow docking of microcontinents from the west that added the Okanogan highlands, the area now covered by the North Cascades, the San Juan Islands, and the Olympic Peninsula? With the rise of the Cascades only a couple of million years ago? With the arrival, 15,000 years ago, of the great glacier that carved Puget Sound, pushed south of what is now Olympia, and buried what is now Seattle under 3,000 feet of ice?

Or does it make more sense to start with people? The oldest sign of man's presence in Washington was found at the Manis site, near Sequim, on the Olympic Peninsula. There, quite by chance, a backhoe excavating a farmer's duck pond unearthed the 12,000-year-old remains of a mastodon. Embedded in one of the hairy elephant's massive ribs was a bone spear point. Other ribs showed marks of butchering. Artifacts up to 10,000 years old have been found at the Marmes rock shelter in eastern Washington, not far from Palouse Falls. There is evidence that people were catching and eating salmon beside the Columbia River 9,000 years ago.

■ EARLY SETTLERS AND EXPLORERS

No one really knows who those early salmon eaters or mastodon killers were. We do know that before European culture arrived, the Makahs at the tip of the Olympic Peninsula paddled long cedar canoes into the open Pacific to hunt whales, the Nez Percé of eastern Washington bred horses, tribes along the Columbia speared salmon above the rapids at Celilo and Kettle Falls, and the Snoqualmies ran a trade route through the Cascades. Tribes in the eastern Cascades set slow fires in the fall, after the high season of forest fires had passed, to clear the forests of underbrush, making it easier to hunt among the pines, and encouraging the growth of edible Indian carrots, camas, huckleberries, and chokecherries. We also know that these people spoke a variety of different languages, including Coast Salish around Puget Sound and Sahaptin along the mid-Columbia River, that none of them carved the great Northwest Coast totem poles—those were actually produced farther north, along the coasts of British Columbia and southeast Alaska.

Chief Joseph John poses in ceremonial clothing at Tofino on Vancouver Island for photographer Edward Curtis in 1931. (Washington State Historical Society, Tacoma)

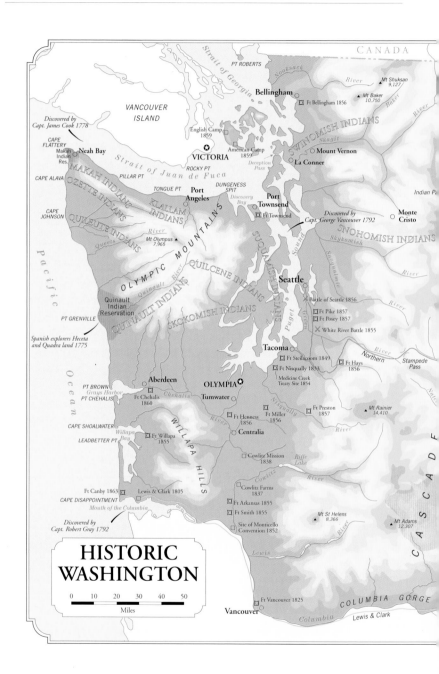

CANADA

PT ROBERTS

Nooksack

River

Mt Shuksan
9,127

Bellingham

Mt Baker
10,750

Baker River

☐ Ft Bellingham 1856

VANCOUVER
ISLAND

*Discovered by
Capt. James Cook 1778*

CAPE
FLATTERY

English Camp
1859

SWINOMISH INDIANS

Skagit

Makah
Indian
Res.

Neah Bay

Strait of Juan de Fuca

VICTORIA

American Camp
1859

Mount Vernon

CAPE ALAVA

ROCKY PT

La Conner

PILLAR PT

TONGUE PT

Port
Angeles

DUNGENESS
SPIT

*Discovery
Bay*

*Deception
Pass*

Indian Pt

Port
Townsend

*Discovered by
Capt. George Vancouver 1792*

Monte
Cristo

CAPE
JOHNSON

MAKAH INDIANS

OZETTE INDIANS

KLALLAM
INDIANS

☐ Ft Townsend

SNOHOMISH INDIANS

QUILEUTE INDIANS

River

Queets River

Mt Olympus
7,965

OLYMPIC MOUNTAINS

QUILCENE INDIANS

SUQUAMISH INDIANS

Skykomish

*Skykomish
River*

Snoqualmie

River

Pacific

Quinault River

QUINAULT INDIANS

SKOKOMISH INDIANS

Seattle

Snoqualmie

Quinault
Indian
Reservation

✕ Battle of Seattle 1856

Puget

Green River

PT GRENVILLE

☐ Ft Pike 1857
☐ Ft Posey 1857

✕ White River Battle 1855

*Spanish explorers Heceta
and Quadra land 1775*

Sound

River

Ocean

PT BROWN

Grays Harbor

Tacoma

☐ Ft Steilacoom 1849

Northern

River

Stampede
Pass

PT CHEHALIS

Aberdeen

☐ Ft Nisqually 1833

Ft Hays
1856

☐

OLYMPIA ✪

Medicine Creek
Treaty Site 1854

Mt Rainier
14,410

CAPE SHOALWATER

☐
Ft Chehalis
1860

Tumwater

Chehalis

WILLAPA HILLS

Ft Henness
1856

☐

Ft Miller
1856

☐ Ft Preston
1857

Nisqually

LEADBETTER PT

*Willapa
Bay*

☐ Ft Willapa
1855

River

Centralia

River

CASCADE

Cowlitz Mission
1838

*Riffe
Lake*

Ft Canby 1863 ☐

Lewis & Clark 1805

Cowlitz Farms
1837

Cowlitz

River

Mt St Helens
8,366

Mt Adams
12,307

CAPE DISAPPOINTMENT

Mouth of the Columbia

☐ Ft Arkansas 1855

☐ Ft Smith 1855

*Discovered by
Capt. Robert Gray 1792*

Site of Monticello
Convention 1852

Lewis

River

HISTORIC
WASHINGTON

0   10   20   30   40   50
Miles

☐ Ft Vancouver 1825

COLUMBIA   GORGE

Lewis & Clark

Vancouver

Columbia

Strait of Georgia

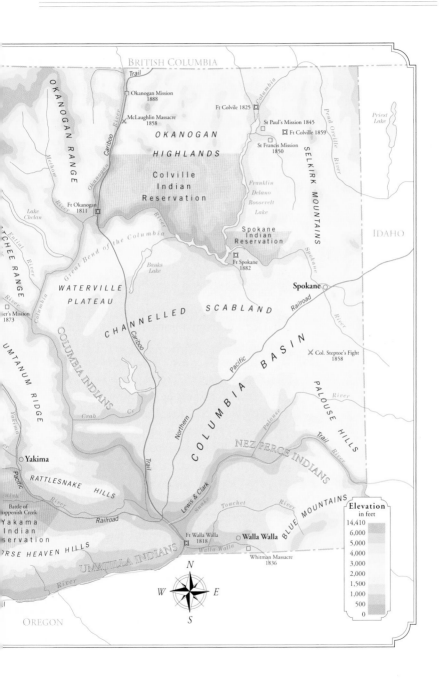

BRITISH COLUMBIA

OKANOGAN RANGE

Trail

Okanogan Mission
1888

Columbia

Ft Colvile 1825

Priest Lake

McLaughlin Massacre
1858

St Paul's Mission 1845

Pend Oreille

River

Cariboo River

OKANOGAN

Ft Colvile 1859

St Francis Mission
1850

SELKIRK MOUNTAINS

HIGHLANDS

Methow

Colville
Indian
Reservation

*Franklin
Delano
Roosevelt
Lake*

IDAHO

Okanogan

Lake
Chelan

Ft Okanogan
1811

River

Spokane
Indian
Reservation

CHEE RANGE

Great Bend of the Columbia

Banks
Lake

Ft Spokane
1882

Spokane River

er's Mission
1873

Columbia

WATERVILLE
PLATEAU

Cariboo

Spokane

Railroad

River

COLUMBIA INDIANS

CHANNELLED   SCABLAND

UMTANUM RIDGE

COLUMBIA   BASIN

✕ Col. Steptoe's Fight
1858

PALOUSE HILLS

Yakima

River

Northern

Pacific

Grab   Cr

Palouse River

Trail River

Yakima

Yakima

RATTLESNAKE   HILLS

NEZ PERCE INDIANS

BLUE MOUNTAINS

Battle of
oppenish Creek

Pacific

Railroad

Lewis & Clark

Touchet   River

Snake

*Yakima
Indian
servation*

Trail

River

ORSE HEAVEN HILLS

Ft Walla Walla
1818

Walla Walla

UMATILLA INDIANS

Walla Walla

Whitman Massacre
1836

River

OREGON

N
W · E
S

Elevation
in feet

14,410	
6,000	
5,000	
4,000	
3,000	
2,000	
1,500	
1,000	
500	
0	

Pioneer settler James Swan, who spent time among the Makahs in the mid-nineteenth century, reported that Makah children's "chief pleasure is to get into a little canoe, just large enough to float them, and paddle into the surf." Their elders were whalers; Swan suggested, "they are . . . to the Indian population what the inhabitants of Nantucket are to the people of the Atlantic coast." He observed that a "pastime of the boys is to imitate the killing of a whale. One will select a kelp stem of the largest size, and trail it along the beach. The other boys, armed with miniature harpoons with wooden buoys attached, follow after, and dart their harpoons into the kelp until it is full or split, when they get another, and keep up the game with eagerness for hours."

We also know that Spaniards sailed along the coast in the eighteenth century—and possibly as early as the sixteenth—establishing a short-lived post at Neah Bay and leaving some place names. We have detailed records of Capt. George Vancouver's visit, when he explored the coast for England, naming Mount Baker, Mount Rainier, Puget Sound, and any number of other mountains, islands, and points for shipmates and friends. Later, New England merchant captain Robert Gray, trading northwestern sea otter skins with China for Boston investors, took the first sailing vessel into the mouth of the river that bears the name of his ship, *Columbia Rediviva.*

The best-known explorers of the future were Meriwether Lewis and William Clark, sent west by President Thomas Jefferson to "explore the Missouri river, & such principal streams of it, as by it's course & communications with the waters of the Pacific Ocean, may offer the most direct & practicable water communication across this continent." The pair entered Washington along the Snake River in 1805 and reached the Pacific that fall at what is now Fort Canby State Park. Lewis and Clark, 29 and 33 years old when they started their two-year journey, were men of very different personalities and interests. "Although Lewis enjoyed eating dog meat and Clark hated it, and Lewis craved salt and Clark dismissed it as a luxury, and Lewis liked eating black currants and Clark favored yellow ones, the two leaders otherwise formed a perfectly harmonious relationship," Frank Bergon has written in an introduction to their journals. "Clark had more experience in actual battle, against the Creek and Cherokee Indians, but both men were archetypal American frontiersmen, whose characters had been forged in confrontation with the wilderness."

Jefferson wanted them to record the appearance and nature of the wilderness they passed through on this journey and the people who lived in it. No one knew who those people were. Jefferson wrote to Lewis, "As it is impossible for us to foresee in what manner you will be received by those people, whether with hospitality or hostility, so is it impossible to prescribe the exact degree of perseverance with which you are to pursue your journey. We value too much the lives of citizens to offer them to probable destruction."

Soon after Lewis and Clark passed through what was for them totally unknown country, fur traders employed by the British Hudson's Bay and North West companies trekked regularly between what is now the interior of British Columbia and the mouth of the Columbia River.

There is often no clear division between the past and the present. The Makahs were still whaling from dugout canoes at the turn of this century; in fact, Asahel Curtis photographed Makah whalers in the early 1900s. Yakamas and other inland tribes were still dipnetting salmon from platforms above Celilo Falls until 1957,

Makah Indians land a whale through the surf at Neah Bay. Sealskin floats hinder the whale's diving and keep him afloat after death. (Washington State Historical Society, Tacoma)

when The Dalles Dam flooded the falls. The first non-Indians who sought and finally found a route across the Cascades used Indian trails and Indian guides, and Interstate 90 basically follows that route today. As late as the 1950s or 1960s, one old woman on the Colville Indian Reservation was still setting fires in the pine forests to clear away the brush; when people from the Bureau of Indian Affairs put the fires out, she'd tell them they were ruining the forest, wait until they left, then torch the underbrush again.

Still, those early explorations, those millennia of fishing and whaling and knowing the land, did not in any organic way develop into the cities and agriculture and industry that exist in Washington today, or that existed here a century ago. Native Americans can claim some continuity with that past, but for society as a whole, links with the pre-European past are largely imaginary.

A rare basketry hat made of split spruce root and black-dyed cedar bark depicts a whale hunt scene.

■ AMERICANIZATION OF WASHINGTON

Modern Washington starts with the Missourian Michael Simmons setting up the territory's first sawmill at Tumwater Falls in 1848; with the pioneer Borens and Dennys shivering through the winter of 1851 in log cabins at Alki Point in what would soon become Seattle; with oystermen living in shacks on Willapa Bay in the early 1850s; maybe even with Marcus and Narcissa Whitman setting up their mission near Walla Walla in 1836.

In 1846, the United States and Great Britain settled the boundary of the Oregon Country, giving the United States clear title to the current states of Washington, Oregon, Idaho, and part of Montana. Washington Territory split off as a separate

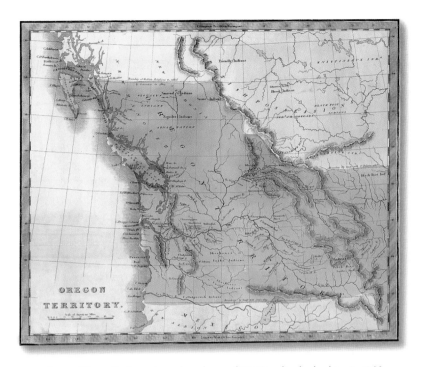

A map of Oregon Territory prior to the settlement of U.S.-Canadian border claims in 1846.
(University of Washington Libraries)

entity in 1853. The first territorial governor, Isaac Stevens—who had finished first in the West Point class of 1839 and fought at Chapultepec in the Mexican War (and who was subsequently killed at the Second Battle of Bull Run)—negotiated treaties with the Indians that gave the United States title to most of the land in 1854, 1855, and 1856. The treaties were negotiated in the Chinook jargon, a Northwestern trade language with very few words, and it is not clear just what the Indians thought they were getting. Whatever they thought, Indians who didn't like the treaties or their results were defeated in sporadic fighting from 1855 to 1858.

People grew crops and raised livestock in Washington from the beginning—indeed, the Hudson's Bay Company ran a farm at Fort Nisqually, just north of the Nisqually Delta, and the company's Fort Vancouver on the Columbia River may have been the first place in Washington where people raised apples or grapes. But

∎ History Timeline ∎

1592 A Greek navigator, sailing for Spain and using the name Juan de Fuca, claims to have discovered a vast strait. Two centuries later Bruno Heceta and Juan Francisco de Bodega claim the Washington coast for Spain.

1778 In search of the fabled Northwest Passage, British explorer Captain James Cook sights and names Cape Flattery.

1787 Strait of Juan de Fuca entered and named by Captain Charles W. Barkley.

1792 British sea captain George Vancouver explores Washington waters and names waterways and landmarks, many in honor of his crew members—Peter Puget, Peter Rainier, Joseph Whidbey, Joseph Baker. The same year, Bostonian Robert Gray is the first to sail into the mouth of Columbia River. He names it after his ship, the *Columbia Rediviva*.

1805 American explorers Lewis and Clark enter Washington from the east and follow the Columbia downriver to the Pacific Ocean.

1812 Fort Spokane established by John Jacob Astor's Pacific Fur Company.

1819 Spain relinquishes all claims to Oregon Country.

1825 British doctor John McLoughlin establishes Hudson's Bay Company's Fort Vancouver.

1828 Jedediah Smith leads fur traders from California to the Columbia River.

1836 Marcus and Narcissa Whitman establish a mission near the Walla Walla, which they run until they are massacred by the Cayuse Indians in 1847.

1846 England agrees to set the border between western Canada and the United States at the 49th parallel.

1852 Seattle founded by the Denny party.

1853 Washington Territory established with a population of 3,985.

1854 Medicine Creek Indian Treaty signed.

1856 Seattle besieged by Indians. Governor Stevens declares martial law on Puget Sound.

1858 Colonel Steptoe defeated by Indians. Colonel Wright defeats Indians in eastern Washington. Indian Wars end.

1864 Asa Mercer travels east and convinces marriageable women to settle in Washington Territory, where men are eager for wives.

1873 Tacoma chosen as western terminus of Northern Pacific Railroad.

1889   Washington State is admitted to the Union. Fires devastate Seattle, Spokane, and Ellensburg.
1897   Gold is discovered in Alaska and Seattle becomes main terminus for Klondike miners.
1900   Frederick Weyerhaeuser starts his Northwest operation.
1906   The Mountaineers founded—an outdoors club devoted to preserving and exploring mountains, forests, and rivers of the Pacific Northwest.
1916   After crashing his newly purchased plane, Bill Boeing, Sr. builds his own pontoons—the first Boeing aircraft is assembled.
1938   Bonneville Dam is completed.
1942   Jimi Hendrix is born in Seattle.
1962   The world's fair in Seattle draws over 9,600,000 people and establishes the city's most recognizable landmark, the Space Needle.
1980   Mount St. Helens erupts.
1987   Bill Gates takes Microsoft public.
1993   Seattle hosts the Asia Pacific Economic Cooperation conference with 15 world leaders in attendance.

WASHINGTON HABITABLE? NEVER!

Not everyone was enthusiastic about extending U.S. territories to the Pacific Coast, as this address to the U.S. Senate in 1843 illustrates:

*D*oes any man seriously suppose that any state which can be formed at the mouth of the Columbia River, or any of the inhabitable parts of that territory, would ever become one of the states of the Union?…Even in the most sanguine days of my youth I never conceived the possibility of embracing within the same Government people living five thousand miles apart….Have you made anything like an estimate of the cost of a railroad running from here to the mouth of the Columbia? Why, the wealth of the Indies would be insufficient….To talk about constructing a railroad to the western shore of this continent manifests a wild spirit of adventure which I never expected to hear broached in the Senate of the United States.

—Sen. George McDuffie, address to the
U.S. Senate, January 25, 1843

mostly, Washington was founded by people who mined the territory's natural resources and sold things.

Ships' crews and early settlers cut old-growth trees beside the salt water of Puget Sound, sawed them into lengths, and loaded the logs onto sailing ships, which hauled them south to San Francisco Bay. In 1853, the Pope and Talbot Company built a mill at Port Gamble, on Hood Canal, just to cut lumber for the San Francisco market.

The early loggers stayed close to salt water—or to rivers that could float logs to salt water. Ox teams dragged the segments of Douglas fir trunks along tracks of peeled and greased logs called skid roads. Oxen couldn't drag an old-growth log far, and they couldn't drag one up a steep hill at all. Forest fires became more frequent when people started working in the woods, and in 1883, a sawmill manager wrote that "The weather is very dry and the whole country seems to be on fire.... [I]f the fire continues we shall be short [of logs] in the fall. After the fire has passed over the ground it is some time before the logger dares to drive his oxen over it for fear of burning their feet, as the fire remains in the roots."

The coal that people discovered in the 1850s and '60s was at least as difficult to

INDIAN CUSTOMS

*O*n arriving among [the Indians ashore] we were exceedingly surprised to see that they had almost all flattened heads. This configuration is not a natural deformity, but an effect of art, caused by compression of the skull in infancy. It shocks strangers extremely, especially at first sight; nevertheless, among these barbarians it is an indispensable ornament: and when we signified to them how much this mode of flattening the forehead appeared to us to violate nature and good taste, they answered that it was only slaves who had not their heads flattened. The slaves, in fact, have the usual rounded head, and they are not permitted to flatten the foreheads of their children, destined to bear the chains of their sires.

The Indians of the Columbia are of a light copper color, active in body, and, above all, excellent swimmers. . . .The men go entirely naked, not concealing any part of their bodies. Only in winter they throw over the shoulders a panther's skin . . . .

[The women] anoint the body and dress the hair with fish oil, which does not diffuse an agreeable perfume. Their hair (which both sexes wear long) is jet black; it is badly combed, but parted in the middle, as is the custom of the sex everywhere, and kept shining by the fish-oil before-mentioned. Sometimes, in imitation of the men, they paint the whole body with a red earth mixed with fish-oil. Their ornaments consist of bracelets of brass, which they wear indifferently on the wrists and ankles; of strings of beads of different colors (they give a preference to the blue), and displayed in great profusion around the neck, and on the arms and legs; and of white shells, called *Haiqua*, which are their ordinary circulating medium . . . . Although a little less slaves than the greater part of the Indian women elsewhere, the women on the Columbia are, nevertheless, charged with the most painful labors . . . .

—Gabriel Franchére, *Narrative of a Voyage to the Northwest Coast of America in the Years 1811, 1812, 1813, and 1814*

(left) The Battle of Seattle *on January 26, 1856 between Indians and early settlers as depicted in a painting by Emily Inez Denny. (Museum of History and Industry, Seattle)*

haul. To bring out the first load of coal from Issaquah, now 20 minutes by freeway from downtown Seattle, in 1864, a Seattle blacksmith built a scow, hired a crew of Duwamish Indians, poled up the Duwamish and Black rivers, sailed across Lake Washington, cut his way through logs and brush up the Sammamish Slough, sailed the length of Lake Sammamish, loaded the coal, then turned around and followed the same tortuous path back to Seattle. The trip took 20 days.

In the 1870s, when people discovered that wheat would grow in the hills around Walla Walla and farther east, transporting grain proved equally laborious. The first rails laid in Washington were used primarily to haul logs, coal, or wheat to the water's edge. They made it dramatically easier to haul heavy loads long distances—and enabled loggers to cut forests farther from Puget Sound. But they had nothing like the impact of the first transcontinental railroads, which transformed Washington's economic relationship with the rest of the country and made it possible to develop vast areas east of the Cascades.

■ RAILROADS

From a late twentieth-century perspective, it's hard to appreciate how important—or how powerful and corrupting—the railroads were. "The generation between 1865 and 1895 . . . was mortgaged to the railroads," wrote Henry Adams, "and no one knew it better than the generation itself."

Washington cities were as eager as Congress to reward—or bribe—the railroad builders. Seattle offered the Northern Pacific Railroad 7,500 lots, 3,000 acres, and a quarter of a million dollars in cash and bonds if it would lay tracks to Elliott Bay. Tacoma offered the railroad two miles of waterfront and 2,700 acres in a solid block if it would lay them to Commencement Bay instead. Tacoma won.

But Tacoma's days of glory didn't last long. Seattle had already become the supply center for mill towns and logging camps all around Puget Sound, and had started supplying Alaska. Even when Tacoma got the railroad, Seattle never lost its crass frontier optimism. After most of downtown Seattle burned in the great fire of 1889, the city rebuilt itself in brick. (Most of downtown Spokane burned in the same year, and Spokane, too, rebuilt itself with brick.)

Seattle soon had a railroad of its own. The Midwestern tycoon James J. Hill completed the Great Northern Railway from St. Paul to Seattle in 1893, just in time for a deep, four-year nationwide depression. During the depression, Hill gained control of the Northern Pacific—and its vast government land grants—and since Hill had already picked Seattle as his main western terminus, that marked the end of Seattle's relative eclipse.

The railroads brought some places into the economic mainstream and turned others into backwaters. Once rails became the preferred means of transportation, the Olympic Peninsula, which had been so easily accessible by ship, was cut off from most of the action.

On the other hand, rails soon made it feasible to mine coal in the eastern Cascades at Cle Elum and Roslyn. Miners migrated to the eastern Cascades from much of Europe and parts of Asia. Early in this century, Roslyn's population included Austrians, Belgians, Chinese, Croatians, Czechs, Dutch, English, Finns, Germans, Hungarians, Irish, Italians, Lithuanians, Montenegrins, Norwegians, Poles, Russians, Scots, Serbs, Slovenes, Swedes, Syrians, and Welshmen.

Farther east, the rails—combined with irrigation and cold storage—made it feasible to grow apples commercially and ship them to markets in the Midwest and East. Wheat country was transformed, too. Spokane became a transportation hub for the surrounding farm area and a key supply point for mining booms

The laying of the last rail on the Great Northern Railway's main line just west of the Cascade summit in December 1892. (Museum of History and Industry, Seattle)

farther east. Eastern Washington wheat that would once have gone down the river to Portland was loaded onto trains bound for Tacoma, where it was shipped to ports all over the world.

■ STATEHOOD AND A NEW CENTURY

Washington became a state in 1889. Eight years later, the steamer *Portland* arrived in Seattle with a "ton of gold. . . ." The Klondike Gold Rush was on. At least two thousand people were waiting at Schwabacher's Wharf to greet the miners who had struck it rich in the Klondike, and within ten days, the first 1,500 people had left Seattle for the gold fields. Overnight Seattle had become a gold rush boomtown. Already a supply center for western Washington and Alaska, now the main terminus of the transcontinental railroads, and not shy about self-promotion, Seattle became the main jumping-off point for Alaska-bound miners. Men and supplies streamed north on just about any ship sound enough to make the voyage. Gold and discouraged prospectors streamed back. Merchants who supplied the miners did very well for themselves, as did people who built or operated ships. "The Klondike excitement will put everything that can be floated into use," wrote a Puget Sound lumber

IMMIGRANT INQUIRIES, 1872

*T*he first inquiries which a person desiring to change his residence from one State to another would naturally be, what advantages does the State to which I wish to emigrate possess over my own? Is it more fertile, more healthy, does it possess a more genial climate, are its resources and commercial and manufacturing advantages greater? Is it easier for the poor laborer to earn a livelihood or the poor farmer to obtain land? What facilities are offered for education and attending church? And finally, what is the character of the population, in order that I may know who are to be my future neighbors and what class of persons I shall mingle with? The person thinking of changing his home should make these inquiries, and if the advantages are in favor of the State to be adopted, one should avail himself of them. There is no portion of the country, perhaps, that offers all the advantages to an immigrant equal to this Territory.

—*Puget Sound Business Directory,* 1872

Would-be fortune hunters crowd onto a steamer bound for Alaska during the Klondike Gold Rush of 1897. (Museum of History and Industry, Seattle)

baron, "and in fact some of the boats have made on one trip almost the cost of building them." Inevitably, sin flourished, saloons proliferated, and Seattle became a center of the white slave trade.

In 1899, the new generating plant at Snoqualmie Falls, the first large hydroelectric project in the state, started selling electricity to Seattle and Tacoma. In 1900, the railroad builder Jim Hill sold 900,000 acres of land grant timberland—given by Congress to the Northern Pacific and subsequently acquired by Hill—at six dollars an acre to his St. Paul neighbor, the midwestern lumber baron, Frederick Weyerhaeuser. The sale was the largest private land deal in American history and the start of the Weyerhaeuser empire in the Northwest. The first automobiles crossed the Cascades over the ruts and rocks of the wagon road across Snoqualmie Pass five years later. At around the same time people started putting gasoline

Soapy Smith

*I*t was along the Skid Road that the most famous of Alaska's bad men, Soapy Smith, rounded up the gang that eventually operated the town of Skagway as its private enterprise. Soapy Smith—like Erastus Brainerd—was a part-time genius. He took a weird bunch of individualists, men who went by the names of Fatty Green and Kid Jimmy Fresh, Yank Fewclothes and Jay Bird Slim, and organized them into a syndicate that not only ran all the gambling and robbery at the southern end of the gold trail, but even took over the United States Army Recruiting Station at Skagway during the Spanish-American War and assigned men to pick the pockets of the recruits who were taking their physicals. Soapy did not profit personally from his endeavors. When he was killed in a duel with the civil engineer who had laid out the town (and who, like Soapy, felt a proprietary interest in Skagway) Soapy's estate was a hundred dollars in cash and a satchelful of marked cards.

—Murray Morgan, *Skid Road,* 1981

Mill Street, the original "Skid Road," so called because of the log skids placed in the street to enable timber to be moved easily to the docks. The street is now called Yesler Street after the mill that operated here at the time of this photo in 1874. Pioneer Square now exists where the flagpole appears in photo. (Museum of History and Industry, Seattle)

engines into fishing boats. When the great earthquake of 1906 destroyed San Francisco, Washington mills cut lumber to rebuild the city; in effect, Washington lumber built San Francisco twice.

To celebrate all this heady progress, Seattle staged the Alaska-Yukon-Pacific Exposition, on what is now the University of Washington campus, in 1909. President William Howard Taft attended, and the exposition marked the finish line of a cross-country auto race. The A-Y-P, as it was known, left a legacy of buildings and landscaping at the University of Washington; Drumheller Fountain, better known as Frosh Pond, and the broad walk that seems to lead straight to the snow-capped peak of Mount Rainier, were created for the exposition.

■ NEW DEAL ERA

As automobiles began to dominate transportation, county and state governments started paving roads. Puget Sound salmon fishermen started making annual trips north to Alaska. Beside the Sound, forest products companies started building pulp mills, giving Washington its first real manufacturing industry. And throughout eastern Washington, the Grange started pushing for public ownership of electric utilities.

Even more monumental were the changes brought by the New Deal, President Franklin Roosevelt's plan to jumpstart the country out of the Great Depression. The federal government started building the huge concrete dams on the Columbia River that would transform the river into a chain of lakes, turning nearly a thousand square miles of eastern Washington desert into the irrigated Columbia Basin Project, and giving Washington residents electricity so cheap that they used it to heat their houses. The first big federal dam, Bonneville, was completed in 1938. The largest, Grand Coulee, was finished in 1941. The dam building continued into the 1970s. It was a mixed blessing. In addition to generating power, irrigating the desert, and enabling barges to haul wheat from Idaho, it flooded the ancient Indian fishing sites at Kettle and Celilo Falls and reduced the river's wild salmon runs—once the greatest chinook salmon runs in the world—from 15 or 16 million fish in a good year to 200 or 300 thousand.

At the time, the bargain seemed a good one. Richard Neuberger—later a U.S. Senator from Oregon—wrote in 1938 that the beneficiaries would include "thousands of farmers who pump by hand, read by kerosene lamp, cook on wood stoves, and watch their wives and daughters stoop for hours over washboards and churns." Rural families started getting electric lights, electric appliances, electric milking machines. A whole new industry, aluminum manufacturing, which required vast quantities of cheap electricity, was drawn to the Northwest.

■ WORLD WAR II AND BOEING

When World War II started, Washington's aluminum industry was available to smelt metal for the military planes produced by Boeing and other aircraft manufacturers. Even before the United States entered the war, Boeing had started hiring workers and turning out more planes. In 1939, the company employed 4,000 people. That was many more workers than any pulp or lumber mill, but a bare hint of what was to come. The war made Boeing an industrial giant, employing up to 44,000 people and turning out as many as 362 B-17 bombers in a single month. And the war spawned the world's first plutonium factory built at Hanford, in the desert of central Washington. Hanford provided the plutonium for the first nuclear explosion and for the bomb that destroyed Nagasaki.

Thousands of soldiers and sailors passed through Washington to train at Fort

WARTIME 1942

*H*ere are vast soldier cities that shelter 50,000 men. Here, too, are lonely island posts manned by veterans of another war, veterans with tattooed arms, gold teeth and rheumatism. Cheerfully and lively, they scan the sea and sky for advancing enemies, betimes playing bagpipes or throwing rocks at wild bears that rob camp kitchens....This Pacific Northwest, by the Great Circle route through the Aleutians, is only about 4,700 miles from Tokyo. Its army posts, naval bases, docks, airplane factories, ship and lumber yards, mines and forests, railway terminals and fishing fleets are all possible objects of enemy attacks.

After the Aleutian thrust, Japanese U-boat shelling of Vancouver and Oregon coasts was no surprise. Portland, Seattle, Tacoma, Vancouver are all exposed to the risk of air raids. But now their all-out defense works, and grim evidence of aggressive warfare meets you at every turn....

—Frederick Simpich, Sr., "Wartime in the Pacific Northwest,"
National Geographic Magazine, October 1942

*The 5,000th B-17 rolls off the assembly line at Boeing in 1943. The aircraft bears the
signatures of all the company employees. (Underwood Archives, San Francisco)*

Lewis and other military posts, and to board the ships that would take them across
the Pacific.

Ten years after V-J Day, in August of 1955, a huge crowd of aerospace executives from around the world gathered on the shore of Lake Washington to watch
Seattle's Seafair hydroplane races. Boeing's chief test pilot, Tex Johnston, brought
the company's prototype 707 in low over the lake and did a full barrel roll at 500
feet. Boeing's president hadn't gotten over his shock before Johnston brought the
big plane back and did it again. Jets had clearly arrived. The symbolic event
launched Boeing's first commercial jet and started the company's rapid rise to
domination of commercial aircraft manufacturing.

The 1960s put Seattle, and Washington, into the national spotlight. The 1962
world's fair in Seattle was followed in short order by the completion of the I-5 freeway from Canada to the Columbia River, the arrival of the state's first major-league
sports team—the Seattle Supersonics of the NBA—and the construction of downtown Seattle's first skyscraper taller than the 1914-vintage Smith Tower.

■ MOUNT ST. HELENS ERUPTS

The 1980s started with a bang—the eruption of Mount St. Helens. The mountain exploded on Sunday morning, May 18, 1980, with a force equal to 27,000 Hiroshima bombs, killing 57 people, vaporizing whole forests, choking the Toutle River and ultimately the lower Columbia with mud, darkening the skies of many eastern Washington farming communities and filling their streets with ash.

The eruption, which focused the world's attention on Washington for a little while, was only one of the shocks that the new decade brought. The recessions of the early 1980s hit Washington harder than they hit many other parts of the United States. The forest products industry lost more than 100 Northwestern mills and took advantage of the slowdown to "restructure," eliminating one-third of its pre-recession jobs. Statewide unemployment climbed to 12 percent, and in some timber-dependent rural areas, it lingered above 20 percent.

But despite the forest products layoffs and the near-collapse of Seafirst, the state's largest bank, things didn't stay grim for long. The mid- and late 1980s soon brought a lot of growth, glamor, and national notoriety to the state.

By the end of the decade, Boeing's Puget Sound work force topped 100,000, and people in the Seattle area worried about the effects of unrestricted growth. Boeing wasn't the only local company making money hand over fist. Microsoft, founded by two Seattle guys and headquartered in Redmond, became the dominant company in the increasingly huge personal computer software industry.

■ HIGH TECH BOOM

Microsoft is one of the country's great high-tech success stories. Two local teenagers, Bill Gates and Paul Allen, met at Seattle's Lakeside Academy. Both went off to college but dropped out and modified the BASIC computer language so that it could be used on small computers sold as hobby kits by a New Mexico firm. They returned to Seattle, where IBM approached them about creating an operating system for personal computers. They bought a system from a company called Seattle Computer Resources and made it into MS-DOS, which became the heart of most personal computers sold all around the world. Allen left the company; Gates stayed. After Microsoft went public in 1987, he became the world's youngest

(previous pages) A Boeing 707 prototype with its wing inverted while doing a barrel roll during the 1955 Seafair Gold Cup Hydro races. Pilot Tex Johnston wanted to impress a gathering of international aeronautical executives gathered for the event. (Boeing Company Archives)

billionaire and one of the nation's richest men. Today, his company is worth more than IBM.

With Microsoft and literally hundreds of smaller companies, the Seattle area became a center of software development. It also became a center of the new biotechnology industry. Seattle and Bellevue both developed high-rise skylines. Washington wines started winning medals in international competition. Seattle acquired a reputation as the coffee capital of the United States. Seattle-based factory trawlers began to dominate the enormous bottomfish fishery off Alaska. Tacoma, with lots of vacant land and great rail connections on its waterfront, became a major container port virtually overnight, rivaling Seattle. Puget

Microsoft magnate, Bill Gates.
(Courtesy Microsoft)

Sound had always been the main supply point for Alaska, and ships from Japan had unloaded freight in both cities in the nineteenth century; now, as Pacific Rim trade boomed, Seattle and Tacoma had the advantage of being the closest major American ports to Japan. Most of the foreign cargoes passing through their harbors came from Asia, and most—garments, electronics, automobiles, and other products—continued on by rail or truck to the Midwest and East. Together, Seattle and Tacoma were soon shipping as many containers as the Port of New York. National magazines started calling Seattle the best city in the country to do business or the nation's most livable city. And inevitably, people started complaining about the newcomers moving in, driving up real estate prices, clogging the roads.

■ FISH AND FORESTS

In the 1990s, Washington found itself part of the nation's main environmental battleground. The controversy with perhaps the broadest biological and economic ramifications involves the fate of wild salmon. The great wild salmon runs tie the mountains to the coastal lowlands, the sage steppe of the interior to the rain forest of the coast. The runs have been depleted all over Washington. Many have reached the brink of extinction.

Commercial and recreational fisheries have been sustained for years by fish hatcheries, but hatcheries have yielded diminishing returns, and they have only masked and exacerbated the destruction of the wild runs.

And then there are Washington's magnificent old-growth forests. "In biomass alone," Keith Ervin has written, "the Pacific forests are rivaled by no other forests on earth. The rain forests of the tropics are small things by comparison."

As early as 1884, the acting manager of the huge Port Blakely mill wrote that "The timber contiguous to the Sound is nearly exhausted." In the 1920s, Clarence Bagley, who had first seen Washington forests in the 1860s, wrote that "our boasted heritage of inexhaustible forests is nearly dissipated. Unless the Federal government or the state takes over the gigantic task of reforesting, the lumber industry of Washington will ere long become a matter of past history."

Timber companies started reforesting during World War II, but it takes time for corporate tree farms to start paying off. When private land couldn't provide enough timber to feed Washington's mills, heavy logging began in the national forests. Whole communities came to depend on public timber. The old-growth forest kept shrinking. Generations of environmentalists were appalled, but aside from preserving specific areas as national parks or wilderness, they couldn't do much about it.

Until the spotted owl came along. Of course, the northern spotted owl had been there all along, but little was known about it until the early 1970s, when research indicated that it lived in old-growth forests, that its habitat was disappearing rapidly, and that the bird itself might not be long for this world. Under pressure from the courts, the federal government listed the owl as threatened in 1990. A group of environmental organizations sued to block federal timber sales in spotted owl territory. In 1991, after hearing arguments in his Seattle courtroom, U.S. District Court Judge William Dwyer enjoined all federal timber sales in western

Soleduck Falls in Olympic National Park.

Washington, Oregon, and northern California, observing that "the records of this case...show a remarkable series of violations of the environmental laws." The injunction lasted until 1994, after the Clinton administration presented a controversial plan to protect old-growth habitats.

■ TODAY'S PLEASURES

The environmental battles would not be raging if there were not a lot left worth fighting over—and a lot of people who cared about saving it. Literally within an hour of Seattle (when traffic is light) one can be hiking in a federally protected wilderness area or skiing in alpine terrain. The same is true of Bellevue, Everett, Bellingham, or Tacoma. In Spokane, the wilderness is a little farther away, but it's wilder. People here relish conversations about trails and camp sites. A person who doesn't hike or ski or climb may feel like a social misfit. It doesn't seem entirely coincidental that REI, Eddie Bauer, and other sellers of outdoor clothing and gear have flourished in Seattle.

Nature intrudes even when one does not make a special effort to go out and find it. Looking up from a city street and seeing the snow on Mount Rainier or Mount Baker or Mount Adams has to affect one's point of view. The sublime is forever being juxtaposed against the tacky. On a country road near Seattle, an old, upholstered chair and bench with patched plastic covers lie among the weeds in a roadside ditch. Somebody saved a few dollars by not taking them to the dump. But look up from them, straight up, and you may see an eagle soaring overhead. Go a mile down the road, look south, and there, rising beyond the pastures, stands Mount Rainier.

Until recently, the outdoors constituted the region's chief—some might say its *only*—attraction; except, of course, for the prospect of steady employment whenever Boeing was on a roll and the West's old appeal of an open society and a fresh start. In the late 1940s, the English orchestra conductor Sir Thomas Beecham called Seattle a "cultural dustbin." Those days are long gone. Not only do Seattle and other Washington cities have the requisite theaters and opera and symphony orchestras, they have acquired a certain cachet. People who are not drawn primarily by the chance to hike or climb or work at Boeing have been moving here from all over the country. Most of the current attention has focused on Seattle, which has become known as the espresso capital of the country, the center of grunge rock, a cool place to be. The city has certainly earned its reputation for coffee. Not only are the cafes and espresso carts ubiquitous; one actually sees a city bus idling at the curb while its driver runs inside for a double latte to go. Even dry cleaners and car washes serve espresso. Not long ago, the *Seattle Times* ran a long article about the subculture of *barristas,* the mostly young people who make espresso at the city's many cafes and sidewalk carts.

But neither the coffee nor the music is exclusive to Seattle. The Seattle rock band Nirvana actually got its start playing in Olympia, and even the depressed Olympic Peninsula logging town of Forks has a drive-in espresso stand.

A lot of people associate Washington with rain and the months of gray, damp weather can get some people down. But when the sun comes out and the mountains appear, it all seems worthwhile. People head for the mountains and fill the sidewalk cafes.

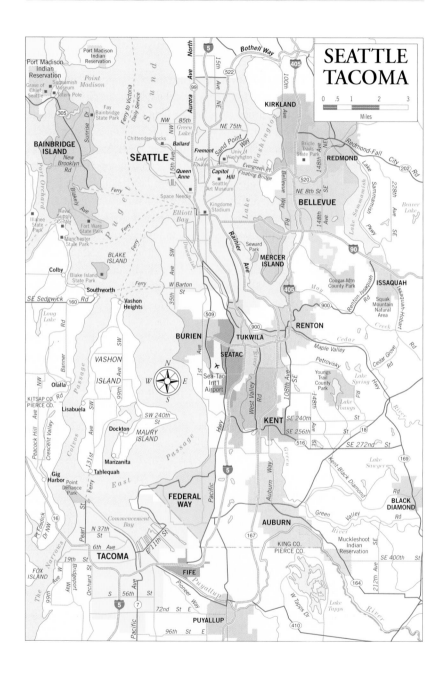

S   E   A   T   T   L   E

IF YOU TRAVEL TO SEATTLE BY CAR FERRY, you'll find the bow of your boat turning into Elliott Bay as you approach the city, then heading eastward toward Colman Dock and Seattle's old downtown waterfront. If you look up at the city's skyline, you'll see the snowcapped Cascades looming above the city's skyscrapers, and the 14,410-foot snow cone of Mount Rainier towering over orange container cranes at the south end of the harbor. Other Puget Sound ferries steer swiftly past, bound for Bainbridge Island and the Kitsap Peninsula. Tugs, their bows pointed out into the open sound, wait for an inbound container ship. Home from the Bering Sea with their catches of bottomfish, blue-hulled factory trawlers moor here and there along the shore.

On a very clear day you can pick out 10,750-foot Mount Baker, to the north, and 10,430-foot Glacier Peak—centerpiece of the half-million-acre Glacier Peak Wilderness—to its right. In front of Baker, at the north end of the visible city, rises the Space Needle, the trademark structure built for the 1962 world's fair, an event that drew both John F. Kennedy and Elvis Presley. For a lot of the country, the 1962 fair put Seattle on the map. At the south end of downtown sits the concrete lump of the Kingdome, Seattle's indoor sports arena, which houses major-league football and baseball, and has housed major league basketball and soccer—to say nothing of rock concerts and dirt-bike races.

The forested bluffs and waterfront condos of Alki Point mark the southern edge of the harbor entrance, on the right. Seattle's first white settlers hauled their belongings across a stony beach here to the spot on Alki where they spent their first wet and miserable winter. Now, this beachfront drive is a favorite spot for summer cruising and swimming.

Beyond Alki, you can see the high span of the bridge across the **Duwamish River** that links West Seattle to the rest of the city. It's harder to spot the mouth of the Duwamish River, where salmon still swim past barges, warehouses, cement plants, the back of Boeing's main headquarters, a shipyard where state ferries are repaired, and a boatyard that launches 110-foot luxury yachts.

North of the Duwamish, a little left of the Kingdome, you can pick out the white, 42-story spire of the **Smith Tower**, which was the tallest building west of the Mississippi when it was completed in 1914 (and it remained the tallest building in Seattle for 55 years). Now, it is dwarfed by highrises, the result of an office building boom in the 1980s that transformed the look and feel of Seattle's downtown. The city's contemporary highrise skyline stretches north from the Smith Tower, and includes a more recent "tallest building west of the Mississippi," the 76-story **Seafirst Columbia Center.**

Despite the building's scale and high-tech coldness, it contains a pleasant and much-used public space featuring a large sculpture by Seattle glass-blower Dale Chihuly. Sometimes, just at sunset, when a red sun is about to drop behind the Olympic Mountains, the convex face of the building catches the light just right and the whole 76-story monolith looks like it's on fire.

Your ferry lands directly down the hill from the Columbia Center at nonde-script Colman Dock, officially Pier 52, the Washington State Ferry Terminal. An earlier Colman Dock on the same site served as the headquarters of the "Mosquito Fleet," the flotilla of boats that ferried passengers and freight around Puget Sound from the mid-nineteenth century through World War II, making Seattle the hub

Smith Tower under construction behind the Grand Trunk Pier where Puget Sound ferries, known as the "Mosquito Fleet," docked. (Puget Sound Maritime Historical Society)

of local trade. Then, every little community had its own dock; double rows of vestigial gray pilings still march, two by two, into deep water at spots where steamboats used to call.

■ DOWNTOWN

When you disembark at **Colman Dock,** it's only a short uphill walk to the central business district. The downtown waterfront where you first set foot on pavement is no longer Seattle's economic focal point, but the proximity of salt water remains vital to the city's character and history. The *Portland* unloaded its "ton of gold" near this dock in 1897, setting off the Klondike Gold Rush. A plaque now marks the spot.

The flat land along the waterfront wasn't put there by nature. The settlers who wintered on Alki in 1851 found that in bad weather or at low tide, the exposed, sloping beach was a lousy place from which to load or unload ships. They consequently moved the community to the bluffs that then dropped steeply into the sheltered inner curve of Elliott Bay.

Henry Yesler, who built and ran the sawmill that was the new city's main industry, used rocks carried as ballast on inbound ships to build a wharf hundreds of feet out into the bay, so that the largest ships could load and unload on any tide. The site of that first wharf is marked by a plaque near Colman Dock.

Many of the old piers along the downtown waterfront have been transformed into shops, museums, restaurants, and amusements. Harbor tours depart from Pier 55 every weekday and Pier 57 on the weekends. Many visitors stroll the mile and a half north to Pier 70, now a commercial complex, detouring over the harbor on the boardwalks and fishing piers of **Waterfront Park,** and returning on a vintage 1927 **Waterfront streetcar.**

Next to the fireboat dock on Pier 54, children may enjoy seeing the small **firefighting museum,** and watching the fireboats stage weekly pumping drills. On Pier 59, they can get a sense of life beneath Puget Sound in the underwater dome of the **Seattle Marine Aquarium,** or take in a film on the **Omnidome's** wraparound screen.

Photographs of downtown Seattle 100 years ago reveal a landscape very different from today's. Then, the steep, overgrown hillsides that rose above the bay were cut by deep ravines; springs flowed down from the bluffs and out across stretches of

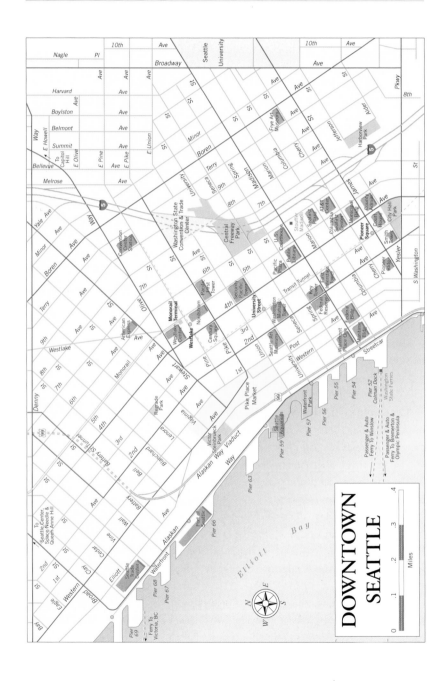

DOWNTOWN SEATTLE

sandy beach, and vast tideflats spread like a muddy apron at the young city's feet.

In 1969, shortly before his 100th birthday, Joshua Green remembered that "when I came to Seattle [in 1886] there were hardly roads at all. The roads just went out of business in the winter time with the mud."

In 1889, most of Seattle's 40,000 inhabitants lived and worked in the 50-plus blocks of one- and two-story clapboard buildings that then comprised downtown. Twice a day, at high tide, the waters of Elliott Bay would force the contents of the city's primitive sewer system up and oozing out into the streets. Seattle stank, and it wasn't built to last. It didn't last, either.

On the afternoon of June 6, 1889, in a cabinet shop at the foot of Madison, an unwatched glue pot bubbled over, and sparked the Seattle fire of 1889. By midnight, most of Seattle had burned to the ground.

The work of rebuilding began immediately. The new downtown that rose from the ashes of the old was made of brick, and its streets were elevated a full story above their previous level to solve the city's chronic sewage problem. Elevating the streets trapped many ground-floor storefronts below ground, and created "Underground Seattle," which is now a major tourist attraction.

A microbrewery pub in historic Pioneer Square.

SEATTLE MAIN ATTRACTIONS

■ UNIQUELY SEATTLE

Pike Place Market. A bustling marketplace that sells everything from fine local produce to fresh fish to handcrafted jewelry. Food stalls and produce stands are tightly packed together beneath a covered arcade. Surrounding the main arcade specialty shops, art galleries, and street performers add to the vibrant atmosphere. *First Avenue and Pike Place; (206) 682-7453.*

Pioneer Square Historic District. A restored neighborhood of red brick buildings converted into restaurants, art galleries, and boutiques. Evenings in and around Pioneer Square attract a crowd of all ages to the many bars and music clubs. Tours of **Underground Seattle** meet at the square and lead visitors through the subterranean streets and storefronts which comprised the commercial center of the city in the late nineteenth century. Call (206) 682-4646 for tour information. Nearby at 117 Main Street, the **Klondike Gold Rush Museum** presents demonstrations, films, and exhibits to explain Seattle's role in the 1897-98 Gold Rush. *Greater Pioneer Square is bounded by the waterfront, Third Avenue, Yesler Way, and King Street.*

Space Needle. Perched 500 feet above ground, the observation deck in this gleaming, futuristic structure provides a stunning panorama of the city. *Fifth Avenue and Broad Street inside the Seattle Center; (206) 443-2100.*

Waterfront. A front row look at the intricate workings of a commercial harbor. Restaurants and souvenir shops line the stretch from Pier 48 to Pier 70, where the view of Elliott Bay is unparalleled. The **Seattle Aquarium**, at Pier 59, offers a fascinating introduction to Puget Sound marine life. *(206) 386-4320.*

Hiram Chittenden Locks. Watching tugs, commercial ships, and pleasure boats pass through the locks, part of the eight-mile Lake Washington Ship Canal, is a star attraction in the city. Viewing windows provide close-up encounters with migrating salmon and steelhead as they make the transition through a fish ladder. To reach the locks visitors stroll through landscaped grounds—packed with picnickers on warm days. The adjacent Carl S. English Jr. Botanical Gardens is also worth a visit. *3015 NW 54th Street; (206) 783-7059.*

■ NEIGHBORHOODS

Capitol Hill. One of the city's prettiest old neighborhoods, offering an eclectic array of mansions, tree-lined avenues, and vintage clothing stores. Broadway, the main thoroughfare, is laden with ethnic restaurants, bars, and interesting shops and is the center of the city's gay life. *Along Broadway, extending from Pine Street to E. Roy Street, and 15th Avenue East.*

Fremont. The Republic of Fremont, across the ship canal from dignified Queen Anne Hill, is Seattle's quirkiest neighborhood. Counterculture haunts like the Still Life Coffeehouse mix well with more upscale establishments like the Trolleyman Pub at the Redhook Ale Brewery. Call (206) 548-8000 for tour information. Citizens of Fremont tout their Sunday public market, summer outdoor cinema, and annual, slightly risque Solstice Parade.

International District. Less congested than most Chinatowns, the "ID" is a 40-block cluster of herbal medicine shops, acupuncturists, Chinese, Japanese, and Korean restaurants, and housewares stores. The **Nippon Kan Theater** stages Asian and Asian-American performances. *628 Washington Street; (206) 467-6807.* The **Wing Luke Museum** focuses on Oriental history and culture. *4076 Seventh Avenue South; (206) 623-5124.* The ID's center is around Jackson Street and Fifth Avenue.

University District. Flanked by Union Bay on one side and Portage Bay on the other, brick buildings and wooded paths adorn the University of Washington campus. On the northwestern corner of the campus at 15th Avenue NE and NE 45th Street, is the **Thomas Burke Memorial Museum,** Washington's natural history and anthropology museum. At 15th Avenue NE and NE 41st Street, the **Henry Art Gallery** presents nineteenth- and twentieth-century paintings and textiles. The adjacent **Washington Park Arboretum** is a serene expanse of flowers, plants, wildlife, and the lovely Japanese Garden where tea ceremonies are performed periodically. Student life revolves around the coffeehouses and shops on University Way NE ("the Ave"). *Visitors Information Center is on University Way NE and NE Campus Parkway; (206) 543-9198.*

■ MUSEUMS

Seattle Art Museum. A monumental terra-cotta-trimmed structure with a grand marble interior. Guarding the entrance is the enormous "Hammering Man" sculpture. Exhibits include Native American, African, Oceanic, and pre-Columbian art. The extraordinary Asian collection is housed in a separate building located in Volunteer Park at 14th Avenue and E. Prospect. *100 University Street (between First and Second); (206) 625-8900 or (206) 654-3100.*

Museum of Flight. Full-size aircraft from every period in the history of aviation are on exhibit here. Boeing's original building, the Red Barn, is also on the premises, displaying historical photographs, artifacts, and aircraft. Visitors may sit in a cockpit, examine rare fighter planes, watch aviation videos, and construct model airplanes. *A 15-minute drive south of downtown on I-5. From exit 158 turn right on E. Marginal Way South. 9404 E. Marginal Way South (Boeing Field); (206) 764-5720.*

In Seattle's transformation from frontier backwater into twentieth-century metropolis, hills have been scraped away or hosed into the bay, gullies and tidelands filled, seawalls built, and finally, most of the city paved and stitched together with new streets and elevated freeways.

Today, glass and steel monoliths rise from thick, gray fog banks, seagulls drift like ghosts between the downtown office towers and disappear in the low cloud mass. The lugubrious whale-honk of a ferry horn sounds somewhere beyond the shrouded waterfront as clean-cut citizens in Eddie Bauer raincoats clutch briefcases and paper cups of cafe latte, and wait for traffic lights to change.

From the ferry landing at Colman Dock, it is a very short walk to the original nineteenth-century center of the city, **Pioneer Square**—a name given both to the triangular cobblestone park on First Avenue, where James Street meets Yesler Way, and to the core of ornate brick and stone buildings at the south end of downtown, built mostly in the decade following the Seattle fire of 1889. The triangular "square" itself marks the site where Henry Yesler built the first steam-driven sawmill on the shore of Puget Sound (before landfill drove the waters of Elliott

The regrading of St. James Street allowed for the construction of a cable car system. (above, Museum of History and Industry, Seattle). The Space Needle, built for the 1962 world's fair, has come to symbolize Seattle's growth since World War II (right).

Bay back to their present line of entrenchment). First Avenue, then called Front Street, was the waterfront in those days, and logs cut from settlers' claims on the forested ridge above town were skidded down what is now Yesler Way to the mill. There, they were sawed into boards that built the embryonic city of Seattle.

Yesler Way was the original Skid Road, a name that most of the country has long since corrupted to "skid row." ("Skidroad was and is that part of any Western town that caters to the needs and urges of loggers, miners, fishermen, harvest hands, and all other itinerant workers," Stewart Holbrook explained in a 1956 book entitled *The Columbia.* "It was usually near the railroad depot and the waterfront, a place of employment offices, small hotels, flophouses, burlesque theaters, saloons, missions, fancy-houses, and a Wobbly Hall.")

Although Yesler's mill was never a great financial success, it was the heart of early Seattle, and most of her settlers' sole source of cash. Seattle's pioneers sold timber cleared from their land claims to the mill, and many earned a living there, working alongside their neighbors, men of the local Duwamish and Suquamish tribes. Yesler's cookhouse—a squat, shake-roofed structure of heavy, dove-tailed timbers—was built beside the mill in 1853, and served as Seattle's first community center, courthouse, jail, and church.

From the years of the Great Depression until the early 1970s, this area was a squalid and neglected district where the city's castoffs congregated. In the late 1960s, "developers" planned to level these old buildings—many by then abandoned and decrepit—and turn Pioneer Square into a downtown parking lot. Fortunately, citizens' groups pressured the city to create the Pioneer Square Historic District and established legal guidelines for restoring and preserving the old face of the city.

Today, Pioneer Square is one of the most vital and interesting places in the city. Its immaculately preserved historic front gives a sense of continuity, of historical connection to an area packed with art galleries, bookstores, and missions serving the needy (thus, a high concentration, too, of homeless people and panhandlers). Office workers process forms between walls built by the city's pioneers, and winos sleep on park benches, while locals and tourists buy pints of microbrews in buildings that once housed saloons frequented by prospectors bound for the Klondike. Elliott Bay Book Company, at the corner of First and Main, is one of the area's most venerable hangouts: five rooms of books, two stories of exposed brick walls, creaky wood floors, literary readings nightly, and a downstairs cafe, make this one of the most popular places in the area.

Visitors who want a taste of local color can sign up for the private tour of **Underground Seattle,** which starts at Doc Maynard's Public House at First Avenue and James Street, across from Pioneer Square.

The **totem pole** that stands today in Pioneer Square is a replica of the original which was stolen from a "deserted" Tlingit village on Tongass Island, in southeast Alaska, by a "goodwill committee" of prominent Seattle citizens in 1899. A souvenir-hunting expedition, sponsored by the Seattle *Post-Intelligencer,* forayed up the coast aboard the steamer *City of Seattle,* and while the residents of the Tongass village were away fishing, three of the ship's crew put ashore and hacked down the beautifully carved 60-foot pole ("just like you'd chop down a tree") from its place in a line of totems facing the beach at the edge of the village.

When the pole was destroyed by a Seattle arsonist 40 years later, its charred

This shantytown (or "Hooverville") was a result of poverty caused by the Great Depression. The photo was taken in 1937. (University of Washington Libraries)

The ornate shelter leading to an underground restroom in Pioneer Square.

body was returned to Alaska, where Tlingit artists carved a replacement.

Near the pole on the south edge of Pioneer Square, an ornate steel-framed shelter with an arched roof of glass panels was built in 1905 to shelter the entrance of a great underground restroom. The shelter was renovated in 1973 with funds from United Parcel Service (UPS). (UPS, incidentally, was founded in 1907, at the site of nearby Waterfall Garden, at Second Avenue South and South Main Street, where the sight and sound of falling water shut out the rest of the city.)

At the edge of cobblestoned **Occidental Park,** on Occidental Avenue South between South Washington and South Main streets, two lascivious wooden figures several meters high face each other across an enclosure of shrubs. The welcoming spirit of the Kwakiutl, cedar breasts sagging, stretches out her arms to Bear, who stands before her like an enormous begging dog.

Visitors intrigued by Seattle's role in the Gold Rush of 1897 will enjoy the exhibits at the Seattle unit of the **Klondike Gold Rush National Historic Park,** in the Union Trust Annex, built in 1901 at 117 South Main Street.

A few blocks south on South King Street, the **Kingdome** usually stands alone in its wasteland of chain-link-fenced parking lots, but when the Mariners are playing baseball or the Seahawks are playing football, the lots fill up and on-street parking disappears.

Inland from the Kingdome and Pioneer Square, the **International District** holds the city's largest concentration of Asian restaurants, food stores, and social services. Asian Americans and even most Asian immigrants live elsewhere now—

and Asian restaurants can be found all over the city—but some of the older, chiefly Chinese, social institutions remain. People still pour in to visit local restaurants and shops. International District businesses have been expanding eastward in recent years. Many of the new stores, restaurants, and professional offices are Vietnamese.

A short walk north from Colman Dock along First Avenue takes you to the new **Seattle Art Museum,** a flashy post-modernist design by Robert Venturi. The grand entrance hall is connected to state-of-the-art galleries by an approach that makes you think you've wandered through the service entrance. The tall, perpetual motion sculpture outside, *Hammering Man,* was made by a Connecticut sculptor who has a kind of Hammering Man industry. It has had its share of adventures. When the museum was first installing it, the huge steel form toppled over— fortunately not flattening any workers or pedestrians, but doing enough damage so that the sculpture had to be shipped back to Connecticut for repairs before the installers could try again. Then, in a guerrilla raid in the dark of night, local artists fastened a huge ball and chain to one leg. Some people liked the idea, but the museum promptly removed the fetters.

Actresses from the Hwa-Shen Peking Opera dressed in full costume during a visit to the city.

Beyond the museum (and First Avenue's few remaining pawn shops), **Pike Place Market** brings farmers and artisans, stores, and restaurants together in an institution justly considered the soul of downtown Seattle. The market began in 1907 as a way to bring farmer and buyer together without enriching the middleman. It almost ended around 1970, when the city of Seattle decided to replace the market—vital but run down—with a big urban renewal project. These plans were derailed by the single-minded opposition of a local architecture professor, Victor Steinbrueck (who is now memorialized by a grassy park at the market's north end) and a grassroots citizens' campaign. In 1971, Seattle voters passed an initiative to save the market.

At that time, the market was seedy, as well as vital, and some people had trouble adjusting to the new era of civic concern. Shortly after the market was saved from urban renewal, but before it was renovated, two elderly women who ran market businesses were chatting at the counter of a cafe on the east side of Pike Place. The counter and a row of old stools took up most of the space. Irene, who owned the place, made Swedish pancakes for breakfast. At lunch, she served roast beef sandwiches; each morning, she put a sirloin tip roast in the oven and cooked it slowly, at 275 degrees, until noon, when she cut thick slices and served them on bread,

Pike Place Market in 1915. (Museum of History and Industry, Seattle)

The market remains the best place to buy fruits, vegetables, and fresh seafood in the city.

accompanied by home-canned vegetables she grew herself in a big garden south of town. In the spring, when the young plants in her garden were vulnerable to slugs, she'd go home after a long day on her feet, pick up a flashlight and an old kitchen knife, and go out in the dark to kill the slugs, one by one. Irene and her friend, who sold cut-rate poultry nearby, were discussing the fact that the Market had just been made into a historical district. They were incredulous. "Hell," snorted one, "there ain't nothing historic down here . . . except *us!*"

The renovated market—today covering seven acres—is flourishing. Shoppers and browsers wander in and out of the enclosed shops and fresh air stalls (no national chains allowed!) or hike the Pike Place Hillclimb from First and Pike to the waterfront. Piles of fruits and vegetables, cut flowers and bonsai plants, butcher shops and fried chicken stands, French, Russian, Greek, and Turkish pastries, coffee by the pound and coffee by the cup, taverns and cafes hardly exhaust your possibilities. Street musicians and cops on bicycles dot the crowds. Amid careful arrangements of fish and crabs, hardy fellows toss whole salmon back and forth. If the immigrant ladies in black dresses who once shopped here for dried codfish are mostly gone, their modern counterparts now shop for an array of old-world olive oils, wines, and cheeses as well as wild mushrooms and Asian greens. Despite all of the changes and new vitality, the market has retained a few of its old shops. **Three Girls Bakery,** founded in 1912, sells wonderful breads and pastries, while **De Laurenti Specialty Foods Market,** founded in 1928, is a classic Italian deli. Newer arrivals include **Jack's Fish Spot,** where you can pick up steamers at the counter, and **El Mercado Latino,** which offers 25 kinds of peppers. Pike Place Market remains the main attraction—indeed, except for the museum and the turn-of-the-century architecture of Pioneer Square, one of the most appealing attractions—in downtown Seattle.

Just a few blocks up Pine Street from the market lies Seattle's shopping and hotel district, with popular **Westlake Park** at its heart—at Fifth and Pine. Seattleites gathered at the park's proscenium arch when Bill Clinton came in 1994; they come here more commonly to stroll through the "waterfall" fountain.

■ THE REGRADE AND BELLTOWN

North of Pike Place Market, the streets run almost level to Seattle Center and steep, primarily residential Queen Anne Hill. The Regrade hasn't always been so flat. It hasn't always been the Regrade.

Seattle is a city of hills, streets climbing steeply or plunging unexpectedly down to the waters of Elliott Bay, Lake Union, and Lake Washington. At the turn of the century, the passengers of horse-drawn streetcars often had to get out and push to make it up the steeper parts of streets like Madison and Jackson. In those days, the rounded cone of Denny Hill rose 140 feet above what is today the flat Regrade neighborhood of Belltown.

The missing hill is a non-monument to city engineer Reginald Thomson, who wanted Seattle's downtown to stretch to the base of Queen Anne Hill and become one continuous, accessible business district. Unfortunately, Denny Hill was in the way, so in 1902 workmen began sluicing Denny Hill—then a well-developed residential area crowned with a luxury hotel—into Elliott Bay, with water pumped from Lake Union.

From 1902 to 1930, 50 million cubic yards of dirt were hosed away, or scooped up and carried by conveyor belt to barges, then dumped into Puget Sound. After the first eight years of the project, the land north of Stewart Street and west of Westlake Avenue looked like the Dakota Badlands in miniature. Stark spires of earth thrust from the raw, flat ground like 100-foot stalagmites; abandoned houses perched on many of the unstable spires, teetering over the abyss before the hoses brought them tumbling down.

From 1911 to 1928, work on the Regrade stopped, and in that 17-year interim, what remained of the hill (east of Fifth Avenue) was a quiet island, floating above the city. No cars could get up there, and the grand old schoolhouse, the Catholic church, the funky houses, and unpaved streets surrounding wooded Denny Park (which then stood about 40 feet above its current location), existed in a sort of time warp.

The work of demolishing Denny Hill resumed in 1928, this time with steam shovels, and was finished less than two years later—just in time for the Great Depression. Despite Thomson's vision, downtown Seattle never has spread that far north. Today's Belltown—bounded by Queen Anne Hill, Pike Place Market, and First and Third avenues—is worth a visit, especially if you enjoy hippish boutiques, nightclubs, or taverns.

Beyond the Regrade, the **Seattle Center** was built for the 1962 world's fair.

A few property owners fought against the Regrade, with the result that their properties were left atop sluiced-away pinnacles. (Washington State Historical Society)

This 74-acre cluster of buildings and gardens has something for everyone. Sophisticated locals go there to attend plays, operas, and concerts at the new **Bagley Wright Theater.** They take their kids to hands-on exhibits, the IMAX theater, and big traveling shows at the **Pacific Science Center,** to the **Seattle Children's Museum** in the basement of the Center House, and to the carnival rides at the **Fun Forest** amusement park. They take prom dates and out-of-town visitors up the **Space Needle** to eat in the revolving restaurant, or just to admire the view. They go to pro basketball games at the **Coliseum** and join the crowds at the **Northwest Folklife Festival** and the annual **Bumbershoot** musical extravaganza. The Center is at its best for festivals—it was, after all, built for crowds—and Bumbershoot is the best of the festivals, bringing a tremendous variety of music to the Center for the entire Labor Day weekend. The Folklife Festival, perhaps the largest

Seattle glass artist Dale Chihuly (foreground, right) is known worldwide for his glass sculptures. (photo by Russell Johnson, courtesy Dale Chihuly)

Seattle master yacht builder Frank Prothro and his grandson work on a boat hull.

in the United States, fills the Center every Memorial Day weekend.

The **monorail,** hailed at the time as the transportation system of the future but never developed as more than another carnival ride, carries people between the Seattle Center and Westlake Mall, on the northern edge of downtown, in 90 seconds.

■ FIRST AND CAPITOL HILLS

East of downtown, across the freeway, rise First and Capitol hills. One pleasant way to walk across to either is through the shrubbery, flowers, and waterfalls at **Freeway Park,** a garden sanctuary built atop hectic Interstate 5.

The more southerly **First Hill** is sometimes called "Pill Hill" because it holds the city's largest concentration of hospitals, clinics, and medical offices. The **Frye**

Art Museum stands on the western slope, Seattle University covers a good deal of the eastern slope, and there are plenty of apartments, but the dominant character for many blocks is medical.

First Hill hasn't always been like that. John Robinson, writing in the *Seattle Weekly,* has described the turn-of-the-century neighborhood as:

> *A* peaceful, quiet enclave of unpaved, tree-lined streets, where lily ponds flourished, rose gardens bloomed, and children could safely ride their ponies at full gallop. Here, in vast, drafty wooden houses, which they had begun to build after the fire levelled most of the town below, lived the city's ascendancy. . . . Families knew each other almost too well. . . . It was a slow-moving life of tennis parties and Sunday night buffet suppers.

One of the few surviving artifacts of that time is the **Stimson-Green mansion,** built by the pioneer lumberman and downtown real estate developer C. D. Stimson. Like many other people who started Washington forest products companies in the late nineteenth century, Stimson came from a Midwestern lumber family. He built a mill in Ballard, across the ship canal from Queen Anne Hill, and at first he lived on Queen Anne, riding to work every morning across a low wooden bridge with his lunch behind him on the saddle. He and his family moved into the First Hill house in 1900. Stimson—who had only one arm but still managed to drive the first automobile in Seattle and tip his hat to people simultaneously—eventually built a house in the exclusive Highlands area farther north, and the banker Joshua Green bought the mansion on First Hill. Green lived there for the rest of his life—and he lived to be 100. The mansion has been restored and is now run by one of C. D. Stimson's granddaughters for weddings and other social functions.

(Stimson's daughter, Dorothy Bullitt, who lived in the mansion as a girl, acquired Seattle's—and the Northwest's—first television station in 1949. She founded and for many years ran the King Broadcasting Company, which eventually owned television and radio stations in Seattle, Portland, Spokane, Boise, San Francisco, and Hawaii, and cable systems scattered through the west and Midwest. Her daughters, who've endowed many environmental organizations, finally sold the company in 1992.)

Capitol Hill, just north of First Hill, is in many ways Seattle's most interesting neighborhood. Capitol Hill offers some of Seattle's nicest old tree-lined residential streets, some of its best espresso, and Broadway, which for several blocks is the city's liveliest and most eclectic thoroughfare—and perhaps the only place in Seattle where restaurants are often packed at 9 P.M. on a weeknight. A variety of local institutions stand on the hill, including Seattle Central Community College, the Cornish School of the Arts, and REI's main store. REI, the giant outdoor gear and clothing retailer, was founded in Seattle in 1938 by a local climber who wanted to make good European climbing gear affordable to himself and his friends. Its original inventory rested on spare shelves in a downtown garage. It is now the largest cooperative in the United States.

Another outdoor clothing giant, Eddie Bauer, is also a Seattle firm. The original Eddie Bauer was running a Seattle sporting goods store in the 1920s when he got chilled on a fishing trip and nearly died of hypothermia. He figured it would be a good idea to have clothing that was lightweight but very warm, so he started making garments filled with down. By the late 1930s, he once told a reporter, he was "putting money away ass over teakettle," and after World War II, he started selling garments through the mail.

The excellent **Seattle Asian Art Museum** and a turn-of-the-century conservatory stand in **Volunteer Park,** well north of REI. The park also contains a reservoir and a climbable old brick water tower, and it provides great views west over Puget Sound. The big old house standing near the park at 712 11th Avenue East is today a bed-and-breakfast, but was once the home of Bertha Landes, who in 1926 became the first woman elected mayor of a major American city. Previously president of the city council, Landes pushed for control, if not abolition, of the prostitution, gambling, and other vice that flourished in the red-light district around the current site of the Kingdome, and for strengthening the publicly owned electric utility and streetcar system. She only lasted one term.

Martial arts movie megastar Bruce Lee lies in the large **Lakeview Cemetery** north of the park, and just north of Lakeview, in the little Grand Army cemetery, Civil War veterans are buried.

St. Mark's Cathedral, a blocky brick and concrete fortress with high, arched windows and a shiny copper roof, perches on the northwest edge of Capitol Hill, above a steep, ferny embankment studded with ivy-choked maples. Its bare, cavernous interior—soaring, vaulted ceilings, walls of raw concrete—is impressive and austere in its massive dimensions, and inspires an awed hush. The interior was left unfinished to preserve the brilliant acoustics for which the building is known.

Near the Montlake Bridge on the Southern bank of the Lake Washington Ship Canal, the **Seattle Museum of History and Industry** preserves pioneer artifacts, Boeing's first aircraft, and historical pictures of nineteenth-century Seattle. Nature trails branch out from here along Lake Washington's shore, and to the **Washington Park Arboretum.**

■ LAKE UNION

West of St. Mark's, between Queen Anne and Capitol hills, lies Lake Union. Once a center of ship building and repair, the lake is still home to commercial shipyards, a lot of marina space, and hundreds of houseboats, as well as some pretty generic waterfront restaurants. The Ship Canal, leading west from the lake to Puget Sound and east into Lake Washington, put the "union" in Lake Union, which provided a bridge between Seattle's two largest liquid bodies in the days when water was the shortest distance between two points, and everything moved by boat. Today, the Ship Canal remains a viable commercial waterway, but to most, the lake is an aesthetic pleasure: a waterfront view. Restaurants, shipyards, office buildings, and private marinas crowd the shore, while fishing boats, yachts, federal research vessels, and luxury houseboats share moorage. Tiers of condominiums climb the hillsides on both sides of the lake. The houseboats moored along the eastern shore, once a kind of floating low-rent district, have gotten more upscale, but there are still patches of weeds and blackberries along the lakefront.

The city government has been encouraging the development of south Lake Union into a center of high-tech industry. The new headquarters of the Fred Hutchinson Cancer Research Center, one of the nation's leading cancer research centers, stands on Eastlake Avenue. "The Hutch" is best known for bone marrow transplants, for which people come from all over the world. In 1990, the Hutch's longtime research director, E. Donnell Thomas, shared a Nobel Prize in medicine for developing bone marrow transplantation.

At the north end of Lake Union stand the massive, rusted pipes and cracking towers of **Gas Works Park.** The dark cluster of derelict industrial forms rises from a peninsula of golf-course-green grass that makes the park an emerald island in the dark waters of the lake. The old gasworks was built in 1904 to convert bargeloads of coal into gas that was used to light Seattle's streets and homes. It ran until 1956.

(right) Japanese garden in the Washington Park Arboretum.

SEATTLE SOUNDS AND SCENES

Before 1990 or so, Seattle's biggest claim to fame among rockers and other rebels was that Jimi Hendrix was born there—in 1942. The music and nightclub scene was small if not quiet, attracting little outside notice. Then Sub Pop records signed Nirvana, and—fueled on the energy of Seattle's frustrated twenty-nothings and a lot of microbrew (no lattes, please)—the Seattle sound, "grunge," took off.

So what about this word, "grunge"? Some aficionados will tell you the term's been haphazardly applied to almost every rock band—as long as it's loud—out of the Pacific Northwest, especially Seattle. Soundgarden, Nirvana, Pearl Jam, Candlebox, Mudhoney, to name but a few. Others in the know, like Seattle bassist Duff McKagan, saw something in common among these bands. Not a grunger himself (he plays with Guns & Roses), McKagan nonetheless explained the sound in a 1992 interview with *Rolling Stone*: "Seattle's grungy. People are into rock & roll and into noise, and they're building airplanes all the time, and there's a lot of noise, and there's rain and musty garages. Musty garages create a certain noise." Listening to Nirvana's "Smells Like Teen Spirit" will give you an idea of the driving and aggressive but muddied sound McKagan was talking about. Or perhaps "grunge" refers to the grime left on your jeans after you visit Jimi Hendrix's grave. In any case, Seattle bands probably didn't mind being lumped together as "grungers" because, in addition to describing a sound, the word seemed to rankle against their city's then squeaky clean image.

The word stuck. Record labels and promoters latched on to the handle, chatted up the "grunge phenomenon," and brought national attention (and dollars) to the Seattle music scene. Fortunately, the national media spotlight (made even larger by Kurt Cobain's 1994 suicide) didn't sap the city's energy or encourage derivative bands—it fostered enthusiasm among musicians and audiences alike for new groups and innovative sounds. According to Tower Records buyer Damon Schroader, the music scene in Seattle is thriving, post grunge hype. Musicians whose bands are already signed with major labels sometimes mix and match to perform—take the Mad Season, which includes Alice in Chains' Layne Staley and Pearl Jam's Mike McCready—or have side projects, like Mudhoney guitarist Mark Arm and Bloodloss. Local hotshots can often be spotted at their colleagues' shows.

Even better, crowds attending lesser-known acts, whether rock, reggae, or rap, are likely to be larger today than they would have been a few years ago. And as bands become more diverse, so do audiences. Especially noteworthy are the all- or mostly female bands, who pull in hordes of "riot grrrls" (recognizable by their plastic barrettes and hobnail boots) from the city and nearby colleges.

To catch the newest-latest Seattle band (or just rub elbows with them), check out the following clubs and taverns. For more information on local bands and shows, pick up an issue of *Rocket* magazine.

Comet Tavern. A youngish, flannel-shirt crowd fills the boardinghouse tables, throws darts, shoots pool, and (for some reason) pins dollar bills to the high ceiling of this smoky pub. 922 E. Pike St.; (206) 323-9853.

Crocodile Cafe. This may be your best bet to catch an up-and-coming band. And it's cheap. Touring musicians are sometimes in the crowd, too, so keep your eyes peeled. 2200 Second Ave.; (206) 441-5611.

Frontier Room. It seems there are way too many people squeezing into the tables at this Seattle scenester hang-out. If you want a drink, you'd best belly up to the bar. 2203 First Ave.; (206) 441-3377.

The Off Ramp. Where Seattle's hopefuls hope to get a gig. A spacious room with a cafe in front; 50-cent breakfast at 1:30 (A.M.). 109 Eastlake Ave. East; (206) 628-0232.

Re-bar. Live music once a week, other nights the DJ rules. A gathering place for musicians and hipsters alike. 1114 Howell St.; (206) 233-9873.

RKCNDY. Say "Rock Candy." The city's best warehouse-style club, where big local and medium-big touring bands play. 1812 Yale Ave.; (206) 623-0470.

In addition to alternative rock clubs and hang-outs, Seattle is also home to some great dance clubs. The city's lesbian and gay community has several hip spots.

Neighbours. A largely gay dance club now becoming universally popular. This club (like some others) acquired its liquor license by calling itself a restaurant. Hence the free buffet. Great for after hours. 1509 Broadway East; (206) 324-5358.

Night Mary's. Very hip and mostly for women—but men are allowed. Live music (even ballroom occasionally!) midweek. 401 Broadway East; (206) 325-6565.

Vogue. Belltown's first groovy club, with an interesting mix of patrons. Live music midweek, dancing on weekends. 2018 First Ave.; (206) 443-0673.

Weathered Wall. Cool nightclub in an interesting space—it's a hotel district storefront. Originally a gay club; now it's pretty mixed. 1921 Fifth Ave.; (206) 448-5688.

—Julia Dillon

In the early 1970s, some residents who had lived with the smoke and stench wanted the by-then-silent gasworks torn down, but instead, the city of Seattle made it into a park. Soon a popular playground for children, Gas Works Park came under a cloud when toxic by-products of its original incarnation were found in the soil. The park's future was in doubt for a while, but the contaminated soil was dug up, trucked away, and replaced. Today, toxic waste is hardly even a memory. Children play on a covered jungle gym formed of machinery from the defunct gasworks, painted bright red and blue and orange. Above a grassy knoll in the park, dragon kites loop and plunge and stream skyward, climbing the wind that comes racing up the lake. Sailboats, yachts, and tugs cruise by. Across the water, the downtown skyline rises beyond the southern shore.

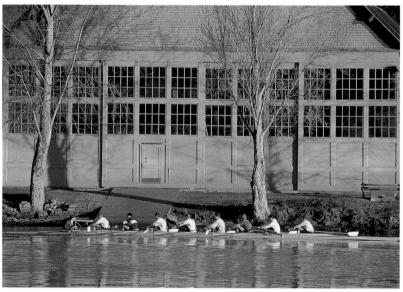

University of Washington crew team practices on Lake Washington (above). Flying kites in Gas Works Park with the original gas works towers in the background (right).

■ NORTH OF THE SHIP CANAL

Beyond the locks (officially the **Hiram M. Chittenden Locks**) that raise boats
from sea level to the level of Lake Union, lies **Ballard,** once a separate city populated largely by Scandinavian immigrants. It also remains a center of the fishing
fleet; you can see boats from the streets of downtown Ballard. Actually, the largest
single number of boats is tied up at Fishermen's Terminal, just across the ship
canal, but marine supply houses crowd the industrial areas of Ballard. Seattle is the
center not only for fishing boats that chase the dwindling salmon populations of
Puget Sound, but also for the Alaskan fishing fleet, which has voyaged north
annually to catch Alaskan salmon since the end of World War I. Halibut boats
make the northward voyage, too, as do crabbers and the big bottom trawlers that
scoop pollack from the depths of the Bering Sea.

The colorful neighborhood of **Fremont,** east of Ballard and across the ship
canal from lovely Queen Anne Hill, has been somewhat "countercultural" for

The launching of a new lumber trade schooner, the Minnie A. Caine, *was captured in the
lens of photographer Asahel Curtis in 1900. (Washington State Historical Society, Tacoma)*

decades: the community's motto, in fact, is "De Libertus Quirkus"—the freedom to be peculiar. It hosts a small concentration of clubs, restaurants, cafes, clothing stores, and probably the best-known street sculpture in Seattle. The bronze pedestrians of *Waiting for the Interurban* have been waiting at a bus stop near the Fremont Bridge since the 1970s, and the more recent Fremont troll munches Volkswagens under a freeway overpass.

Beyond Fremont and gentrifying Wallingford lies the **University District**, home of Washington's largest school, the **University of Washington**. The commercial streets run heavily to used bookstores and Asian fast-food outlets. The campus is lovely, albeit less bucolic than it was when the ratio of buildings to trees was lower. Once a kind of glorified high school on a hill in what is now downtown Seattle (an 1881 ad for the school touted its invigorating climate and assured prospective students that there was no malaria), the modern UW (or "U-Dub" as it's commonly called) rakes in more federal research and training money than any other public university in the United States. Its more sterile lower campus, between the main campus and the water, is where a lot of the research action takes place: the hospital, the excellent medical school, and marine studies department are all there. The university is considered one of the best places in the country to study nursing or acting. Its professors include Nobel Prize–winning scientist Hans Dehmelt, the first person to actually observe a "quantum shift"; and National Book Award–winning novelist Charles Johnson (*Middle Passage*). Pulitzer Prize–winning poet Theodore Roethke, who taught here from 1948 until his death in 1963, has been followed by a succession of other first-rate poets including the late James Wright, and Richard Kenney, who in 1994 won a $50,000 Latham Prize. The departments of molecular biology, neurophysiology, and atmospheric sciences are all considered strong. The university also is known for large basic classes, big-time college football, and highly publicized athletic scandals.

■ LAKE WASHINGTON AND EASTERN SUBURBS

Whenever network television covers a University of Washington football game, the camera pulls back at some point and gives the national audience a panoramic view of Lake Washington shimmering in the sunlight, its blue waters dotted with sailboats and yachts. The lake was carved by the same great glacier that gouged out the basin of Puget Sound. Completion of a ship canal to Puget Sound in 1916 was

supposed to make Lake Washington a center for building and repairing ships. It didn't, although wooden ships were built there during World War I and even later, and a small fleet of Alaskan whalers wintered in Kirkland for a number of years. Now, the lake is used primarily by pleasure boats, and it forms a kind of watery front yard for swank houses. One can't see the old-growth forest (dislodged by an ancient earthquake) that stands under the deep water by the eastern shore. And one can no longer see the sea-monster that was spotted occasionally by water-skiers and others in the 1970s and early 1980s. The mystery of the monster was solved when people found the carcass of a huge, ancient sturgeon floating in the lake. Sturgeon are long-lived, as well as large, and this one had evidently been turned loose at the end of the Alaska-Yukon-Pacific Exposition, where it had been displayed in a pond in 1909.

Across the now-monsterless lake from Seattle, **Bellevue** is still stigmatized by many Seattle residents as the epitome of bourgeois suburbia. There's plenty of pleasant suburban housing in Bellevue and nearby communities—plus some very elegant houses along Lake Washington—but pure suburbia marked a relatively brief interlude in Bellevue's existence. Originally, Bellevue was a farming community east of the lake, locally famous for its annual summer strawberry festival.

Nearby Newcastle was a coal-mining center in the 1800s, and while the big mining operations pulled out after the turn of the century, independent miners kept working the seams of coal into the early 1960s. Cougar Mountain, at the eastern edge of modern Bellevue, was honeycombed with mine tunnels.

When the first floating bridge was completed across Lake Washington in 1940, pastoral Bellevue, at the eastern end of the bridge, was suddenly on the main line. After World War II, suburban housing blossomed in the fields and pastures, and Bellevue became a classic Eisenhower-era bedroom suburb. It is still growing tract houses and mini-malls, but in the 1980s it also became a major employment center with its own highrise office buildings, and large numbers of people started commuting *to* Bellevue to work. The skyscrapers still have a rather odd, disconnected look—there's no conventional city around them—rather like Phoenix with trees, but Bellevue is the state's fourth largest city and the center of the software and other high-tech industries that have developed east of the lake.

The heart of the local software industry is, of course, Microsoft's headquarters campus in **Redmond**. There isn't much to see, even if you drive through, but Microsoft makes Redmond the absolute epicenter of world software development.

(previous pages) A stunning vista of downtown Seattle across Elliott Bay.

A group of miners poses at the entrance of a Renton Cooperative Coal Mine in 1895.
(Museum of History and Industry, Seattle)

At the south end of the lake lies **Renton**, a nineteenth- and early twentieth-century coal town that has become a late twentieth-century Boeing town. Mining started there in 1873 and continued through World War I. Early in this century, a 150-foot-high slag heap caught fire and smoldered for years, putting the community under a permanent cloud. Boeing started making planes there during World War II and has done so ever since at a plant on the southern shore of Lake Washington.

The first coal mined at Renton was taken down the Black River to the Duwamish and then to Elliott Bay. Salmon ran up the Black, and both Indians and early generations of non-Indian settlers used it as a thoroughfare. The Duwamish Indians had a winter village beside the river, an outlet from Lake Washington. When the Lake Washington Ship Canal opened in 1916, however, the lake suddenly had a lower outlet. Water gushed out, the lake level dropped nine feet, and the head of the Black River was left high and dry. The river simply disappeared. Fish flopped desperately in pools of water in the otherwise dry river bed; people gathered them in gunny sacks. Today, there is virtually no sign that the Black River ever existed—and most people probably don't know that it ever did.

■ BOEING

Between I-5 and US 99, on the banks of the Duwamish River stands the headquarters of Boeing, the world's largest manufacturer of aircraft. Boeing started in 1916, when William Boeing, an heir to Midwestern lumber money who had set up shop here to finish a yacht, decided to build airplanes. He built wood-and-fabric aircraft at first—his very first was a seaplane that made its maiden flight from Lake Union.

He also founded United Airlines, which the federal government forced Boeing to unload for antitrust reasons. Boeing's passenger jets are flown all over the world; the company is the state's largest employer, dominating Seattle's economy.

Boeing's back yard makes an ideal site for an aircraft museum. Even non-museum-goers get a kind of show as they drive by East Marginal Way South, off Interstate 5: freshly painted jets lined up waiting for buyers to fly them away; an occasional bulging AWACS radar plane; new jets going up for test flights over the Cascades and the Sound. If you're game for more, stop by the **Museum of Flight**, at 9404 East Marginal Way South, for a history of U.S. and Pacific Rim flight.

■ ALONG THE DUWAMISH

From Boeing north to downtown Seattle, the setting is mostly industrial. The Duwamish River is still—incredibly—a salmon stream, but its lower reaches are lined with shipyards, warehouses, and cement plants. At the mouth of the river where it enters Puget Sound, the big orange gantry cranes load containers onto oceangoing ships, and container trucks heading to and from the docks join the car traffic that zooms overhead on the high bridge, visible from a ferry deck in Elliott Bay.

The high bridge, completed in the early 1980s, has a remarkable history of bizarre coincidence and outright scandal. In the early 1970s, when all traffic to or from West Seattle crossed two old drawbridges built before World War II, a bond issue to build a high bridge was presented to Seattle voters. They rejected it, but a freighter rammed into one of the open drawbridges, permanently jamming it in a raised position. Senator Warren Magnuson, by then the second most senior member of the U. S. Senate, corralled federal money for a grandiose new bridge.

The new bridge soars grandly over the Duwamish. Below, Indians still set nets to catch returning salmon and other fishermen drop hooks and lines into the murky river mouth to catch bottom fish.

From the bridge that soars above the river mouth, on a clear day you can see the Olympic Mountains rise a mile and a half above Puget Sound's western shore, and you may ponder the porpoises that occasionally play in the bow waves of state ferries, or the pods of killer whales that sometimes swim down from the San Juans. On a rainy day, the mountains disappear and you see only shades of gray. If the sky is merely overcast, as it often is, the mountains may appear and disappear in the mist. The trees look dark on the slopes of West Seattle and Queen Anne Hill. A cold wind blows off the water. Whether you're up on the bridge or on the deck of a ferry heading toward Colman Dock, it's probably a good day for a cup of coffee.

Sunset over Puget Sound and the Olympic Mountains.

OLYMPIC PENINSULA
AND PACIFIC COAST

THE NORTHWESTERNMOST PART OF THE CONTINGUOUS UNITED STATES, the Olympic Peninsula juts north between the Pacific Ocean and Puget sound. Heavily glaciated, never crossed by any road, the Olympic Mountains form the peninsula's 8,000-foot-high spine. Short, swift rivers radiate from the mountains to the Pacific on the west, the Strait of Juan de Fuca on the north, and Hood Canal on the east. In west-facing valleys, the continent's only major temperate rain forests grow within a day's hike of glacial ice and the weathered rock of Pacific beaches. Olympic National Park, which protects the mountains and rain forests of the peninsula's core, also contains the nation's longest wilderness beach outside Alaska.

If you travel to the Olympic Peninsula from downtown Seattle, a car ferry will take you to Bainbridge Island or Bremerton on the western shore of Puget Sound. Here you drive off the ferry, and begin your trip north and west.

It's hard to believe that **Bainbridge Island,** now chiefly a high-rent suburb, was a logging and shipbuilding center in the late nineteenth century, and that its Port Blakely sawmill was perhaps the largest mill under one roof anywhere in the world. The *Politkofski,* an old Russian gunboat that became American when Alaska did in 1868, towed 110-foot logs to Port Blakely from the southern Sound, and schooners anchored near the mill to load lumber for ports all over the world.

Bainbridge Island, a half-hour ferry ride across Elliott Bay, is a popular and relaxing day's excursion from Seattle. The quiet harbor town ("Cabot Cove without the bodies," a "Murder She Wrote" fan calls it) and its main attractions, **Bainbridge Island Winery** and **Eagle Harbor Waterfront Park,** are easily explored by foot. Taking the car along the ferry is warranted, however, for drives to the island's two state parks and beaches and to the **Bloedel Reserve,** a 150-acre private sanctuary of landscaped gardens and nature trails.

On much of the island, homes are far between, and the road—dotted with leisurely cyclists—travels through a thick forest of fir, alder, and maple. The island offers **Fay Bainbridge State Park** in the northeast and **Fort Ward State Park** in the south; both have beaches and picnic areas.

A high climber tops a tree which will be used as a spar pole for cable logging in this 1923 Asahel Curtis photograph. (Washington State Historical Society, Tacoma)

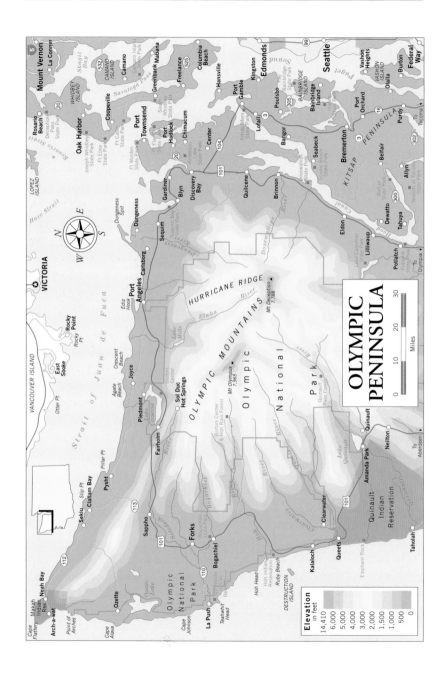

OLYMPIC PENINSULA

Elevation
in feet

14,410
6,000
5,000
4,000
3,000
2,000
1,500
1,000
500
0

Miles

0   10   20   30

■ KITSAP PENINSULA

Cross the Agate Pass bridge from Bainbridge Island and you'll find yourself on the Kitsap Peninsula. The **grave of Chief Seattle**, for whom Seattle was named, overlooks Puget Sound at Suquamish on the Port Madison Indian reservation. As a boy, the future chief saw Capt. George Vancouver's ship, *Discovery,* sailing down Puget Sound, and as a tribal leader, he welcomed the first white settlers to Alki Point 59 years later. A few years later, in the city named for him, he made—or is supposed to have made—perhaps the greatest speech ever delivered in the Northwest. Seattle was speaking primarily to territorial governor Isaac Stevens. His speech was translated on the spot into the simplified Chinook jargon, from which it was translated into English 33 years later by Dr. Henry Smith, who had heard the original. Presumably, the ideas were Seattle's but at least most of the language was Smith's. "Undeniably majestic as it is," historian David Buerge has written, "Seattle's speech does not conform to what we know of the native speaking style of the Puget Sound region." Nevertheless, the speech attributed to Seattle is a masterpiece. The best-known passage reads:

> Every part of this soil is sacred in the estimation of my people. Every hillside, every valley, every plain and grove, has been hallowed by some sad or happy event in days long vanished. Even the rocks, which seem to be dumb and dead as they swelter in the sun along the silent shore, thrill with memories of stirring events connected with the lives of my people, and the very dust upon which you now stand responds more lovingly to their foot steps than to yours, because it is rich with the blood of our ancestors and our bare feet are conscious of the sympathetic touch. . . .

Chief Seattle is also known for promptly freeing his slaves when Abraham Lincoln issued the Emancipation Proclamation in 1863.

Nearby, along **Liberty Bay,** the town of **Poulsbo** plays up its Norwegian immigrant history. Its name means "Paul's Place" in Norwegian, and the town sponsors a Viking Fest in mid-May, the Skandia Midsommarfest in June, and the Yule Log Festival in November.

A fleet of abandoned gray warships rides perpetually at anchor in **Bremerton,** a Navy-yard town since the late nineteenth century. Its downtown retail shops have mostly fled to the huge mall at Silverdale, but the shipyard still repairs Navy vessels, and the mothballed fleet still rides at anchor in Sinclair Inlet. A direct car ferry connects the town with Seattle.

The old mill town of **Port Gamble** looks over the glacial fjord of Hood Canal on the far side of the Kitsap Peninsula. The New England character of the white frame buildings evokes the Maine backgrounds of the founders of the Pope and Talbot Company, which sold lumber in Gold Rush San Francisco and—looking for a West Coast source of raw material—built the first mill and the town of Port Gamble itself in the 1850s. The graveyard is filled with headstones of men who left New England or northern Europe to work and die on the shore of Hood Canal.

As you drive northwest on the floating bridge across the flat, blue water of Hood Canal, it's hard to imagine that 80-mile-per-hour winds sank this bridge's predecessor in 1979. As you head toward the tranquil, wooded shore and a hint of mountains to the west, it's even harder to believe that deep beneath the canal's surface, the ultimate military doomsday machines, Trident submarines, slip out to sea.

■ NORTHWEST OLYMPIC PENINSULA

The far shore belongs to the Olympic Peninsula, with its timber towns and the rain forests, mountains, and beaches of Olympic National Park. North lies **Port Townsend.** Everybody seems to like Port Townsend: the bookstores and restaurants in the late nineteenth-century brick buildings downtown; the ornate Victorian houses, many made into bed-and-breakfasts, on the bluff above; the picturesque old military post of **Fort Worden**—setting for *An Officer and a Gentleman*—where the officers' quarters and parade ground overlook the Strait of Juan de Fuca. The late science fiction writer Frank Herbert, author of the fabulously popular *Dune* series, lived here for years surrounded by *Dune* memorabilia, and for a while rumor had it that he had achieved self-sufficiency on six acres at the edge of town. He once said, "I love Port Townsend. It's just about the right size. People are very supportive. Extreme political views don't last long." Herbert was not the only writer attracted to Port Townsend; the town has a literary reputation, as well as an end-of-the-earth feeling fostered by the windswept bluffs and the long views out over the Strait.

The drive west from Port Townsend is alternately beautiful and depressing. Beautiful, because you can still glimpse the awesome forest landscapes of Washington's primeval past. Depressing, because the peninsula's modern inhabitants have harvested most of the big trees, and more recently have succumbed to the strip-mall development aesthetic. Stands of massive old cedar and fir still crowd the

---

SMALL FARM IN THE OLYMPICS

I'm not sure whether it was the cherry tree or the purple carpet of sweet violets flanking the funny silvery woodshed, or the fact that the place was so clean, not a scrap of rubbish, not a single tin can, but it suddenly lost its sinister deserted look and began to appear lonely but eager to make friends. A responsive little farm that with a few kindnesses in the way of windows and paint and clearing might soon be licking our hands.

—Betty MacDonald, *The Egg and I*, 1945

---

highway in places, and on a cloudy day, when their dark, shaggy forms loom in the fog, tendrils of mist swirl in your headlights and the sky is shrouded in gray, you could be motoring into a primordial jungle. In autumn, the red and yellow leaves of vine maple show among the evergreens; the carpet of fern and bunched grasses beneath the trees is glazed with moisture.

Other spots along this road resemble Christmas tree lots; signs proudly proclaim model tree farms. Clear-cut and reseeded a decade ago, these patches of scrappy fir and alder are choked with salal and bracken, and spotted with jagged stumps. In half a century or so they may indeed yield new crops of harvestable trees, but in the short term, all seems to be desolation.

The larger towns along US 101, scattered with Quickie Marts and fast food joints, can be distinguished from highway towns elsewhere in the West only by their proximity to the dark waters of the Strait of Juan de Fuca, to the north, and the steep Olympic peaks to the south.

Following side roads toward the mountains, you get a better sense of the area in bygone days. Modern ranch-style homes and bungalows are common, but so are the silvered cedar fence posts and decrepit, shake-roofed farm buildings of old-time homesteads. Rain-soaked pastures are punctuated here and there with ancient stumps six feet in diameter.

In addition to its unpronounceable name, **Sequim** (say "skwim") is noted for its burgeoning retirement population and its dry climate (it sits in the rain shadow of the Olympics). **Dungeness Spit,** claimed to be the largest natural sandspit in the world, juts into the Strait of Juan de Fuca. On a clear day, you can see Vancouver

Island to the north across the dark, frigid waters of the Strait. When it's cloudy, the sky, the waves, and the sand are painted in shades of gray, and the sun is a blurred, moon-size disk behind the fog. The spit extends northeast, curving in toward the eastward bay like the mandible of a giant beetle. Sea birds bob in the sheltered water. Sea lions cruise along the exposed western shore. Raked by the wind even on a sunny day, the huge sandspit runs five and a half miles from its base to the lighthouse at its tip. The coastal forest near the base and adjacent tidal zones are now under protection as part of the **Dungeness National Wildlife Refuge,** which today hosts some 250 bird species.

Pulp mills stand at the water's edge in **Port Angeles.** Logs are piled beside the main waterfront street, and logging trucks whip past on nearby highways. More blue-collar and less charming than Port Townsend, Port Angeles nevertheless attracted the late short story writer Raymond Carver and the poet Tess Gallagher. It stands right on the Strait, contains some good places to eat and stay, and serves as the main gateway to Olympic National Park and Vancouver Island.

Clam digging along Dungeness Spit (left). Deserted wharves and warehouses line the shores of the Olympic Peninsula (above).

■ OLYMPIC NATIONAL PARK

Olympic National Park encompasses more than 1,300 square miles of wilderness surrounding the Olympic Mountains—a massive, crumpled wall of rock forced up nearly 8,000 vertical feet from the sea. The slow and brutal collision of continental plates pushed the mountains upward, inch by inch, over millennia.

The land around the Olympic Mountains was first set aside as forest reserve in 1897. Twelve years later, President Theodore Roosevelt, in his last days in office, established the Mount Olympus National Monument as a sanctuary for the later-named Roosevelt elk. They had been hunted nearly to extinction for their teeth, which were used as watch fobs.

Under pressure from logging and mining interests, President Woodrow Wilson reduced the protected area by half in 1915, re-opening much of today's park to logging and homesteading. That ended in 1938, when Congress created the Olympic National Park, at the urging of local environmentalists and of Franklin Roosevelt, who had visited the area and had been shocked by what he called the "criminal devastation" of the forests. Since then, the park has been expanded to include the Queets and the Hoh river valleys. More recently, Congress added the coastal strip, the longest stretch of wilderness beach outside Alaska.

■ VISITING OLYMPIC NATIONAL PARK

In addition to its vast size and stunning scenery, Olympic is the most geographically diverse of our national parks. Crowned by 7,965-foot Mount Olympus, clad in glaciers and towering over steep, green valleys, the Olympic Mountains exude a sense of grandeur. Along with the peaks and valleys of the Olympic Mountains, the park also embraces 57 miles of pristine seacoast, large swaths of lush, temperate rain forest, and a splendid array of wildlife, including black bears, mountain sheep, bald eagles, and more than 5,000 Roosevelt elk. With more than 600 miles of footpaths, but absent a road traversing the park, the heart of the Olympics reveals itself best to travelers on foot or horseback. Fortunately for auto-bound travelers and campers, a few spectacular roads probe fleetingly (never more than 20 miles) into the borders of the park, granting sublime mountain vistas of the distant Olympics, as well as access to alpine, beach, and rain forest trailheads. Motorists planning to visit Olympic will have to do some backtracking, especially if they visit more than one section of the park.

STOLEN THRILL

*T*here is a kind of stolen thrill, something unearned and simply granted, about the presence of the Olympics. The state of Washington makes its margin with the Pacific as if the region west of the Cascade Mountains had all been dropped heavily against the ocean, causing wild splatters of both land and water: the islands of Puget Sound and the San Juan group, streaky inlets everywhere, stretched stripes of peninsula such as Dungeness and Long Beach, the eighty-mile fjord called Hood Canal, and a webwork of more than forty sizable rivers emptying to the coast. Amid this welter the Olympic Mountains stand in calm tall files, their even timbered slopes like black-green fur to shed the wet. The region's history itself seems to step back and marvel at these shoreline mountains. The coastal Indians appear not to have troubled to travel much in them. Why wrestle forest when the sea is an open larder? White frontier-probing too went into an unusual and welcome slowdown when it reached the Olympics. Although the range sits only sixty miles wide and fifty long, not until 1889 did a six-man expedition sponsored by a Seattle newspaper traipse entirely across it and leave some of the loveliest peaks of America with the curious legacy of being named for editors.

—Ivan Doig, *Winter Brothers*, 1980

If you intend to hike or camp in the Olympics, plan around the weather. Except in summertime, harsh weather is the rule rather than the exception here. One minute you're driving toward that dangerous black cloud mass, and the next you're in the thick of it. Rain sizzles down in hard, cold lines; huge drops spatter on the windshield and beat like gravel on the roof.

Olympic's beaches, tide pools, and rain forests embellish the west side of the peninsula, where the heaviest rains in the continental United States (up to 140 inches per year on average!) water massive forests of immense cedar, spruce, and Douglas fir, many of them draped and thickly bound in mosses of a hundred shades of green. The main roads to the rain forest trailheads follow the Hoh River near Forks; the Queets River near the town of Queets; and the Quinault River, beyond Quinault Lake in the southwest corner of the park. Access roads to the Olympic beaches lead to Ozette Lake, La Push, and the southern stretch of coastline between Ruby Beach and Queets.

Port Angeles, on the northern boundary of the park, is the closest town to Olympic's mountaintops and vistas. The park's grandest entrance winds 17 miles

up from Port Angeles to Hurricane Ridge, where, surrounded by mountains, you can look out over the Elwha Valley into the heart of the Olympics or look north to the Strait of Juan de Fuca. Hurricane Ridge is definitely not backcountry—there's a day-use lodge here, even a snack bar—but you can hike a long way without finding better views of the peaks. The Park Service keeps the road plowed all winter, and people drive up here for cross-country and limited downhill skiing.

A road less traveled leads from US 101 just east of Port Angeles to the trailheads and campground at **Deer Park**. The blacktop of the Forest Service road ends seven miles below the campground, and from here on it's one unpaved lane of steep, rutted switchbacks, with traffic in two directions. Above the tree line, a grassy slope rises to jagged outcrops of dark granite. When it's clear above and cloudy below, you look out over steep, densely wooded valleys, where tidal waves of white clouds curl and break in slow motion.

West of Port Angeles, the **Elwha River** leads deep into the mountains, where it drains one-fifth of the park. Just before you cross the river on US 101, turn left, up Olympic Hot Springs Road to the lower **Elwha Dam**. Rising in a narrow canyon where moss, ferns, and small cedars sprout from every foothold in the gray rock, the old, 100-foot-high dam has darkened and roughened over time, until it looks almost like it belongs in this canyon—as does the lake formed behind it. Before this dam was built here in 1914, the Elwha flowed uninterrupted from the high Olympics to the Strait of Juan de Fuca, and up to eight species of Pacific salmon and sea-run trout annually swam upstream to spawn. Hundred-pound chinook salmon were often seen fighting the rapids high into the rocky headwaters. In good years, 100,000 or more pink salmon would crowd the narrow stream.

An elderly member of the lower Elwha S'Klallam tribe described what it was like from memory: "The river was filled with fish. When I went out fishing with my grandmother, I would catch 50 fish. She would catch 100. We'd carry them back in a wheelbarrow." When the dams were built, all that changed. Remnant populations remained—and remain to this day—below the dams, but the great fish runs, walled off from their spawning grounds, disappeared. Now, a lot of people would like to see the dams removed, so that fish can spawn far up the river again. The problem is that removing the dams would cost millions of dollars, and so far, Congress shows no inclination to sign the check.

If the dams go, what will the river look like? Probably much as it looks above the second dam, built in the 1920s, which you can see by following the road to

(previous pages) A view of the Olympics from Mount Walker on an unusually clear day. The mountains receive the heaviest annual precipitation on record in the coterminous United States.

Olympic Hot Springs inside the park. There, mist clings to the hills, drifting through the evergreens. Gray-green epiphytes hang from branches. Glowing, yellow-green moss carpets earth, rocks, and logs. Below, the river pours through the rocks in a constant succession of rapids. The sound of rushing water fills the valley.

Further west along US 101, travelers pass through low forests to scenic **Lake Crescent**, a lake surrounded by hills and perhaps best known to fishermen for its trout. Close at hand are the fireplace cottages of **Lake Crescent Lodge**, which were built for Franklin Roosevelt's 1937 visit. Even more relaxing than a day of fishing may be had by "taking the waters" in the three mineral water pools at **Sol Duc Hot Springs**, 12 miles south of Lake Crescent along a paved road.

■ ALONG THE WESTERN STRAITS

Beyond Port Angeles, State Highway 112 rolls west along the Strait of Juan de Fuca to some of the most remote coastline in the country. To the north, Vancouver Island is visible in ghostly outline behind the low clouds and mists of the Strait. South and east, a luminous blanket of winter snow caps the crumpled ridges of the Olympic Mountains, rising starkly from their surrounding forests. The road is narrow and winding. As you follow it along the coastline, curving around rocks, cautiously taking a single lane around major washouts, you get a sense of how rugged this coast is and how remote it used to be. Even now, the route gives a driver little room to pass Winnebagos or avoid log trucks. Don't be in a hurry. You won't want to rush anyway, because this is one of the finest coastal drives in the Northwest. Near Pysht, huge, mossy spruce trunks crowd the blacktop and along the Pysht River, epiphytes drip from maple limbs like Spanish moss in some Louisiana bayou. Farther west, you see rocky headlands, sea stacks, and waves breaking on a stony beach.

The destination is **Neah Bay,** a rather shabby commercial and sport-fishing village, although the boats tied up in the harbor give it a certain appealing coastal color. This has been a fishing center for a long time. For centuries the Makahs paddled dugout canoes into the Strait and the Pacific to hunt whales and halibut. They later adapted larger, American-style vessels to this use. In 1889, a federal fisheries researcher told the *Seattle Post-Intelligencer* that Makahs were operating five fishing schooners at Neah Bay and were in the process of building another 40-ton boat.

Neah Bay was the site of the first European settlement in Washington State. In 1791, Spanish colonists from San Blas, Mexico, arrived aboard the frigate *Princesa* at the bay they called Nuñez Gaona, after a Mexican archbishop. They built a fort and a bakery and planted a small garden, but abandoned the settlement after five months.

The first white men to stay came here in 1850, and a few years later a smallpox epidemic swept the village; dead bodies littered the beach for miles. Eventually, two-thirds of the Makah people died of diseases brought by Europeans.

The **Makah Cultural and Research Center** displays artifacts recovered from the Ozette village site at Cape Alava (see the essay, "Makah Whale Hunters"), and replicas by contemporary craftsmen of traditional tools and clothing. The grooved rocks used for fishing weights suggest how much work it took to make simple things—and how careful one presumably was not to lose them. The people who made these objects certainly were not stingy with their labor—even fish clubs and other utilitarian objects are ornamented. In part, the exhibits form a kind of hymn to cedar. Makahs used it for straight-sided boxes and for the wide, flat planks of their longhouses. (A modern reconstruction of a longhouse stands in the

Makah Indian petroglyphs on the coast south of the Ozette Indian ruins (above). Makah sisters with grandchild in Neah Bay (right).

MAKAH WHALE HUNTERS

The original inhabitants of the north coast called themselves Qwidicca-atx (Kwee-DITCH-chuh-ahtl)—loosely translated as "people who live on the cape by the rocks and seagulls." Europeans found the Klallam word Makah—"generous with food"—easier to pronounce, and the name stuck. The Makah and their ancestors have inhabited the narrow margin between the Olympic rain forest and the Pacific Ocean for perhaps the last 5,000 years. Culturally closest to the Indians of present-day British Columbia, the Makah forged out into the Pacific Ocean in canoes to hunt the 40-foot-long, 20-ton grey whale.

Early Makah whalers followed elaborate rituals to remove their human taint and purify their bodies for the whale spirit. The morning of the hunt the harpooner rose at dawn, bathed in the icy water of a lake or pond, and rubbed a handful of twigs over his body until the twigs were covered with blood. He repeated this three more times, then dove beneath the surface of the water and imitated the movements of a whale, slowly, as he hoped the whale would during the hunt. Some whalers dove into the water with a corpse or skeleton strapped to their backs, offering prayers to the dead spirit, asking for help in the hunt.

Fortified with spiritual power and courage, Makah men then put out to sea in dugout canoes to stalk the whale. Paddlers brought the canoe in behind the whale, keeping out of its field of vision; when the narrow wooden boat was directly above the beast, the harpooner standing in the bow hurled his shell-tipped harpoons.

Once the first harpoon was driven in, inflated seal bladders attached to the spear kept the whale from diving too deep. When it surfaced to draw breath, more spears were thrown. When the behemoth was dead, its mouth was sewn shut to keep the gases that gave it buoyancy in, and keep seawater out. The whale was towed back to shore, and butchered on the beach. Its meat was eaten, its blubber was rendered for oil, and its bones were made into war clubs and woodworking tools.

The last whale hunt took place in 1913.

museum.) Cedar bark gave them material for woven mats, blankets, and hats. The wood was made into graceful, tapered canoe paddles; and above all, it was made into the canoes themselves. The museum contains modern versions of the smaller cedar canoes once used for seal hunting and daily travel, and the long canoes with flat bottoms and high prows used for whale hunting on the Pacific.

Perhaps the most startling display case holds a row of knife blades, some slate, some shell, and one of rusted metal. Metal! Five hundred years ago, Makah crafts-people were making blades out of metal. Where did they get it? Presumably from ships that drifted across the Pacific from Japan.

In the mid-nineteenth century, early settler James Swan found the Makah using copper taken from Asian shipwrecks. It is unclear how often living mariners—people from another world—drifted ashore with their wrecks, but a documented case of Japanese sailors surviving a shipwreck here happened in the early nine-teenth century. Charles Wilkes, an American naval officer who led a voyage of exploration to this coast in 1841, wrote in his diary that:

> Near this spot . . . the very remarkable occurrence of the wreck of a Japanese junk happened in the year 1833. The officers of the Hudson's Bay Company became aware of this disaster in a singular manner. They received a drawing on a piece of [rice] paper in which were depicted three shipwrecked persons, with the junk on the rocks, and the Indians engaged in plundering. This was sufficient to induce them to make inquiries; and Captain M'Neil was dispatched to Cape Flattery to obtain further information, and afford relief should it be needed. He had the satisfaction to find the three Japanese, whom he rescued from slavery; and the Hudson's Bay Company with characteristic liberality, sent them to England.

Was that the Makahs' first close encounter with Asian culture? Similar "remark-able occurrences" may have been happening for hundreds of years.

On the far side of Neah Bay, **Cape Flattery**, the westernmost point of land in the coterminous United States, juts into the Pacific. From high ground west of town you can look south along the misty coast, over the dark forest and the white

Makahs harvest a whale. Ancient traditions dictated the division of the whale, the harpooner receiving the largest share. (Asahel Curtis photo, Washington State Historical Society, Tacoma)

line of breakers at the edge of the continent, to the distant sculpture garden of sea stacks at Point of Arches.

On the way back, it's somehow not surprising to see a rainbow arc over the green waters of the Strait of Juan de Fuca.

■ OZETTE LAKE AND NORTH OLYMPIC COAST

West of Sekiu on State Highway 112, a branch road winds southwest, following the Hoko River through heavily logged hills toward Ozette Lake. Most of the land along this road is clear-cut to low stumps and slash piles as far as the eye can see, and Cat tracks crisscross the bald hillsides like sutures on a raw wound.

The road ends at a ranger station on the north end of 10-mile-long Ozette Lake. You have just entered the coastal section of Olympic National Park.

One hundred years ago, the land around Ozette Lake was home to a few hundred homesteaders, mostly Scandinavian families, who cut old-growth trees with handsaws, pulled the massive stumps with mules or blasted them out with

The trunk of a felled tree serves as a bungalow in this 1907 photo.
(Museum of History and Industry, Seattle).

A fallen old-growth fir tree in the Olympic rain forest reveals its age as 380 years.

dynamite, and built their homes here. Lars Ahlstrom, a homesteader who settled here in 1902, worked his claim alone until 1958. His decades of toil are commemorated in **Ahlstrom Prairie,** a broad marsh crossed by the Cape Alava trail. Around the lake, the forest has swallowed all traces of the farms that thrived here for a few brief years. Even on Ahlstrom Prairie seedling evergreens are beginning the long work of reclamation.

Two three-mile boardwalk trails from Ozette Lake to the long wilderness beach cut through thick rain forest, where columns of sunlight split the dense canopy high overhead, and a soft, green light seems to emanate from the trees and the earth itself.

Between the Makah reservation, which occupies the extreme northwestern tip of the peninsula, and the big Quinault reservation, south of Kalaloch, the whole Pacific coastline is part of the Olympic National Park, except for three small pockets of land occupied by the Ozette, Quillayute, and Hoh reservations. The ancient forests grow down to the shore. Near the water, pale lichens beard the scaly boughs of Sitka spruce. At low tide, the broad, sandy beach stretches out to small, wooded islands and surf-sculpted outcrops of rock that dot the shore. Some of these land forms would look more at home in the Arizona desert than in the shallows of the Pacific Ocean. In places, exploding breakers have worn the rock to the pitted consistency of wormwood. One wonders how many times one drop of spray must have hit the stone just there to wear that half-inch hole.

Waves deposit spongy beds of sea grass and red-brown kelp—four feet deep in places—along the tide line, and plant stiff stalks of bullwhip kelp like flag poles in the sand. Hurled by a storm above the high tide line and stranded after a journey of untold miles and years, a drift log seven feet thick, its skeletal root mass spreading like giant tentacles, testifies to the power of this ocean.

Tracks of deer and raccoon show clearly in the sand, and black cormorants spread their wings to dry in the sun atop wave-shaped seastacks. The hoarse cry of a great blue heron splits the air as the bird rises with a few impossibly slow beats of its enormous wings. Mats of slick, red kelp pop underfoot, and a young bald eagle flies northeast with a fish hanging limp in its talons, a pleading gull in pursuit.

Cape Alava was the site of a Makah village for at least 2,000 years, and was abandoned only in the late nineteenth century after the U.S. government ordered village children off to school in Neah Bay. Like many long-inhabited sites, from Troy to Monte Albán, the Ozette village was built in succeeding layers. An early layer, sealed in by mud slides centuries ago and exposed by winter storms in 1970, provided one of Washington's most important archaeological sites—a Northwest coast Pompeii. Wooden artifacts and woven baskets dating to the 1400s, perfectly preserved in their airless tomb, gave a clearer picture of traditional Makah life. The archaeological excavation of the Ozette village eventually ran out of money and shut down. The artifacts are preserved at the tribal museum in Neah Bay, and a replica cedar longhouse now marks the village site.

■ LA PUSH

Fourteen miles west of the US 101 town of Forks lies the fishing village of La Push, close to the mouth of the Quillayute River on the tiny Quillayute Indian Reservation. Its name, La Push, is a corruption of the French word for mouth, *la bouche,* after it found its way into the Chinook jargon. The road to La Push heads west off US 101, crossing and recrossing the Soleduck River on green-girdered bridges. The

SCENT OF CEDAR

The gray log lies high up on the rocky beach, weathered until it resembles the trees behind it less than the stones on which it rests. Grab a sliver of pale wood and rip it back. Beneath the surface, it shines a rich orange-red. From it rises a pungent odor, something you might smell after opening a jar of an exotic spice. The wood is western red cedar, grown in some damp valley of this Northwest, cut, bucked, and rafted, then washed loose from a log boom years or decades ago.

If you travel inland from the beach, through a dense forest of fir and hemlock, you may come to one of those valleys. Picking your way through a swamp, you might find a long, fluted cylinder, half-submerged and covered with moss, solid to the step or touch, like a Roman column somehow transported to these woods. It too is cedar. Beyond it a living tree rises from a fluted base three feet thick. Bark coats it in thin, shaggy vertical strips. The branches dip and curve like the lines of a Japanese temple. The foliage is flat and multibranched, like layer on layer of horizontal bracken fern. Nearby, like an obelisk, soaring straight as a die from the forest floor, a dead cedar trunk reveals the naked, skeletal shape. Even thicker at the base than the living tree, it transcends the leaning alders around it and even the spar-straight second-growth Douglas fir on the hill above, rising to a needle point.

It doesn't take much imagination to see this gray column as a totem in the woods. In fact, the totem poles and other magnificent wood carvings of this coast were made from cedar. The Indians used cedar not only for carving. They split cedar to make walls and roofs for their houses. They twisted strands of shredded bark to make rope and fishing line, and hollowed cedar logs to make their great, seagoing canoes.

snowy ridges of the Olympics form a majestic backdrop for the shingle mills and clear-cut patches that follow the road.

The coast here is magnificent: wind-warped cedar and hemlock, and stands of lichen-whitened alder stand on steep clay banks overlooking the endless Pacific. Waves curl and break, and rush hissing up the broad sandy beach, slapping and rolling massive, bleached drift logs as the tide rises. Offshore, sea stacks—weird hives and spires of dark basalt—rise from the surf. Seals bob in the swells beyond the breaking waves, and seagulls cry and wheel overhead. **Second Beach** and **Third Beach** are reached by half-mile trails leading down from the road about a mile before town.

The town of La Push lies on **First Beach**, a site occupied by the Quillayute for unknown centuries. Their mile-square reservation was not established until 1889; the isolated tribe was overlooked by Governor Stevens and his agents when the treaties of 1855 were drafted. Don Pullen, a white fur trader, had built a house and trading post here and claimed 1,500 acres of land at the mouth of the river in the 1880s. His claim fell within the reservation boundaries established in 1889. In an epic display of spite, he waited until the Quillayutes made their fall journey east to work the hop fields near Puyallup, and then burned their village to the ground.

Today, La Push is a collection of shabby, weathered houses, with one store, an old Shaker church, and a small harbor where a fleet of fishing boats bobs. Salmon fishing is the chief livelihood of the Quillayute people, as it has been for millennia. Charter boats leave from the harbor, too. Ubiquitous satellite dishes and new pickup trucks contrast oddly with the general funkiness of La Push. The new tribal schoolhouse, next door to the salmon-processing plant, is a dapper building, painted with grinning animal figures in red and black.

Sunset off the coast near La Push (above).
Hiking in Olympic National Park—one of the world's few temperate rain forests (right).

■ RAIN FORESTS

People come from all over the world to see the rain forest, and with good reason. Actually, you can see little bits of it all over western Washington—little valleys or hollows into which the prevailing winds funnel so much moisture that moss covers the ground, rocks, and rotting logs, epiphytes drip from all the tree branches, and the air is filled with the sound of running water. The rain forest valleys all catch the prevailing winds from the Pacific, which bring rain and mist up the Hoh, Queets, Quinault, and Bogachiel rivers to the big spruce and cedar trees, the lichen-whitened alders, the ferns, the mosses, the shrubs, the epiphytes. Everything is green—innumerable hues, shades, textures, and overlapping layers of green. Straight rows of young trees grow from the mossy corpses of "nurse logs" on the forest floor, while colonnades of larger trees grow over the spaces where rotting nurse logs used to lie. There are no hard edges; everything is softened, enveloped, illuminated by moss. A thick carpet of moss covers the ground where exposed roots radiate out from a huge spruce trunk. The roots create ripples in the green, and waves of moss seem to flow toward the spruce. In the rain, the wet greens take on an extra glow. In fall, you may hear the surprisingly high, tinny "bugling" of Roosevelt elk or see one of the big buckskin creatures slip through the trees.

The rain forest may be the best place to appreciate the beauty and complexity of an old-growth forest. As if you were standing in the nave of Chartres or Notre Dame, you're aware of massive columns leading up into the filtered daylight, of a vast, enclosed space far above.

The canopy of branches overhead is made up of multiple layers. In places, light penetrates, allowing a dense understory of brush and small plants to develop on the forest floor. Some old trees die and remain standing as gray, weather-bleached snags. Others fall and decay slowly, releasing nutrients for centuries. Literally hundreds of plant and animal species, including the northern spotted owl and marbled murrelet, are found in Washington's old-growth forests.

Trees can, of course, be planted, grown, and cut on regular rotations like alfalfa or corn. Tree farms develop trees more rapidly than nature does, but they produce single-species, even-aged stands, cut for narrow boards and paper pulp. An old-growth forest is something very different.

On US 101, just south of Forks at **Bogachiel State Park,** one can head east into the Bogachiel Valley rain forest. Past the Bogachiel River, North Hoh Road leads inland to the **Hoh Rain Forest Visitor Center,** where the best-known rain forest trails begin.

Farther south, US 101 leads east to Lake Quinault, where you will find trailheads, campgrounds, and outside the park, old Lake Quinault Lodge. This handsome retreat was built in 1926 and later restored with its high ceilings, wide French windows overlooking the lake, and a large lobby complete with a grand fireplace.

■ GRAYS HARBOR

Curving inland around the Quinault Indian Reservation, US 101 heads south to the estuary and mill towns of Grays Harbor. From Seattle, it's a lot quicker and easier to reach Grays Harbor by driving south to Olympia and then turning west, and unless one is circumnavigating the peninsula, that's the more sensible way to go.

Grays Harbor itself is one of the largest estuaries on the Pacific Coast north of San Francisco. The towns of **Aberdeen** and **Hoquiam,** which stand beside the estuary, have always been forest products centers—cutting lumber, making pulp, shipping lumber, shipping logs. Old pilings driven into the bottom to hold log booms rise from the water's edge. Stacks of logs and heaps of sawdust stand by the shore. The towns themselves have obviously seen better days.

This is timber country, hit hard by the logging ban in state or federally owned old-growth forest, by pulp mill closures, automation, and the depletion of the forests. The harvest peaked in 1929.

The towns have hung on, though. People still work in the woods and mills. The port still ships logs. A tall-masted sailing ship built with state economic development money draws some tourists. Oysters grow in the shallow waters on the south side of the estuary, toward the coast. **Westport,** at the southern edge of the estuary's mouth, remains a center for commercial fishing and crabbing fleets, as well as for charter boats that take people into the ocean to catch salmon, catch bottomfish, and watch the whales that migrate up the coast every spring.

Westport and the other nearby coastal communities are geared primarily to sport fishermen and whale-watching expeditions. Nature lovers taking a stroll along the water's edge may end up feeling more indignant than refreshed when they see the locals driving their cars up and down the beach.

Elevation
in feet

14,410	
6,000	
5,000	
4,000	
3,000	
2,000	
1,500	
1,000	
500	
0	

SOUTH
COAST

0   5   10   20

Miles

People do visit Westport, though—some even bring wetsuits and surf in the cold Pacific. Also, they visit the **Grays Harbor National Wildlife Refuge**, at the northern edge of the estuary, to see the birds. The refuge accommodates up to one-half of the million or so shorebirds that visit Grays Harbor at peak times. It's a good place for birds because it's a good place for eelgrass and other seaweeds, which birds eat, and for algae, invertebrates, and small fish, which depend ultimately on nutrients that the eelgrass releases when it dies—making eelgrass the nutritional foundation for the whole system. Eelgrass produces more dry matter per square meter per year than any terrestrial food crop except sugar cane, and it dies down completely every year. The estuary serves as a nursery for young salmon not yet ready to venture into the open sea, and for young crustacea. The other great coastal estuaries of Washington—Willapa Bay, just south of Grays Harbor, and the Columbia River mouth, farther south—serve similar functions. The best months to visit the refuge are April and May, and best times of day are one hour before and one hour after high tide.

■ WILLAPA BAY

Willapa Bay has been called the cleanest large estuary anywhere in the United

States outside Alaska. A quick detour on the short drive south from Grays Harbor takes you into the depressed logging town of **Raymond**, where a tall wooden statue of a logger stands in a pleasant little park, and a big Weyerhaeuser mill looms at the edge of downtown.

Farther south, US 101 runs along the waterfront of **South Bend** which bills itself as "the oyster capital of the world." In fact, Willapa Bay produces more oysters than anywhere else in the United States and is at least one of the top five oyster-producing spots in the world. Huge piles of oyster shells stand beside metal packing houses at the water's edge, and are hauled away by the truckload. (For more on oysters, see following chapter, "HEAVENLY OYSTERS.")

In the early 1850s, men built shacks on the west side of Willapa Bay and gathered the native oysters for sale to Gold Rush San Francisco, where people had the money and inclination to pay for delicacies. James Swan arrived here at the end of 1852 to find 14 settlers and shoals "covered with shell-fish." Schooners from San

Discarded oyster shells from a cannery are ground up and used for fertilizer.
(University of Washington Libraries)

Francisco would pull into the shallow bay, settlers would paddle out with heavy baskets of oysters, the oysters would be hauled on board, and the captains would pay for them in gold. The oysters sold for a dollar a basket, and a schooner often took 1,200 to 2,000 baskets—a sizable investment at that time and one that would not necessarily reach San Francisco alive.

People have been selling Willapa Bay oysters ever since. Production is still measured in millions of pounds, and the industry provides a powerful incentive for local communities to keep the water clean. The main threats to the industry in recent years have been non-native spartina grass, which covers submerged areas on which oysters could otherwise be grown, and ghost shrimp, which literally undermine the oyster beds.

On the residential hill above South Bend's main drag, the 1910 **Pacific County courthouse,** with its dark, spreading dome, its ornate, arched upper windows, and its two-story pillars flanking the grand entrance, looks out over the shallow bay.

Parts of Willapa Bay have been protected since 1937 as a national wildlife refuge. The refuge provides winter habitat for black brant, a stopping place for up to 150,000 northbound shorebirds every spring, and up to 100,000 southbound waterfowl every fall. Near the refuge headquarters, below South Bend, Long Island supports a 4,000-year-old grove of western red cedar.

To reach the rest of the refuge, you have to drive around the southern edge of the bay to the tip of **Long Beach peninsula,** which separates Willapa Bay from the ocean. On the way, you cross slow, winding rivers and sloughs, an old dock with a venerable dredge in the shallow water beside it, and a mountain of oyster shells on the shore.

North along the peninsula, there are plenty of real estate signs, but no significant views of the ocean. You do get a glimpse of Willapa Bay at **Nahcotta,** where you can find a packing shed with the obligatory heap of shells, and you can see it again at **Oysterville,** where some of the houses date from the 1860s and 1870s. Oysterville also boasts a church with a small, ornately shingled steeple, a 1906 schoolhouse no longer in use, and a sign that marks the site of the first Pacific County courthouse—the seat of local government until South Bend boosters stole the records and built a courthouse of their own.

This is the area in which early settler James Swan and pioneer oystermen lived in the early 1850s. Washington wasn't even a separate territory then, but it was very much part of the United States, and the oystermen were as enthusiastic as anyone in their celebration of the Fourth of July. In the summer of 1852, Swan wrote:

(previous pages) Sea stacks and a sunken ship mast pierce the coast along a wilderness beach south of Cape Flattery. (Photo by Ed Cooper)

It was announced to me that the boys, as the oystermen were termed, intended celebrating the 4th of July at my tent. [The morning of the Fourth] was ushered in by a tremendous bonfire, which. . .was answered by every one who had a gun and powder blazing away. Toward two o'clock; they began to assemble [at Swan's tent for a pot-luck dinner], some coming in boats, others in canoes, and a few by walking round the beach, which they could easily do at any time after the tide was quarter ebb. [After dinner and some patriotic readings,] it was proposed to close the performances for the day by going on top of the cliff opposite, and make a tremendous big blaze. . . .some six or eight immediately crossed the creek and soon scrambled to the top of the hill, where we found an old hollow cedar stump about twenty feet high. . . .We. . . soon had the old stump filled full of dry spruce limbs, which were lying about in great quantities, and then set fire to the whole. It made the best bonfire I ever saw; and after burning all night and part of the next day, finally set fire to the forest, which continued to burn for several months, till the winter rains finally extinguished it.

Leadbetter Point State Park, beyond Oysterville but before the refuge land at the extreme tip of the peninsula, gives you the chance to walk along a bay that remains much as it was when early oystermen first came here. Sunlight gleams on the water and on the wet sand. Rafts of shorebirds rise, skim the water, flash white undersides as they turn, and settle up the beach. Hundreds of little birds huddle along the shore; the air is filled with their twittering. Across the water, dark hills rise above pale strips of cloud. A white oyster dredge is working far out in the bay.

The peninsula provides plenty of opportunities to pull out onto the beach and drive along the sand. When **Long Beach** boosters advertise the world's longest beach drive, they aren't kidding. Things can get pretty funky out there on the shingle with cars cruising along the tide line, people sitting on lawn furniture beside parked pickups, kids buzzing along the water's edge on mopeds, and all the walkers and sunbathers you'd expect on a popular beach out enjoying themselves, and maybe even horseback riders. Yet a couple of blocks from the resort carnival atmosphere of downtown Ocean Shores, for example, you can be walking on a wide, unspoiled beach. You can look out over tawny, wind-whipped beach grass to wet sand to gray water that runs all the way to Asia.

■ THE COLUMBIA

The surf at **Fort Canby State Park** may seem innocuous enough when you squint in the sun of a summer day, but in the winter, you're conscious of the acres of driftwood driven high above the normal tideline by Pacific storms, and of small trees, sculpted by the west wind, growing almost horizontally along the sand. North beyond an unbroken swath of wet sand, a lighthouse clings to an outcropping of dark rock; a light has pierced the frequent coastal fogs on that site for more than 100 years. Other dark outcroppings rise from the mist behind the beach grass. Offshore, the gray sky looks almost white where it meets the sea as filtered sunlight reflects from the spray whipped constantly from the wave crests.

This was the beach on which American explorers Lewis and Clark first walked beside the Pacific in 1805. The scene was even wilder then, and not far from here, a member of the expedition killed a condor with a wingspan of more than nine feet.

Fort Canby was built on a rocky headland during the Civil War and fortified heavily after the Spanish-American War. A fine interpretive center here contains journal excerpts from the Lewis and Clark expedition and photo murals of places

The oldest standing cannery in Washington sits on the Cathlamet waterfront along the Columbia River (above). A glowing sunset over Willapa Bay (right).

SPYING THE COLUMBIA, 1792

In 1792, Boston fur trader Capt. Robert Gray commanded the first sea voyage into the mouth of the Columbia River. He named the harbor after himself and the vast river after his ship, the Columbia Rediviva, *or* Columbus Reborn. *John Boit, a crewman, recorded his impressions:*

*T*his day saw an appearance of a spacious harbour abrest the Ship, haul'd our wind for it, observ'd two sand bars making off, with a passage between them to a fine river . . . . The River extended to the NE as far as eye cou'd reach, and water fit to drink as far down as the Bars, at the entrance. We directed our course up this noble river in search of a Village. The beach was lin'd with Natives, who ran along shore following the Ship. Soon after above 20 Canoes came off, and brought a good lot of Furs and Salmon, which last they sold two for a board Nail. The furs we likewise bought cheap, for Copper and Cloth. They appear'd to view the Ship with the greatest astonishment and no doubt we was the first civilized people that they ever saw.

Shifted the Ship's berth to her Old Station abrest the Village Chinoak, command'd by a cheif name Polack. Vast many Canoes full of Indians from different parts of the river where constantly along side.

This day left Columbia's River, and stood clear of the bars, and bore off to the Northward. The Men at Columbia's River are strait limb'd, fine looking fellows, and the women are very pretty. They are all in a state of Nature, except the females who wear a leaf Apron (perhaps 'twas a fig leaf). But some of our gentlemen, that examin'd them pretty close, and near, both within and without reported that it was not a leaf but a nice wove mat in resemblance! and so we go—thus, thus—and no Near!—!

—John Boit, crewman aboard *Columbia Rediviva,* 1792

on the explorers' route. You can walk through the crumbling concrete of old coastal gun emplacements and look out over the north jetty, which guards the mouth of the Columbia River. Waves smash against the black boulders of the north jetty, throwing spray to the uppermost rocks. Beyond, the river's freshwater flow enters the sea. There is no sign of the currents that sweep the freshwater plume north in winter and south in summer, no hint of the treacherous Columbia River bar that has wrecked so many ships that have tried to cross it.

■ EAST UP THE COLUMBIA

If you drive east from Fort Canby up the Columbia, you'll notice dark rock—a basalt flow older than the mountains—pushing through the soggy ground along the river bank. Old pilings stand in the shallows. Cattle stand in wet pastures. Abandoned houses and barns dot the land. A sign marks the site at which Lewis and Clark camped for ten days in November 1805, and evidently first saw breakers driven upriver from the open sea. (The explorers actually thought they had seen the ocean before this, when they sighted the broad expanse of Grays Bay.) Between November 8th and 12th, Clark wrote in his diary:

> *We* are all wet and disagreeable, as we have been for Several days.... The flood tide came in accompanied with emence waves and heavy winds, floated the trees and Drift which was on the point on which we Camped and tosed them about in such a manner as to endanger the canoes...with every exertion and the Strictest attention by every individual of the party was scercely sufficient to Save our Canoes from being crushed by those monsterous trees maney of them nearly 200 feet long and from 4 to 7 feet through.
>
> [We were awakened by a] tremendous wind from the S.W. about 3 oClock this morning with Lightineng and hard claps of Thunder, and Hail. [A few hours later, it] rained with great violence until 12 oClock, the waves tremendious brakeing with great fury against the rocks and trees on which we were encamped...we took advantage of a low tide and moved our camp around a point to a Small wet bottom, at the Mouth of a Brook...It would be distressing to See our Situation, all wet and colde our bedding also wet (and the robes of the parich compose half the bedding is rotten) in a wet bottom scercely large enough to contain us our baggage half a mile from us, and Canoes at the mercy of the Waves.

Beyond the sign that marks a happier campsite, you pass small, sluggish rivers and sloughs, old churches, and the green superstructure of the old suspension bridge across the river to Astoria. A big mill still stands at the edge of **Cathlamet,** a charming hamlet with white clapboard Victorians and storefronts. The mill's not far from the turnoff to the **Julia Butler Hansen National Wildlife Refuge for the Columbian White-Tailed Deer.** Lewis and Clark found plenty of the deer all along the lower river, but they are now an endangered species. The refuge's namesake, Julia Butler Hansen, was a state congresswoman from Cathlamet for many years. She was tough: a Washington historian once referred to her "longshore personality."

Just as Cathlamet is still a mill town, this is still logging country. When the river road climbs over rocky outcroppings, you get long views through the drifting clouds of hills that have been thoroughly scalped by chainsaws. The wonder is there are still any trees left. When Swan sailed up the coast from San Francisco on a brig in 1852, the morning of November 25 found him "about 30 miles to the westward of the Columbia River, from which a huge volume of water was running, carrying in its course great quantities of drift-logs, boards, chips and sawdust, with which the whole water around us was covered." People have been cutting trees near the lower Columbia ever since.

Naturalist Robert Michael Pyle, who lives in Grays River, has written:

> . . . Creases and wrinkles in the abused skin of the Willapa Hills show the field marks of rain forest: garlands of *Usnea,* pale green old-man's beard lichen, hanging from hemlocks like Spanish moss, tresses of chartreuse club moss padding the boughs of bigleaf maples, swinging from the limbs in the ratta-tatta-tatta rain and luxuriating in the mossehurr. Sprays of licorice ferns sprouting from the collarbones and patellas of the lumpy maples, and vast banana slugs patrolling the fecund forest floor or negotiating the nurse-log greenways.

Garlands of Usnea *(old man's beard) hang from forest boughs.*

HEAVENLY OYSTERS

by John Doerper

EVERY FALL, WHEN THE LEAVES TURN GOLDEN, I know that oyster season is just about to begin. The oysters will stay in season until the water warms up next May or June. I drive south on Chuckanut Drive, from Whatcom into Skagit County, turn right at the Oyster Creek Inn and wind my way down the narrow draw of Oyster Creek to the shore of the bay and the low headland, covered with oyster shells and occupied by the **Samish Bay Shellfish Farm**—an aggregation of shucking sheds, cabins, and cottages which makes the farm look almost like a small shoreside village. I am in luck. The oysters spawned early this year, fattened on the detritus of summer, they are back in season, plump and flavorful. But before I buy, I take a good whiff of the air.

The sea breeze is pregnant with aromas: the refreshing scent of fir boughs wafts down to the beach from the cliffs; a sharp tang of salt and kelp and marine life hovers above the tide flats; an earthy bouquet of fragrances rises from the mud of the tide flats. Thinking of the old adage that you'll know how the oysters in a given bay taste if you take a good whiff of the beach at low tide, I'm getting hungry. This bay smells great. I long to become part of the shore and the sea, to imbibe it, to take some of this mystical experience home with me, and I know I can come closest by eating an oyster, which is the one tangible part of all of this I can ever hope to share.

Sharing is what oysters are all about. Oysters have ever been a sociable food. In Dickensian London, diners stood at bars, eating oysters raw, enhanced perhaps by a touch of cayenne pepper and malt vinegar, accompanied by crusty bread, sweet butter, and stout, the drink seemingly created just to heighten the natural flavor of oysters. I am fortunate because I work in an office where just about everyone loves oysters, especially when they come with a good stout or porter brewed by a local microbrewery. Since I have stopped at the oyster farm on my way to work, I buy several dozen oysters in the shell to take with me. But first I need to slurp a dozen oysters in the shell, right at the farm.

Eating an oyster freshly plucked off the beach is the only way I can truly hope to incorporate the sea and the cloud-laden sky, a misty seaside morning or a sunny afternoon by the shore. Eating a fresh oyster on the seashore creates a memory like no other. A good oyster is like a poem of nature—an incarnation of the sea breeze, of the saltwater reflecting the green trees, berry bushes, and herbs of the shore. But while a good oyster contains some of the aromas of the sea surrounding its bed, it transmutes the flavor of the seawater into a magical liquor, the way a poet transforms words. The words themselves are still there, but they have taken on a new, mystical gestalt; a life of their own. Thus the oyster liquor, though more or less briny, depending on how salty the environment is in which the oyster is raised, is not just mere sea water which has remained behind in the shell, it is a truly special liquor.

You can easily test this by reducing both oyster liquor and seawater over moderate heat. The sea water will evaporate and leave nothing but a crust of salt and minerals; the oyster liquor will thicken into an aromatic sauce.

■ HOW AN OYSTER SHOULD TASTE

Every oyster connoisseur knows how an oyster should taste, but defining this flavor with any amount of precision proves just as elusive as describing the flavor of a complex wine or rare tea. Eleanor Clark states, in the classic oyster book, *The Oysters of Locmariaquer*, that with oysters, "the whole point is flavor," but immediately adds that "you can't define it." I asked Kevin Shoemaker, general manager of Elliott's in Seattle, one of the region's top oyster restaurants, and his former chef, Tony Casad, to define the flavor of oysters for me. Shoemaker talked about distinguishing oysters of separate species and from different growing regions by their salinity and by their mineral content (how "metallic" their taste is). Casad agrees, and adds texture and sweetness. Some oysters, he says are a little creamier, like those from **Westcott Bay on San Juan Island**, others, like **Orcas Island's Crescent Bays** are firmer. He also stresses the shape of the shell—whether deep or shallow—the shell color, and the way the shucked oyster looks on the half shell. "When the oysters are shucked properly, they look appealing," he adds. Shoemaker and Casad should know. At Elliott's annual "Oyster Sound Off" held in October, they served more than 35 different kinds of oysters—all of them superbly fresh.

Bill Marinelli, a seafood broker, who supplied about a third of those oysters, describes the flavor of oysters as "incredibly complex," and says you must judge an oyster the way you judge a fine wine. Aside from salinity and texture, you also evaluate the aftertaste, which may be fruity like watermelon, or crisp like cucumber. He describes some of the Pacifics he sells as "smoky." Marinelli insists that, like a wine, an oyster should be judged by the way it relates to other foods.

As I sit on the shore and savor the aftertaste of my farm-grown oyster, I reflect on the obvious, "forward" oyster flavors, which I compare to the cries of the seabirds on the shore and then once again savor the hidden flavor elements, elusive like the song of the hermit thrush hidden deeply within the shore woods, but staying with me and haunting my palate with their memory. Because oysters are so surprisingly delicate, I once compared the evanescence of their aroma and taste to the fleeting existence of a morning glory, which opens in the morning, fully charged with life, but becomes a mere memory by nightfall. Yet, on further study, I discovered that oysters are also surprisingly sturdy. They can live out of the water for up to a week, as long as their shells remain tightly closed. According to Bill Dewey, manager of Samish Bay Shellfish Farm, oysters can freeze solid, through and through, and come back to life when the weather warms, as long as they remain undisturbed in their beds. Despite their delicate flavor, they can hold their own against heavy flavors like vinegar, garlic, onion, chile—perhaps in part because of their brininess. An oyster's shape, size, and flavor are not only determined by its species, but also by its habitat. Oysters growing on rocks or racks, on long lines suspended in deep water, or in suspended trays or lantern nets, will have a cleaner taste than oysters growing in the silt of tide flats. Beach-grown oysters exposed to the elements when the tide runs out will have heavier shells than oysters always covered by water—and may thus stay fresh longer.

■ OYSTER SPECIES AND OYSTER FARMERS

Oyster farmers on the Pacific Coast raise several different species: the native "Olympia" oyster, a tiny, flavorful mollusk which rarely grows larger than 1 1/2 inches in length, the Pacific miyagi oyster, imported from Japan before World War II, but long since gone native, and the European flat oyster ("Euro-flat," "Umpqua flat"), a succulent larger relative of the native Pacific Coast oyster. In addition, a few oyster farms grow a smaller, very tasty sport of the Pacific oyster, the Japanese Kumamoto (though questions have recently arisen if this strain still exists in its pure form or has irreversibly hybridized with the Pacific).

Pacific oysters like company and, if left alone, they will settle on top of each other in dense, contorted clusters. This makes shucking very difficult, a task for experts. For this reason, many Northwest oyster farms have traditionally sold their oysters shucked: the oysters are shucked at the farm, presorted by size, packed into jars, and shipped to restaurants and markets. Most of these shucked oysters are used in cooked dishes.

Shucked oysters being jarred, near the town of Nahcotta on the Long Beach Peninsula.

WASHINGTON OYSTERS

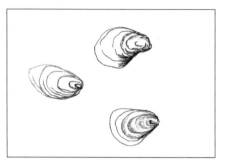

OLYMPIA OYSTER
[Native oyster; U.S. Pacific coast]
Ostrea lurida

A very small, dull-colored oyster that looks much like a tiny, somewhat elongated European flat oyster. Great flavor!

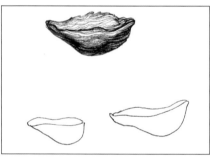

KUMAMOTO OYSTER
Crassostrea gigas, var. *kumamoto*

This is really an odd oyster. It is only a sport of the Pacific and may not be genetically distinct at all. Its claims to fame are a smaller size, better flavor, and deeper cup. Other than that they are not easy to tell apart.

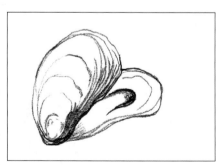

ATLANTIC OYSTER
Crassostrea virginica

Like all oysters, highly variable in shape. Smoother shell than Pacific—though that can vary highly. More elongated than Euro flat. Dark horseshoe shape scar on inside shell is generally a good field sign.

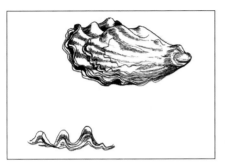

HYBRID PACIFIC OYSTER
Crassostrea gigas, hybrid

Hybrid oysters have a more deeply flutted shell, which can be quite flaky, almost fragile. They were first raised by Bill Webb at Westcott Bay on San Juan Island. Hybrids look much like Pacifics with a "lacier," more fragile shell. Great flavor.

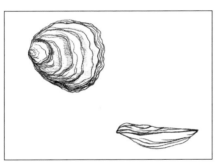

EUROPEAN FLAT OYSTER
["Euro flat, Belon".]
Ostrea edulis

Basically roundish, smooth [for an oyster], with a flattish top shell. Also highly variable.

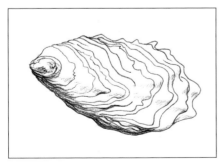

PACIFIC OYSTER
Crassostrea gigas

Roughly fluted shell; highly variable in shape and texture; can be very rough or almost smooth. Can get quite large, but most oysters sold commercially are 2–4 inches in length.

Illustrations by John Doerper

The Kumamoto, Euro-flat, and native oyster have traditionally been sold in the shell and shucked just before being consumed raw. During the last decade, advances in cultivation methods, plus the switch from ground culture, in which the oysters are grown in clusters directly on the bottom of a bay, to suspended culture, where the oysters are grown individually above the ground, has led to the ready availability of "single" oysters which are easy to transport in the shell and should not be shucked until just before they are slurped from the shell.

Some oyster farms, like Samish Bay, grow only half-shell oysters; at others, almost all oysters are shucked on site and sold in jars. After leaving the oyster farm, I stop off the road, settle myself in a clearing which opens onto a view of the San Juan Islands, and sit down to an impromptu picnic. The office can wait.

■ WHAT TO DRINK WITH OYSTERS

I accompany the oysters with chunks of dark rye bread and with sips from a quart bottle of rich, dark Pike Place stout. I used to insist on dry white wine with my oysters until I learned through a series of taste tests that beer and oysters are the better match.

On the other hand, dry European-style white wines may go better with European flat and native West Coast oysters (both of the genus *Ostrea;* the Pacific oyster and kumamoto belong to the genus *Crassostrea)*. But I also learned something very surprising during these taste tests: that red wine, rather than white, may be the perfect wine for oysters. Bill Marinelli agrees. When I told him I was fond of the Beringer beaujolais nouveau with oysters, Marinelli expressed his fondness for oysters and Saintsbury pinot noir from Northern California's cool Carneros growing region, and for Oregon pinot noirs. But he has also experimented with cabernet franc and merlot, claiming that some make great oyster wines. This pairing is more logical than it seems at first glance, since many oyster aficionados dip their raw oysters into a red wine vinegar mignonette. Back to the tasting room.

It's easier to match drink to cooked oysters than to raw oysters, if only because of the influence that seasonings exert on the flavor of the dish.

■ SHUCKED OR IN THE SHELL?

While I sometimes buy shucked oysters, I buy them only at the oyster farm and carry them home in a cooler, protected by ice. I asked Lee Wiegardt, manager of **Nahcotta's Jolly Roger Oyster Company** and acknowledged dean of Willapa Bay oystermen, about the proper way of buying shucked oysters in the jar. "The oysters have to be coded," says Wiegardt. "Don't buy them if they're not coded." Oyster jars now have a pull date—14 days for most growers.

Wiegardt advises consumers to "buy the one that's farthest from the pull date." He adds that shucked oysters have "no smell when they're absolutely fresh." As they get older, they get a little sharp smell, then a "funky" smell, and then they can get downright stinky. To my nose, oysters that are too old have a whiff of overly ripe Limburger cheese. Wiegardt says shucked oysters should be stored at 28 to 31 degrees F —they contain enough salt to keep them from freezing. He suggests that you take the oysters home right away. Like all seafood, oysters should not just be set into a warm car but should be carried home in an ice chest. It's important to find a seafood supplier you can really trust, adds Wiegardt. But he warns, you can not smell the things that can really hurt you—such as polluted water. **Willapa Bay** is so pure, Wiegardt says, the federal government is using it as the basis for setting new nationwide water standards. Wiegardt warns against using oysters that are too small if you want to fix a dish of fried oysters—they'll taste too much like greasy breading, not enough like oyster, and he claims that our oysters fry up better than East Coast oysters because they're saltier and have more flavor.

■ BAKERS

The hot new trend in oyster cookery is what Wiegardt calls "bakers," large oysters baked or barbecued in their shells and then topped with a variety of sauces and dressings, from barbecue sauce to chile salsa, black bean sauce, or even chicken stock. He recommends taking off the top shell before setting the oyster onto the grill and topping off the shell with beer. When the beer has boiled away, the oyster is ready to eat.

(following pages) Bundled oyster shells to be used for future spawning in Willapa Bay, America's foremost oyster farming area.

■ PURITY

Washington State is now the largest oyster-producing state in the nation (with more than 50 percent of the crop grown in Willapa Bay), and the West Coast is the largest oyster-producing region in the nation: Washington ranks first, with 9 million pounds, over Louisiana, with 7.98 million pounds; Maryland ranked a distant third, with 2.33 million pounds. Regionally, the Pacific Coast region (Northern California, Oregon, Washington, and Alaska but, because of the international border, not British Columbia) ranks first with 10.8 million pounds—or 37 percent of the national harvest of 29.2 million pounds. The Gulf Coast Region (Florida, Alabama, Mississippi, Louisiana, and Texas) came in second with 10.6 million pounds, or about 36 percent; the Chesapeake Region was third with 13 percent of the harvest. According to Tim Smith, Executive Director of the Pacific Coast Oyster Growers Association, this number one ranking is not one the Pacific Northwest will relinquish soon: "There seems to be a general awakening among retailers, restaurants, and consumers, to Pacific Coast shellfish," says Smith. "There are clearly advantages in safety, quality, and supply available in shellfish that are farm-raised in cold pristine waters such as our growing areas on the Pacific Coast. And modern hatcheries and farming techniques should allow us to continue to grow to meet increasing demand—if we can protect our farms against pollution." According to Bill Dewey, a past president of the Pacific Coast Oyster Growers, that's exactly what the oyster growers are doing—and they're succeeding. Who knows, the way things are going worldwide, the Pacific Northwest may soon be the only place in the world with a plentiful supply of great oysters.

■ MY FAVORITES

I've watched the Pacific Northwest oyster industry grow during the last decade, and I've eaten a lot of oysters. My favorites? Umpqua (European) flats from Winchester Bay, the Kumamotos from Hayes in Tillamook Bay, the native oysters ("Olympias") from Willapa Bay, and the Pacifics raised by Bill Webb in Westcott Bay on San Juan Island and by Bill Dewey in Samish Bay. But this is not to say I don't like oysters from other growing regions. My mouth waters at the thought of slurping—from their pristine half-shells, filled with precious liquor, of course: delicate Fanny Bays and

Lasqueti Islands from Georgia Strait, crisp Crescent Bays from Orcas Island, richly flavored Hama Hamas from Hood Canal, assertive Quilcenes from Quilcene Bay, the elegantly flavored—though somewhat large—Pacifics raised by Larry Qualman in Coos Bay, and last but not least, the creamy Willapas from the West Coast's largest oyster-producing bay.

CAPTAIN WHIDBEY INN POACHED OYSTERS

2 cups	Dry white wine
1 tbl	Dried sweet basil
1 tsp	Paprika
1 cup	Unsalted butter
6 pints	Shucked oysters
Toasted french bread rounds	

Combine wine, basil, paprika, and butter in large, heavy skillet and heat until it just boils. Add oysters all at once. Poach until oysters become firm and opaque. Immediately remove from liquid (do not overcook). Serve oysters on rounds of toasted French bread. Carefully skim butter off top of poaching liquid and pour over oysters. Serve with a crisp white sauvignon blanc or semillion. *Serves 8 to 12*

MARINATED OYSTERS

2 pints	Extra small oysters (shucked)
1 cup	White wine vinegar
2 tsp	Fresh French tarragon
3 tbls	Pickling spice
$1/4$ cup	Amontillado sherry

In a large saucepan, simmer oysters in their liquor until curled at the edges (about 3 to 5 minutes). Combine remaining ingredients in a small saucepan and cook over medium heat for 10 minutes. Drain oysters thoroughly and transfer to a bowl. Strain sauce and pour liquid over oysters. Cover and refrigerate for at least 3 hours. Serve well-chilled with crackers. *Serves 6 to 8*

—Courtesy, John Doerper

■ OYSTER FARMS

Following is a select list of oyster growers selling oysters at the farm. Most oyster farms are open from 8 to 5 on weekdays; a few are open on weekends, but call ahead.

Blau Oyster Company. 919 Blue Heron Road, Bow (Samish Island: west of Mount Vernon, east of San Juan Island); (360) 766-6171. Pacifics.

Brady's Oysters. Near Westport, at Elk River Bridge; (360) 268-0077. Pacifics.

Calm Cove Oyster Company. S.E. 481 Fagergren Road, Shelton; (360) 427-5953. Pacifics, European flats, Olympias.

Ekone Oyster Company. 192 Bay Center Rd., Bay Center (near Willapa Bay); (360) 875-5494. Pacifics, delicious smoked oysters.

Jolly Roger Pacific Oysters. Nahcotta Dock, Ocean Park; (360) 665-4111. Pacifics shucked, smoked, in shell.

Samish Bay Shellfish Farm. 188 Chuckanut Drive, Bow; (360) 766-6002. Pacifics, fresh crab, and pink scallops in the shell.

Westcott Bay Sea Farms. 4071 Westcott Drive, near Roche Harbor, Friday Harbor (San Juan Island); (360) 378-2489. Pacifics, European flats.

Sunset over Willapa Bay (above).
Bill Webb, owner of Westcott Bay Sea Farms, poses with some gourmet varieties. (right)

NORTH-CENTRAL
AND THE SAN JUAN ISLANDS

SEATTLE AND THE OTHER CITIES on the eastern shore of Puget Sound are always near salt water and always—on a clear day—in sight of mountains. One of the area's great attractions has always been the ease with which one can reach the mountains—to hike, ski, climb, pick berries, or just look around—or, with a boat or ferry ticket, reach the islands in Puget Sound. From Snoqualmie Pass north to Canada, hundreds of miles of hiking trails wind through the Alpine Lakes, Glacier Peak, Henry M. Jackson, Boulder Creek and Noisy-Diobsud wilderness areas, Ross Lake National Recreation Area, and North Cascades National Park. To the west, killer whales, ferries, kayaks, and sailboats travel through the islands.

■ NORTH CASCADES

The North Cascades start at Snoqualmie Pass, due east of Seattle—although of course the Cascade Range continues south all the way to California. From here north, three paved roads cross the mountains: Interstate 90, the fastest, crosses the

Snowfalls on the rails over Snoqualmie Pass were sometimes so heavy that rotary plows could not operate. In those instances, Chinese coolies were hired to dig the tracks clear by hand, as captured in this 1886 photograph. (University of Washington Libraries)

3,022-foot Snoqualmie Pass; farther north, slower, equally scenic US Highway 2 crosses 4,061-foot Stevens Pass; and farthest north, US Highway 20, the North Cascades Highway—the slowest but most scenic of all, and closed every winter because of deep snow—crosses 5,477-foot Washington Pass.

One can make a long loop through Snoqualmie and Stevens passes or a much longer loop through Snoqualmie Pass and the North Cascades. Smaller roads, many of them unpaved, lead to trailheads, campgrounds, and fishing spots all along the Cascades.

Drive into the mountains on a cloudy day, and the evergreens on the steep slopes look almost black, while the rock walls rising into the clouds seem to go on forever. Hike there in the heat of summer, and the soil of the rocky trail may be dry as dust, while farther up you may still find patches of snow and meadows of flower in full spring bloom. You'll see the outrageous color combinations that only nature can get away with—the bright red-orange of Indian paintbrush against the intense purple of lupine, for example. The higher you climb, the more layers of mountains appear, the more you see of the great, snowcapped volcanoes.

From the Canadian border south to Snoqualmie Pass, lands along the spine of the Cascades have been designated as national park, wilderness, or national recreation areas. The preservation of these 3.5 million acres of mountains and forests and glaciers reflects the decades of effort by Washington environmentalists.

Hikers make their way through all the protected areas in these mountains, as do a variety of critters. The heavy snows of winter, and the rock and ice of the high country, have not made the mountains inhospitable to wildlife. Wolves, once hunted to extinction in the North Cascades, are back. Packs that presumably came from British Columbia have recolonized the northern part of the range. Threatened northern spotted owls and marbled murrelets nest here. Salmon spawn in many of the rivers. And then, there are those formidable North American predators, grizzly bears. The big bears were once relatively plentiful in the North Cascades but were presumed extinct here throughout most of the 1970s and '80s. Hikers periodically reported seeing grizzlies, but biologists couldn't find enough hard evidence to confirm the sightings. Finally, when a hunter reported seeing a grizzly drag an elk carcass across a dirt road, biologists went to the site, found clear grizzly pawprints, and concluded that the bears were back. Actually, they had probably never left; there just hadn't been many of them, and they had stayed out of sight. By now, definite signs of their presence have been found from the Canadian border all the way down past Snoqualmie Pass. The mountains had stayed wilder than anyone had thought.

■ SNOQUALMIE PASS

Most of the transcontinental traffic between Seattle and the Eastern Seaboard gets funneled over the Cascades through Snoqualmie Pass on the fast lanes of I-90. Snoqualmie is the pass for people in a hurry; for those who aren't, there are ample roads to wander just off the main highway. To the north, the half-million-acre **Alpine Lakes Wilderness,** for instance, a haven for hikers, fishermen, and backpackers, comes almost to the shoulder of the road.

Despite its modest elevation, Snoqualmie Pass receives 35 feet of snow a year, and offers skiing for all experience levels. Skiers head for the groomed slopes, Nordic trails, and warm firesides of ski areas like **Alpental, Ski Acres,** and **Snoqualmie Summit.**

Even if Snoqualmie Pass hadn't been the route freeway builders took through the Cascades, it would have geological and historical significance. Geologically, it divides the North and South Cascades. The granite peaks that dominate the crest of the North Cascades are much more rugged and ancient than the great volcanoes that dominate the crest south of the pass. (Great volcanoes, like Mount Baker and Glacier Peak, also rise from the North Cascades, but granite prevails along the crest.)

Well west of the pass, people follow trails through the so-called **Issaquah Alps,** low mountains south of the freeway, and climb the steep southern slope of 4,167-foot **Mount Si,** the crag that looms over the upper Snoqualmie Valley. Nearby, the Snoqualmie River plunges 268 feet over a stone ledge at **Snoqualmie Falls.** The spot has always been sacred to the Snoqualmie Indians, who believe that the mists rising from the catch basin below ascend like prayers to heaven. Today, the site is well known to fans of "Twin Peaks" who recognize the stately Salish Lodge overlooking the falls as the lodge featured in the television mini-series.

A hydroelectric powerhouse carved out of the solid rock below the falls has been producing electricity here since 1899. Children and steam train enthusiasts can ride on the scenic **Puget Sound & Snoqualmie Valley Railroad** between North Bend, at the base of Mount Si, and Snoqualmie, near the falls. Purchase tickets for the ride at the **Snoqualmie Depot Museum** on Railroad Avenue. Call (206) 746-4025 for information.

Farther down the Snoqualmie Valley is **Carnation Farms,** operated as a research dairy since 1910. A large statue near the entrance commemorates one Segis Pieterje Prospect—known to her intimates as "Possum Sweetheart"—who in 1920 set a world record for the most milk produced in a single year. A London dairy magazine called her "the most wonderful cow in the world."

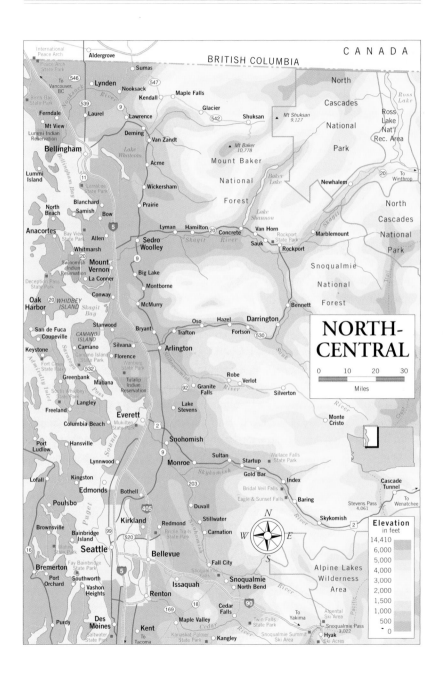

CANADA

BRITISH COLUMBIA

NORTH-CENTRAL

| 0 | 10 | 20 | 30 |

Miles

Elevation
in feet

| 14,410 |
| 6,000 |
| 5,000 |
| 4,000 |
| 3,000 |
| 2,000 |
| 1,500 |
| 1,000 |
| 500 |
| - 0 |

■ EVERETT

Driving north instead of east from Seattle, it's harder to leave the city behind. The Seattle standard metropolitan statistical area embraces Everett, 30 miles north, and the Seattle economy extends at least to the southern edge of Everett, where Boeing manufactures 747s in the largest space under one roof in the world. The weekday tour of the plant, which allows visitors to view the huge aircraft in various stages of assembly, is arguably the premier industrial tour of the state. Call (206) 342-4801 for information.

Historically known not as a Boeing town but as a mill town, Everett lies on the shore of Port Gardner Bay, an inlet of northeast Puget Sound, bounded on the east and north by the dark waters of the Snohomish River. Everett's waterfront is still dominated by lumber mills—its commercial soul since the city's inception a century ago. In years past, motorists were well advised to roll up their windows as they breezed by Everett—the rotten egg smell wafting from the city's pulp mills was legendary. Today, most of those mills have closed, and many jobs have moved to the Boeing plant south of town.

In the late 1880s, as the Great Northern Railway inched westward from Minneapolis, Port Gardner was proposed as the railroad's western terminus. (Trains, including Amtrak's *Empire Builder,* still roll into Everett from the east by way of Stevens Pass—or rather *under* Stevens Pass through one of the nation's longest railroad tunnels.) Sensing the site's economic potential as a processing and shipping center for wood cut in the vast forests linked to the sound by the Snohomish River, local investors teamed up with Tacoma lumber baron Henry Hewitt and a group of eastern capitalists, including Charles Colby and John D. Rockefeller, to form the Everett Land Company (named for Colby's son, Everett). The town was platted as "Everett" in 1890.

After a few years as a thriving mill town, Everett was crippled by the Panic of 1893; Rockefeller and his partners pulled their money out, and the city foundered until the turn of the century, when James J. Hill's Everett Improvement Company started buying up land. Frederick Weyerhaeuser subsequently built what became the world's biggest sawmill on Everett's shore.

In the early decades of this century, the town's thriving lumber mills became a source of bitter labor strife when newly organized mill workers confronted mill owners over wages and working conditions. The shingle weavers, who routinely lost fingers and larger appendages to the steel blades that sliced cedar into roofing, were particularly militant. The "Everett Massacre," which was the bloodiest episode in Everett's long saga of labor conflict, took place during the shingle weavers' strike of 1916. Vigilantes had beaten a group of Wobblies on the outskirts of town, and a boatload of Wobblies traveled north from Seattle on the steamer *Verona* for a protest rally. A crowd of armed deputies was waiting for them on the docks. Shots were fired from both the dock and the steamer. When the shooting stopped, five men lay dead and 31 lay wounded on the boat, two men lay dead on the dock and, presumably, some men—who were never found—lay dead beneath the water of Gardner Bay. Seventy-four Wobblies were arrested and charged with the murder of the two deputies killed on the dock. (No one was ever charged with anything for killing the men on the boat.) After a jury acquitted the first defendant, the rest were simply released.

The labor battles are long gone, along with most of the mills—and the old-growth forests that fed them. Beautiful examples of building styles popular in this century's early decades decorate downtown Everett. Within a few blocks you see the grand old wing of the Spanish mission-style courthouse with its clock and bell

The crew and passengers on an inaugural trip of the Great Northern Railway pause for a photo opportunity in the early 1890s. (Museum of History and Industry, Seattle)

tower; the ornate art-deco brick of City Hall, the patina on the copper steeple of the Presbyterian church; and the massive, Romanesque Federal Building. Many of the fine old mansions built by lumber barons still stand on Grand and Rucker avenues at the north end of town. Several blocks further north on 18th Street are the marina and Marina Village—a string of waterfront restaurants and shops. It's here that you catch the ferry to **Jetty Island** for a day of picnicking, hiking, and bird watching. Other sites in Everett include the **Everett Museum,** housed in a turn-of-the century brick building at 2915 Hewitt at Maple Street and the **Everett Publick Market** at 284 Grand, a two-story structure consisting of shops, galleries, cafes, and an antique mall.

■ CASCADES EAST OF EVERETT

East of Everett, State Highway 92 follows the path of the old Everett and Monte Cristo Railway, built by the Everett Land Company to carry ore from Rockefeller's

Crowded conditions in logging camps as seen in the bunkhouse above, led to labor unrest among the loggers and miners. (Museum of History and Industry) Modern methods, like air-lifting logs out of difficult-to-reach areas, have ameliorated some of the harshest working conditions (left).

silver mine at Monte Cristo to a smelter on Gardner Bay. It strikes the South Fork of the Stillaguamish River at Granite Falls, winds along the river, and enters the Mount Baker–Snoqualmie National Forest. Evergreens, big leaf maples, and alders crowds the river bank. In autumn, maples drop leaves the colors of fire and gold on the thick mat of ferns and salmonberry bushes beneath them. Close to the river, ferns and feathery mosses carpet the trunks of cedar and hemlock, and stands of thin, pale alder picket the shore. The Stillaguamish runs slow and gray, split here and there by narrow islands, or tumbles and breaks on its rocky bed.

The river valley rises to high, wooded bluffs that give way to rocky crags as the valley narrows toward the end of the paved road. At Verlot, State Highway 92 (here known as the **Mountain Loop Highway**) becomes a graveled corridor that curves east and south past Silverton and then winds 20 miles through the thick forests of the Sauk River Valley between the Monte Cristo turnoff and State Highway 530 a few miles south of Darrington. Forest roads lead to trailheads for the **Henry M. Jackson Wilderness** and the **Glacier Peak Wilderness,** the largest wilderness in the state.

In 1889, veins of silver and lead ore were found in the mountains above Barlow Pass. The site was named **Monte Cristo,** after prospector Frank Peabody's remark: "It's as rich as the Count of Monte Cristo." A mine was sunk here, financed by Rockefeller and the Everett Land Company. A town of clapboard stores and saloons sprouted below the mine along Dumas Avenue—a dirt road named for Peabody's favorite author (Alexandre Dumas the elder wrote *The Count of Monte Cristo*). Miners worked in dark, cramped tunnels by day, blew off steam at night in the Burning Stump dance hall on Dumas, and went home to sleep in dormitories near the shafts.

The mine petered out in the 1920s, and by now few traces remain of the old town. Monte Cristo used to be a popular destination for weekend motorists, but the old road washed out and was never rebuilt. These days, few people make the long, steep hike from Barlow Pass.

Darrington lies on the Sauk River, surrounded by cloud-wreathed ridges and knolls. Logging is the community's bread and butter, and mangy clearcuts scar the high hills in all directions. Many of Darrington's early settlers hailed from North Carolina, and a bluegrass festival held here each July celebrates the town's Tarheel roots.

You can also reach Darrington by driving north from Everett on Interstate 5,

Melting snowdrifts remain a common sight well into summer along mountain roads in the North Cascades.

turning east toward Arlington, and following the North Fork Stillaguamish River on State Highway 530. Dairy cattle graze in wet meadows with the crags and spires of the North Cascades rising behind them. New metal roofs gleam on old wooden barns, and weathered metal shows the dull rust of time. Old wooden silos lean from the vertical, rural ruins in the making. Taut cross-fencing divides the pastures of active dairy farms. The open hay mow of an abandoned barn gapes hollowly at the road.

Above Arlington, Highway 530 follows the North Fork Stillaguamish River, whose tributary, Deer Creek, once produced the largest run of wild summer steelhead on Puget Sound. In recent times careless logging practice has destroyed much of the spawning habitat on Deer Creek.

About 40 miles east of Arlington, a hard-to-find gravel road, Forest Road 2010, leads to the small **Boulder River Wilderness,** which protects perhaps the last substantial stand of low-elevation old-growth forest in the western Cascades. As you walk along the Boulder River, you can see it plunge over and around huge boulders. The river's surface is streaked with foam; in places it's totally covered with foam and looks like espresso hidden beneath the froth of a good cappuccino. Alders, their gray bark dappled with white lichen and clumps of moss, rise and slant in a complex rhythm of vertical lines. Backlit, the trunks of larger trees are dark, almost like the dark patches on a negative, while the yellow-green moss on the branches seems to glow. The big trees along the trail are easily six or seven feet across, and the vertical grain of bark on a big cedar could almost be the veined granite of a cliff. The complex, overlapping layers of needles, branches, moss and ferns, all backlit by the fading sun, create a wall of green, a kind of green light. Beams of light diffused in mist create a glow between the columns of massive cedars. Sunlit spider webs glisten iridescently among the dark, mossy branches and great trunks, and within them spiders wait patiently in the green light. Across the river, framed by the trunks of majestic trees, a sheet of water plummets down a sheer rock face, splits, then plunges over wet granite festooned with moss, ferns, bushes, and trees, to the foaming green river.

■ Skagit River

The Skagit River rises in Canada and flows down through the North Cascades, entering Puget Sound in a wide delta southwest of the town of Mount Vernon.

Much of it is protected as the **Skagit National Wild and Scenic River.** At the river's mouth, the **Skagit Wildlife Area** provides habitat for whistling swans, snow geese, and other birds.

Mount Vernon, which most travelers reach via Interstate 5, is the usual point of departure for the famous **Skagit tulip fields.** Straddling the murky jade green Skagit River, the town houses a natural food co-op, a Mexican grocery, two bike shops, a good bakery, and a small bookstore with an entire shelf devoted to UFO abductions. Above the weathered brick buildings of the old commercial district, layers of darkening clouds are superimposed on the gray sky, and away to the east the Cascade foothills disappear in the hovering mist. Men with ponytails drive by in old trucks with gun racks, and businessmen in gray suits sip coffee in the bakery. In the parking lot, high school girls slouch in Puma sneakers and baggy jeans, smoking menthol cigarettes, and listening to Salt-n-Pepa—wishing this was Seattle, or at least Bellingham. Even so, every April Mount Vernon is the sought-after destination for many Washingtonians when the town ushers in the spring with a 10-day Tulip Festival. (See "Festivals and Events" in "PRACTICAL INFORMATION.")

For a look at the Skagit River delta farmlands, turn off the freeway south of Mount Vernon and head west to **Conway.** One hundred years ago, a branch line of the Great Northern Railway ran along the east bank of the Skagit River's south fork, and passed through here. Today, little remains except a white-steepled church built in 1916 and a tavern 20 years older.

Between Conway and La Conner, the delta is spread with farms, laid out in a patchwork of fallow and green. Farmhouses huddle with their smaller outbuildings and huge old barns at regular intervals, and irrigation ditches wind through the green fields like the tailings of giant moles.

Some valley farms produce milk, vegetables, and berries, but the Skagit delta's most famous crop is flowering bulbs—daffodils and tulips that paint the fields with huge squares of yellow, pink, and red in late March and April, and draw sightseers from far and wide. Along the road sit a few immaculately restored farmhouses that are now bed-and-breakfasts. An old store with a gas pump out front advertises: "Bait, Ammo, Cold Beer." To the east, an occasional rough, wooded hump juts up 100 feet or more from the flats, and further off, the foothills of the North Cascades rise from their misty shrouds.

La Conner lies along the eastern bank of the Swinomish Channel, a narrow inland waterway once used as a sheltered passage from Bellingham Bay to Puget

MYSTIC SKAGIT VALLEY

*I*t is a poetic setting, one which suggests inner meanings and invisible connections. The effect is distinctly Chinese. A visitor experiences the feeling that he has been pulled into a Sung dynasty painting, perhaps before the intense wisps of mineral pigment have dried upon the silk. From almost any vantage point, there are expanses of monochrome worthy of the brushes of Mi Fei or Kuo Hsi.

The Skagit Valley, in fact, inspired a school of neo-Chinese painters. In the Forties, Mark Tobey, Morris Graves and their gray-on-gray disciples turned their backs on cubist composition and European color and, using the shapes and shades of this misty terrain as a springboard, began to paint the visions of the inner eye. A school of sodden, contemplative poets emerged here, too. Even the original inhabitants were an introspective breed. Unlike the Plains Indians, who enjoyed mobility and open spaces and sunny skies, the Northwest coastal tribes were caught between the dark waters to the west, the heavily forested foothills and towering Cascade peaks to the east; forced by the lavish rains to spend weeks on end confined to their longhouses. Consequently, they turned inward, evolving religious and mythological patterns that are startling in their complexity and intensity, developing an artistic idiom that for aesthetic weight and psychological depth was unequaled among all the primitive races. Even today . . . a hushed but heavy force hangs in the Northwest air: it defies flamboyance, deflates extroversion and muffles the most exultant cry.

—Tom Robbins, *Another Roadside Attraction,* 1971

Sound. Red and white tugboats often chug by, coaxing rafts of logs between La Conner's marina and the logs stacked on the bare dirt of the scaling yard just across the water on the Swinomish Indian Reservation.

Quaint "olde tyme" boutiques—craft stores and antique marts—occupy the turn-of-the-century storefront buildings along La Conner's First Street, and cater to a booming tourist trade. Visitors browse the trinket shops and dine al fresco at the many restaurants whose decks overhang the channel.

La Conner's reputation as an "artists' colony" dates back to the late 1930s, when seminal Northwest School painters Guy Anderson and Morris Graves took up residence in a dilapidated cabin here. It got a boost in the 1970s when novelist and pop philosopher Tom Robbins became the town's most famous resident.

(previous pages) Mount Vernon in the Cascade Mountains rises above fog settling in over Skagit Valley.

Some fine old Victorian homes and a few interesting churches stand among the houses on the hillside overlooking the commercial district and the channel. The **Skagit County Historical Museum** sits atop the hill, at the end of Fourth Street. The two-story brick wedge of City Hall, built in 1886, rises above Second Street at the south end of town. Between the city hall and the high, orange arch of the painted steel bridge that spans the channel, a few utilitarian, concrete fish-processing plants stand near the water in a confusion of green nylon nets and crab pots.

■ UPPER SKAGIT: NORTH CASCADES NATIONAL PARK

Above the more placid stretches of river in the Skagit Valley, the Skagit tumbles down out of some of the state's most wild and beautiful country. Upstream from the vacation town of **Rockport**, the **Skagit River Bald Eagle Natural Area** attracts some 500 bald eagles every winter, when they come to feed on spawned-out chum and other salmon.

Beyond the eagle refuge, State Highway 20, the **North Cascades Scenic Highway**, follows the river through **Ross Lake National Recreation Area**, a federally administered buffer zone between the northern and southern units of **North Cascades National Park**. Campgrounds, trailheads, privately owned lodges and resorts, and boat launches lie within Ross Lake National Recreation Area and adjacent national forest lands—in some cases right along the scenic highway.

The drive along the highway is distractingly scenic, and one can stop for the views from Goodall Creek Viewpoint and the Diablo Lake, Ross Lake, and Washington Pass overlooks.

Near the **Colonial Creek campground,** a stream cloudy with rock ground to dust by a glacier flows past the bases of cedars and firs four, five, six feet across, while long-dead cedar snags rise from the mud and epiphytes drip from the brush. The North Cascades are generally thought of as a place of rock and ice, but they are also a place for plants. North Cascades National Park is home to 1,700 species, more than botanists have found in any other national park.

The highway's climax is **Washington Pass** (5,477 feet), from which short hikes lead to spectacular views of **Snagtooth Ridge, Cooper Basin,** and the jagged peak of **Liberty Bell.** These higher reaches of the Scenic Highway close after the first snows of November and do not open until the spring melt, in April.

Although you can see the peaks of North Cascades National Park from the highway, the national park itself is a virtually roadless wilderness accessible only by foot. To see much of this country, you have to get out and walk, or take a boat on one of the lakes. You can walk for days without crossing a road. Trails connect the national park and recreation area with the Pasayten Wilderness to the east, and to the Glacier Peak Wilderness and the Lake Chelan National Recreation area to the south. Water taxis take hikers up 24-mile-long Ross Lake to trailheads far north of the road. One trail leads to the nations largest stand of old-growth western red cedar. But there are also short trails that start at campgrounds or the side of the highway, and can easily be covered in a day or a few hours.

Fishermen can rent boats and motors at the Ross Lake Resort or the Diablo Lake Resort. People who bring their own kayaks, canoes, or powerboats can launch them on Diablo Lake. Both Ross and Diablo lakes were created early in this century by Seattle City Light power dams. The extremely scenic trip up Diablo Lake—spent looking up at glaciated peaks and squeezing through a rocky gorge—ends at the foot of Ross Dam.

At the end of the rough Cascade River Road, a four-mile hike will take you to **Cascade Pass** and back. At Cascade Pass, you may be able to look across acres of

A view of Lake Diablo, and the North Cascade Highway winding along its shores (above).
Cultivated tulip fields in the Skagit Valley (right).

lupine and white beargrass at walls of granite and ice. Immersed in the scent of wildflowers, you may hear a rumble like distant thunder as ice—jagged tons of ice compressed by weight and studded with boulders—crashes from the glacier across the way. Water seeps out under glaciers, tumbles over boulders in gray streambeds, and drops down sheer vertical walls. In a nearby cirque filled with fireweed, dozens of nameless waterfalls cascade over granite cliffs.

■ FIDALGO AND WHIDBEY ISLANDS

From La Conner, you can look across the Swinomish Channel to Fidalgo Island, reached by a bridge on its northern side. Despite an overdeveloped highway strip into town, and a massive oil refinery, the Fidalgo Island "capital" of **Anacortes** is visited by most travelers along the Puget Sound coast. In large part this is because it is the terminus for ferries to the San Juan Islands and to Sydney on Canada's Vancouver Island.

Anacortes is an interesting destination in its own right, with several attractive parks and maritime views, the ornate nineteenth-century residential neighborhood of **Causland Park,** and an attractive old downtown area. A refurbished steam engine pulls cars and tourists through the town on the **Anacortes Railway** from the old Burlington Northern Depot. From **Washington Park,** you can look across the straits to the San Juans and the Olympic Mountains. South of town, and accessible by paved road, **Mount Erie** offers wider views to Mount Rainier and Mount Baker.

Across Deception Pass Bridge from Fidalgo Island lies Whidbey Island, the second longest island in the country. Lying in the Olympic rain shadow, Whidbey receives one of the lowest levels of rainfall in western Washington. Sunny summer days here attract many visitors. Farms and woods cover most of this peaceful island, and towns are small, even quaint.

Deception Pass State Park guards both shores of the channel that British navigator Captain George Vancouver sighted in 1792, mistaking it for the entrance to a bay. He was soon apprised of the truth, but memorialized his error by renaming it **Deception Pass.** Today's visitors to the park can hike, swim, fish, or go boating.

Whidbey Island pioneers built blockhouses to protect themselves from anticipated raids by the Skagit Tribe. Some of the log structures still stand in the town of **Coupeville**, founded in 1852 and known for its well-preserved Victorian-era downtown. Another attractive walking town is **Langley**, which offers galleries and restaurants. For four days in late August, its Island County Fair brings together local agricultural exhibits, a parade, and logger competitions. **Fort Casey State Park** preserves fortifications built by the army in the 1890s, the **Admiralty Point Lighthouse**, and an underwater park.

■ SAN JUAN ISLANDS

Lying at the crossroads of Puget Sound and the Straits of Georgia and Juan de Fuca, the San Juans are the summits of a sunken mountain range stretching from the mainland to Vancouver Island. The range's highest peaks are the 172 proper islands of the archipelago; a few hundred others hold their heads just above the water's surface at low tide. Named by the Spanish explorer Francisco Eliza in 1791 for his patron, Señor Don Juan Vicente de Guemes Pacheco de Padilla Horcasitas y Aguayo, the viceroy of Mexico, the San Juans form a maze of islands—some bare, limpet-shaped rocks the size of station wagons, others big enough for a house.

The larger islands are several miles across: some rise steeply from the water to high knolls or hog-back ridges bristling with firs, while others are relatively flat and gently contoured. Lopez, Shaw, Orcas, and San Juan—the four largest—are served by the ferry from Anacortes and from Sydney, British Columbia. The rest can be reached only by private boat or plane. Weathered cabins and new glass-fronted homes are scattered along hidden coves and on tiny islands 100 yards across.

The San Juans receive an average of only 29 inches of rain a year, and some of the islands lie in a "dry belt"—a rain shadow of the Olympic Mountains—where as few as 15 inches fall. Plants such as camas lily and Indian paintbrush, commonly found east of the Cascades, mingle with the Douglas fir and salal characteristic of western Washington. Gerry oak is native to San Juan Island. Even a species of prickly pear cactus (*Opuntia fragilis*) grows here. In places, rugged cliffs rise from the sea to dry, open meadows, where desiccated mosses crunch underfoot, and tiny wildflowers tremble in the slightest wind.

If the rain shadow has created a semi-arid marine climate, it has not made the islands eternally sunlit. Rain clouds pass over as they ride the prevailing current,

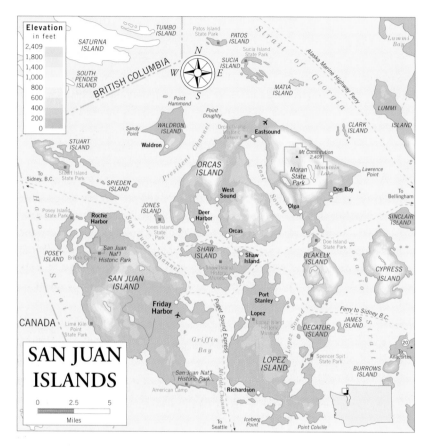

Elevation in feet
2,409
1,800
1,400
1,000
800
600
400
200
0

SATURNA ISLAND

SOUTH PENDER ISLAND

BRITISH COLUMBIA

TUMBO ISLAND

Patos Island State Park

PATOS ISLAND

Sucia Island State Park

SUCIA ISLAND

MATIA ISLAND

Strait of Georgia

Alaska Marine Highway Ferry

Lummi Bay

LUMMI

N
W   E
S

Point Hammond

Point Doughty

Sandy Point

WALDRON ISLAND

STUART ISLAND

Waldron

Orcas Island Historic Museum

Eastsound

CLARK ISLAND

ISLAND

To Sidney, B.C.

Stuart Island State Park

SPIEDEN ISLAND

President Channel

ORCAS ISLAND

Mt Constitution 2,409

Moran State Park

Mountain Lake

Lawrence Point

Haro

Posey Island State Park

Roche Harbor

JONES ISLAND

Jones Island State Park

West Sound

Deer Harbor

East Sound

Olga

Doe Bay

To Bellingham

SINCLAIR ISLAND

POSEY ISLAND

British Camp

San Juan Nat'l Historic Park

San Juan Channel

SHAW ISLAND

Orcas

Shaw Island

Doe Island State Park

BLAKELY ISLAND

Rosario Strait

CYPRESS ISLAND

Shaw Island Historic Museum

SAN JUAN ISLAND

Strait

CANADA

Lime Kiln Point State Park

Friday Harbor

Griffin Bay

Lopez

Lopez Island Historic Museum

Port Stanley

Puget Sound Express

DECATUR ISLAND

Lopez Sound

Ferry to Sidney B.C.

JAMES ISLAND

Strait

Spencer Spit State Park

(20)

To Anacortes

SAN JUAN ISLANDS

0   2.5   5
Miles

San Juan Nat'l Historic Park

American Camp

Middle Channel

LOPEZ ISLAND

BURROWS ISLAND

Richardson

To Seattle

Iceberg Point

Point Colville

which sweeps in from the ocean and curls clockwise down and back on itself. If it is raining in Seattle, the San Juans are probably overcast.

These islands have been inhabited seasonally for about 2,000 years. For many centuries, people of the Lummi, Samish, and Songish tribes used them as summer homes, camping in shelters of woven mats, and as a sort of natural supermarket, taking salmon and halibut from the reefs and harvesting camas root and berries on the land.

The tribes weren't the only people who grasped the advantages of fishing here. At the turn of the century, non-Indian fishermen from Bellingham, Gig Harbor, and settlements on Hood Canal rowed to the San Juans, where they harvested the salmon with seines pulled by pairs of four-man skiffs. At night, each ethnic group had its own favorite beach. Scandinavians camped on Lopez, while "Austrians" from the Dalmatian coast camped on San Juan Island. Fishermen of other ethnic origins claimed different beaches on San Juan.

Fishermen and recreational boaters aren't the only mariners who have been drawn to the San Juans. The maze of narrow channels, the countless sheltered coves, and the proximity to the Canadian border—which cuts a zigzag path down the Straits of Georgia and Haro—have made the archipelago a smugglers' haven ever since the international boundary was established in 1872.

The first contraband to pass through the San Juans' twisted waterways was British wool, brought by canoe from Vancouver Island in the dead of night. The islands' two most famous smugglers were Jim Kelly and Larry Kelly, unrelated men who happened to share a name and the same line of work—running opium and Chinese laborers from British Columbia to Washington—in the 1880s and '90s.

Prohibition brought a new wave of smugglers to the San Juans. In the early 1920s, a Seattle police captain named Ray Olmstead headed a ring of bootleggers

Kayaking off Orcas Island in the San Juans.

here, bringing as many as 200 cases of illegal liquor a day across the border until his arrest in 1925.

Today, it would be naive to assume that none of the sailboats, yachts, tugs, seiners, gill-netters, kayaks, or ferries winding through the islands carry drugs or other contraband.

Lopez Island is the first stop on the ferry run from Anacortes. Named for Lopez Gonzales de Haro, the Spanish captain who sailed under Eliza's command and "discovered" the San Juans in 1791, Lopez is the flattest of the big islands, and its relatively gentle topography has fostered agriculture since white settlers first arrived on the island in the 1850s. Some small farms still thrive on Lopez, but most of the island's large, open parcels are hay fields today. Nevertheless, people raise everything from sheep to llamas, and kiwi fruit to wine grapes.

The local economy leans heavily on the tourist trade. Possibly, some of the island's 1,800 year-round residents find themselves overwhelmed by the number of people who descend on Lopez every sunny weekend, but they do appreciate the money visitors spend. Like the rest of the San Juans, Lopez struggles to hold on to its authenticity and remain a vital community.

Lopez Village, on the island's western shore, features a few good restaurants, a winery, a supermarket, and a great local history museum. From the ferry terminal you reach Lopez Village by following Ferry Road South about five miles. Along the way you will pass two splendid parks. Both **Odin County Park** and **Spencer Spit Park** are ideal spots to while away an afternoon hiking, beaching, picnicking, and even clamming.

Shaw Island, the ferry's next stop and the smallest of the four islands that it serves, is home to a few hundred permanent residents—among them a community of Franciscan nuns who run the ferry dock and the grocery store. Shaw's residents value their seclusion, and have thus far resisted the tourist trade that thrives on the neighboring islands. Shaw offers neither restaurants nor overnight accommodations—the island's community plan forbids both.

On the map, **Orcas Island**—the largest of the San Juans and the ferry's third stop—looks like a pair of lungs wrapped around the long, narrow body of East Sound. Up close, Orcas is lush and steep, and its roads are narrow and contorted. Luxury homes occupy much of the coastline, but along the island's one main road, the landscape remains mostly rural, or thickly forested with second-growth fir and alder. Recent logging has scarred some of the landscape.

At the end of the nineteenth century, fruit orchards and hop fields flourished in the fertile soil of Crow Valley, on the island's western lobe. But all the crops went to market by boat, and as water transportation lost ground to railroads and then trucks, the islands became commercially stranded. After early irrigation projects made the naturally arid Wenatchee and Yakima Valley regions of eastern Washington into fruit-growing centers, most of Orcas Island's orchards were abandoned.

A handful of resorts—from posh Rosario to low-budget Doe Bay—as well as beautiful Moran State Park draw hordes of visitors in summer.

The massive hump of **Mount Constitution,** the highest point in the San Juans, rises 2,409 feet above sea level on the eastern lobe of Orcas Island. A steep, narrow road of white-knuckle switchbacks climbs to the mountain's summit. At road's end, high above the clouds, stands a watchtower built of hand-cut stone by the Civilian Conservation Corps in 1934-36. An open deck on top of the tower affords a spectacular 360-degree view.

To the east, **Mount Baker's** flawless, snowy form rises godlike over the North Cascades. (In the San Juans, Baker is the peak of reference, as Rainier is from Seattle to Olympia.) The jagged ice and granite wall of the Cascades and the Canadian Coast Range forms the eastern horizon. The Olympics are etched on the western sky. Far below, countless islands rise from their dark seabed, and tiny plumes of white smoke climb the sky above Bellingham Bay, east across Rosario Strait. Eagles soar a thousand feet below.

Mount Constitution is surrounded by **Moran State Park,** a forested 3,325-acre tract of land that covers most of Orcas Island's eastern lobe. The park includes isolated lakes, sandy beaches, and scores of campsites, as well as Mount Constitution and Mount Pickett. A few ancient spruce and fir—four or five feet in diameter—grow near the cool, mossy gorge of Cascade Falls, a short walk from the Cold Springs trailhead.

This park was the gift of shipyard tycoon Robert Moran, who served as Seattle's mayor during the fire of 1889, made a fortune building steamships for the Klondike gold rush, then retreated to the San Juans. Moran bought thousands of acres on Orcas, built a 19-bedroom mansion (today the centerpiece of Rosario resort) with two bowling alleys and an indoor pool in 1906, and in 1921, donated most of his land to the state.

During the Great Depression, the C.C.C. cleared the park's campsites and trails and built its stone gazebos, as well as the Mount Constitution Observation Tower

and the stone guard rails along the mountain's treacherous, winding road.

San Juan, the most developed and second largest of the islands, is the last stop in U.S. waters on the ferry run from Anacortes, and the seat of San Juan County government. San Juan's National Historic Park, vantage points for whale-watching, restaurants, hotels, and campgrounds attract droves of fair-weather visitors who disembark at the town of Friday Harbor.

A few ribbons of two-lane blacktop cross the island from coast to coast, winding past the small farms that occupy the cleared bottomland of the San Juan Valley. The roads are confusing and poorly marked, but eventually, they all lead back to Friday Harbor. Traffic—both cars and bicycles—fills them every summer. (There is no public transportation.) Many local cyclists will tell you that the best way to enjoy the islands is to leave your car in Anacortes, take ferries between the islands, then bike and camp at your leisure.

A town of 1,600 on the island's east coast, **Friday Harbor** is the only population center on San Juan Island and the largest community in San Juan County. It was named for Joe Friday—not the "Dragnet" detective, but the Hawaiian shepherd who once lived here. Friday Harbor climbs the hill above the ferry landing and a

Mount Baker (above) forms a vivid backdrop to the San Juan Islands. "River Jim," a well-known decoy artist, lives in Deer Harbor (left).

neighboring marina. The town's brightly painted, remodeled, turn-of-the-century homes house an assortment of chi-chi bistros, health food stores, and gift shops. A jumble of houses old and new, fashionable and funky, surrounds the business district.

Friday Harbor may have more real estate offices than any other town its size in Washington, if not the world. The San Juans were a sparsely inhabited backwater until the mid-1970s, but their population has doubled in the last 20 years, and land prices are astronomical. Unbuilt half-acre lots are advertised at $72,000, and the median home value is close to half a million dollars.

Ironically, a dearth of potable water has (for now) put the lid on residential development. Islanders debate the desirability of desalinization plants to ensure a supply of fresh water, but for now most agree that there are just too many people here.

Friday Harbor's **Whale Museum**, a yellow two-story building kitty-corner from the old brick courthouse on First Street, about three blocks north of the ferry dock, houses skeletons, models, and informational displays. Speakers in the stairwell broadcast what first seem to be the sounds of creaking docks and keening seagulls—in fact they are the recorded voices of local whale pods, often observed at **Lime Kiln State Park** on the island's east side.

American and British troops occupied San Juan Island jointly for 12 years in the mid-nineteenth century, and American Camp, where the U.S. forces lived, and English Camp, the British stronghold on the island's north end, are now both administered as **San Juan's National Historic Park.**

American Camp occupies most of San Juan's southern tail, six miles south of Friday Harbor, and includes an information center, interpretive trails, two restored military buildings, and a few miles of public beach. The open plain around American Camp is honeycombed with rabbit warrens, over which eagles, hawks, and owls glide, looking for dinner.

British Camp overlooks **Garrison Bay**, a sheltered inlet on the island's northeast corner, a 10-mile drive from Friday Harbor. A handful of neat, whitewashed buildings, including a two-room barracks house with brick fireplaces, is scattered across the manicured lawn that slopes down to the bay. A blockhouse built of unpeeled, whitewashed logs stands at the water's edge.

A deep tranquillity hangs over the bay, and one imagines there were worse

THE PIG WAR

In 1858, about two dozen American gold seekers, returning discouraged from the Fraser River rush, settled down to farm on San Juan Island—which was claimed at the time by both the British and the Americans. One settler, a Mr. Lyman Cutler, staked a claim near Bellevue Farm, property of the Hudson's Bay Company and Her Brittanic Majesty. One June day in 1859, when he walked out of his cabin, he discovered a Hudson's Bay Company hog rooting in his potato patch, and he shot the pig dead. Settlers at Bellevue Farm were outraged, and tensions generated by six years of territorial wrangling reached the boiling point.

British authorities threatened Mr. Cutler with arrest, and Gen. William Harney, commander of U.S. forces in the Pacific Northwest, sent 66 men under Capt. George Pickett—who four years later led the famous charge at Gettysburg—to occupy San Juan Island.

British Columbia's governor James Douglas responded in kind. The showdown quickly escalated, and by the end of August, 461 American soldiers had dug in near Bellevue Farm facing five British warships carrying 2,140 men and 167 cannon.

By the time news of the conflict reached Washington D.C., the nation seemed poised on the brink of a war over a pig, at the same time that it was about to break apart over slavery. President James Buchanan relieved General Harney of his Northwest command, and a joint military occupation of the island was negotiated with Great Britain. In 1872, the dispute was finally referred to an independent arbitrator—the German emperor, Kaiser Wilhelm I. The Kaiser ruled in favor of the United States, which is the obscure reason why today, the San Juan Islands are not a part of Canada.

George E. Blankenship in his 1938 history book *Told by the Pioneers* tells the following popular version of the war's outcome:

> *The* Olympia boys were preparing for their trip to Victoria when there was posted upon a bulletin board on a Western Union telegraph blank, the following purported dispatch from Washington: "Emperor William has decided to let the result of the coming baseball game between Olympia and Victoria dictate his decision of the international boundary question." Olympia won, and Emperor William decided in favor of the United States, but it is unlikely that he ever heard of the ball game. But there were those who took the above dispatch as authentic.

places for a Royal Marine to be stationed. The joint occupation was a peaceful affair, and relations between British and American troops were friendly. "Enemy" soldiers often attended holiday parties at each other's encampments. They spent most of their time gardening and hunting, and maintaining their tidy settlements. The amiable nature of the occupation is reflected in the small, formal garden the British planted here—a sunburst of hedges bordering patches of flowering bulbs.

A few structures remain standing here thanks to the preservation efforts of a local named Crook, who homesteaded the land following the departure of British troops. A marker at British Camp says that Crook lived and farmed here until 1965.

A trail leads uphill from the parking lot, across the road and up to the British cemetery on the slope of **Mount Young** (650 feet). Here lie the oak-shaded gravestones of eight Englishmen who died during the joint occupation. These men were casualties not of war, but of boredom. Their chiseled epitaphs recall drowning and hunting accidents.

Above the graveyard, the steep, arid slopes of Mount Young are reminiscent more of northern California than western Washington. Open expanses of tall, golden grasses are dotted with mossy slabs of exposed granite, and ancient oak trees—twisted Andalusian hydras—are scattered over 80 acres.

■ BELLINGHAM

The last big town before the Canadian border is Bellingham, which was cobbled together from four pioneer communities on Bellingham Bay. A water-powered sawmill was ripping logs into boards beside Bellingham Bay in the early 1850s, and Bellingham has been a mill town ever since—but it has not been just a mill town. Coal was mined not far from the water in the mid-nineteenth century; and mines continued operating past World War II. Teachers were trained in the nineteenth and early twentieth centuries at the New Whatcom Normal School, which has long since evolved into the well-respected and architecturally attractive **Western Washington University.** A lively counterculture community grew up around the university in the late 1960s and has helped set the city's tone ever since. More recently, the Bellingham area became a mecca for Canadian shoppers and real

British Camp overlooks Garrison Bay, near the site of the U.S.–British sovereignty conflict that came to be known as the Pig War.

estate investors, who have helped set the tone in different ways. Ships of the Alaska Marine Highway System travel up the Inside Passage to Ketchikan, Wrangell, Juneau, and Haines from a pier on Bellingham Bay. Victorian houses on the hills look out over the bay and down on the brick buildings of the old downtown. The ornate, restored **Mount Baker Theater** still shows films. Most retail business has fled to the malls, but the **Whatcom Museum of History and Art** at 121 Prospect Street is going strong in a massive brick fantasy built in 1892 as the Bellingham City Hall.

From Bellingham, one can proceed to the border and Vancouver, British Columbia, or head east to 10,750-foot **Mount Baker.** Baker offers climbing, downhill skiing and trails through the Mount Baker Wilderness. State Highway 542, which leads to Baker, also leads to trailheads for the northernmost and wildest parts of North Cascades National Park.

FAIRHAVEN

Fairhaven, it has been said by local street-corner sages, is more of a state of mind than a village. Physically, Fairhaven has been part of the city of Bellingham, since the independent town joined with the communities of Sehome and Whatcom to the north in 1903 to form a new city named after the large bay to the west. But, spiritually, Fairhaven has maintained its independence as a liberal enclave in a conservative city. Downtown Fairhaven is a collection of coffeeshops, bookstores, restaurants, and a pub, occupying late nineteenth-century brick buildings. Beyond the core, it's a medley of cottages and gardens, of greenwoods bordering a purling creek, of wildflower meadows and, down along the bay front, sandstone cliffs, tideflats, boat yards, and fishing boats. Here the Alaska ferry docks on the site of the largest salmon cannery in the world and, in summer, passenger ferries carry visitors to the San Juan Islands and Victoria, the capital city of British Columbia, on Vancouver Island. But, as along Monterey's Cannery Road, few cannery vestiges are left. Sea ducks and river otters feed on the mussels covering the abandoned pilings; great blue herons patiently stand in the shallows, waiting for unsuspecting fish to swim by; crows and gulls patrol the shore, digging for clams and marine worms, and bathing in the brackish water of Padden Creek Lagoon. Sea lions and seals float by, their heads raised above the swirls of the tide rip; now and then a bald eagle soars overhead.

Fairhaven is rife with history. Ancient shell middens and stone tools (going far back to the Clovis period) prove that the mouth of Padden Creek has been occupied by man since time immemorial. The Lummi Nation once had a fishing village here, and there are legends of a fierce battle fought between the local tribes and marauding Spanish pirates in Padden Marsh sometime in the 1600s. There's no historic proof of the battle, but pioneers found a Spanish chalice, dated 1640, embedded in a muddy bank.

History records one Indian raid in 1854, when Haidah Indians, visiting from northern British Columbia, swept down on the fledgling community and attacked a log cabin with little success, but paddled off with the heads of two hapless British coal miners. (Sehome to the north had a coal mine.)

Few historic remains of the nineteenth-century waterfront survive, but a local historical society has put down granite plaques throughout the village, marking such historic sites as the city's drowning pool (for dogs only, it says), the place where a freight wagon was swallowed by quicksand, the shore where Fairhaven moored its prison (a barge), and the site of the town pillory. Yes, Fairhaven had a pillory as late as the 1890s. Plaques also tell you where Dirty Dan Harris, the city's founder, built his log cabin, where the bunkhouse of Chinese cannery workers stood, and where a saloon owner died in a main street shoot-out.

Fairhaven's residents are a motley lot: fishermen and college professors, poets and construction workers, ship fitters, painters, and the sons and daughters of hippies who settled here in the 1960s. Most importantly, it's a friendly crowd, meeting at the Southside Café (1303 12th) or the Colophon (1208 11th) for breakfast, enjoying lunch under the spreading horsechestnut tree at the Cobblestone Café (1308B 11th St.), trysting on the bench outside the Eclipse Bookstore (915 Harris), browsing the shelves at Village Books (1210 11th), enjoying a pint of porter at the Archer Ale House (1212 Tenth St.), or crowding into Stanello's (12th & Donovan) for the best pizza in town. In the evenings they congregate at Post Point, to watch the red sun sink behind the San Juan Islands.

—John Doerper

SEATTLE TO MOUNT BAKER

Driving north from Seattle, on your way to Mount Baker, you have tired of the Interstate and decided to take to the back roads. Shortly after you leave Interstate 5 at the Alger turnoff, you enter a green tunnel of arching trees with occasional glimpses of farms and green pastures. At the south end of **Lake Whatcom** you turn east. You'll get a good look at the lake, cutting fjord-like through steep mountains, but soon you're back in the green tunnel. After turning left at State Highway 9, the trees give way to the pretty farmsteads and pastures of the Nooksack middle fork.

After turning right onto State Highway 542, the Mount Baker Highway, you'll drive past more pastures and farms. Beyond Glacier, the scenery becomes wild, the trees grow taller and steep cliffs crowd the road. A few miles south on Glacier Creek Road will bring you to the trailhead for **Coleman Glacier.** A short trail leads to the glacier's snout where the ice pushes into the alders; a longer, steeper hike brings you to the glacier's side where you can look down into the crevasses and listen to the ice as it grinds downhill. Few folks know you can walk right up to a glacier at such a low altitude in Washington State. The scenery is spectacular—as though taken straight from an Alaska tourism brochure. Take a close look at the edges, where the ice meets the land—in midsummer this fertile verge is covered with pink and white wildflowers.

Back on the main road, your next stop is **Nooksack Falls,** reached by a short gravel road through the woods. The tree-girted falls plunge over a rocky ledge 170 feet into a narrow canyon. This is a popular picnic site, but beware—the rock is unstable and there's real danger of taking an irreversible plunge. **Picture Lake,** near the end of the road, high up on the east slope of Mount Baker, makes for a safer picnic site, but, as one of the most photographed spots in the state, it's almost déjà vu. All because of dramatic, glaciated **Mount Shuksan** looming across the valley. The blueberries here are very good, and they ripen from August till late fall. They grow on very low bushes but are worth every stoop. If the snow has melted, you can drive on to the very end of the road and hike along alpine ridges for good views of both Mount Baker and the glacier-cut valley of Baker Creek.

To return, follow the highway to Bellingham and take Interstate 5 south to the northern end of State Highway 11, Chuckanut Drive, at Fairhaven Parkway. At the first traffic light you face a choice. You can turn right into Fairhaven Village, or left to take the winding road south through woods, past precipitous sandstone cliffs, gnarled trees, and intimate, wooded coves with tiny, secluded beaches. It's time for dinner now and you have several choices: a picnic at Larrabee State Park, a simple meal at the Oyster Creek Inn, or an elegant feast at the Oyster Bar. (See "PRACTICAL INFORMATION.") The latter comes with views of the islands and sunset over Samish Bay.

—John Doerper

Picture Lake and Mount Shuksan, one of the state's most photographed scenes.

SOUTH-CENTRAL

THREE OF WASHINGTON'S GRANDEST NATURAL ATTRACTIONS punctuate the Cascade Mountain Crest between Snoqualmine Pass and the Columbia River: the 14,410-foot snow cone of Mount Rainier; the smoking crater of Mount St. Helens, which erupted in 1980; and the Columbia River Gorge, where the rugged Cascade Range grudgingly opens to allow the West's largest river passage to the sea. Less grand but appealing for their low-key ambience and natural beauty are the small islands at the southern end of Puget Sound, and the state's pleasant capital at Olympia.

■ LOWER PUGET SOUND AND VASHON ISLAND

Vashon Island is accessible only by water, although it has been populated for more than a century and was once a tremendous producer of currants and strawberries. It has one sizable industry, the K-2 ski company—founded by the Vashon guys who first figured out how to make fiberglass skis. Today, K-2 is the largest ski manufacturer in the country.

In the summer, **Quartermaster Harbor**, along the island's southern shore, is filled with sailboats, speedboats, and yachts, many of which tie up at **Dockton Park**. In winter, perhaps a couple of dozen pleasure boats are moored at Dockton, along with an old gill-netter and a couple of seiners. Several rows of weather-darkened old pilings stand in the still water below the bluff where Dockton's turn-of-the-century buildings stand. It's hard to imagine that in 1892, this sheltered water held the only real drydock north of San Francisco. Before 1892, if a merchant ship needed repairs and the captain didn't want to take her all the way to San Francisco, he would just run her into shallow water and wait for the tide to go out. In 1950, the WPA guide to Washington found Dockton "a pale ghost, with graying remnants of wharves and ships along its waterfront." Today, you don't even find many remnants. Near the dock to which the seiners are moored, you can see trestle-like wreckage in the water. That's about it.

Across the harbor, you see the dark mass of conifers and the white of scattered houses. Close in, black-and-white scoters skim the surface of the water.

People who live here don't feel much nostalgia for the days when Vashon lay in the mainstream of Puget Sound commerce, and virtually no one wants to see the island enter the modern mainstream. In 1992, when the state of Washington briefly revived the notion of building a bridge that would link Vashon to Seattle and the Kitsap Peninsula, roughly one-quarter of the island's population showed up at a public meeting to protest. So it's still the more leisurely car ferries that take the locals north to Seattle or south to the city of Tacoma.

■ TACOMA

Tacoma's blue-collar image tends to keep people at bay, but the city offers some excellent parks and views, ornate turn-of-the-century downtown buildings, a fine small aquarium and zoo, and traces of an expansive nineteenth-century self-image that once marked the "City of Destiny." The ferry ride from Vashon Island is a far more appealing way to approach the city than Interstate 5. To the left of the ferry dock the black breakwater of the Tacoma Yacht Club shelters sailboats and yachts. To the right of the ferry dock, the wooded peninsula of **Point Defiance Park** juts into the Sound. Miles of wooded roads wind through Point Defiance. A saltwater beach

A Skokomish fishing camp in the lower Puget Sound area was photographed by famed frontier photographer Edward S. Curtis in the 1880s. (Museum of History and Industry, Seattle)

runs below the bluffs. Reconstructed buildings from the Hudson's Bay Company's old **Fort Nisqually** stand there, as do the aquarium and zoo. There are rose gardens, picnic tables, big trees, brushy banks, and ravines. One would be hard pressed to find a more spectacular urban park anywhere in the United States.

A strip of park runs along the water for miles. On a summer day, the paved pathway is crowded with runners, walkers, skaters, cyclists, people pushing baby carriages, people walking dogs. The grass is dotted with picnickers and sunbathers. The parking areas are filled with young people hanging out beside flashy cars. Mount Rainier rises from the Cascade Ridge like the half-melted remains of the last great snowman, heaped to the very clouds, and you get a sense that this city which took something close to the Indian name for Rainier—*Tahoma*—really does have a special relationship with the mountain.

From the ferry landing, a narrow, dripping tunnel leads to an old smelter site and a drive along the water toward Tacoma's downtown. On the tideflats beyond, you can see a pulp mill with its mountain of sawdust, warehouses, an aluminum plant,

Shipyards at Dockton, Maury Island *was painted by Alice Samson in 1907.*
(Museum of History and Industry, Seattle)

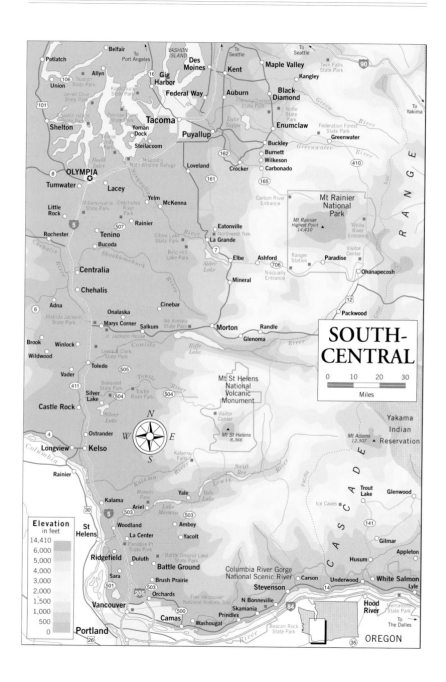

SOUTH-
CENTRAL

0   10   20   30

Miles

Elevation
in feet
14,410
6,000
5,000
4,000
3,000
2,000
1,500
1,000
500
0

and rows of tall blue container cranes. Always a port—shipping wheat and flour to the United Kingdom in the late 1880s—Tacoma today is the nation's sixth-largest container port.

Entering the city from Ruston Way, you pass between the old City Hall and Northern Pacific Railroad headquarters, which stand as portals at the north end of downtown. Just up the hill, the restored 1918 **Pantages Theater** and the restored **Rialto Theater** draw people to plays, concerts, and films. At the south end of downtown, the old, domed **Union Station** has been restored as part of a new federal courthouse. The **Washington State Historical Society** is building new quarters right next to Union Station; for now, the Historical Society is located near Stadium High School at 315 N. Stadium Way. The **Tacoma Art Museum** stands right on the main drag at Pacific and 12th.

It's hard to imagine that downtown Tacoma was ever known as a rowdy town, but it was. During World War II, officials at nearby Fort Lewis declared 16 different places

The Tacoma-Narrows Bridge, unstable and dubbed "Galloping Gertie" from the time it opened in 1940, is shown here in mid-collapse during a windstorm. (University of Washington Libraries)

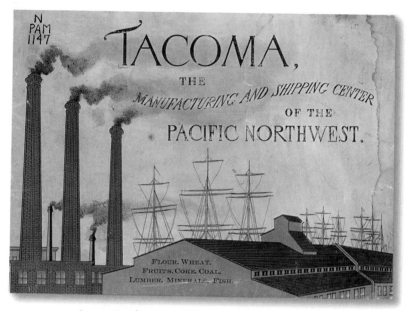

A promotional poster extols Tacoma's industrial opportunities.
(University of Washington Libraries)

off-limits to the troops. Even after the war, "night life in Tacoma meant bookie joints, slot-machines and pin-ball routes, unlicensed drinking spots, and an abundance of brothels, most of them in Opera Alley, between Broadway and Market Street," historian Murray Morgan writes in *Puget's Sound.*

The modern city has made a major effort to restore the **Thea Foss Waterway,** named for the Norwegian immigrant woman who founded what became a huge tugboat company, Foss Launch and Tug, and supposedly served as the model for Norman Raine's "Tugboat Annie" stories which were popular before World War II.

■ NISQUALLY NATIONAL WILDLIFE REFUGE

On the shore of Puget Sound between Tacoma and Olympia, the fields and marshes of the spreading Nisqually Delta are preserved as the Nisqually National Wildlife

(following page) An enormous stack of cedar boards dwarfs a worker at a turn-of-the-century mill near Seattle. (Pemco Webster and Stevens Collection, Museum of History and Industry, Seattle)

WEYERHAEUSER

Weyerhaeuser is the largest forest products company in the Northwest. Aside from its vast land holdings and timber-cutting operations, it is also a potent symbol of the logging industry in arguments over clear-cutting, preserving wildlife habitats, creating parks and hiking trails, exporting logs, and converting forest land to other uses.

Like most of the other men who started Washington timber empires in the late nineteenth century, Frederick Weyerhaeuser, a native of Germany, had been a lumber baron in the Midwest. He saw the pine forests of upper Michigan going fast and decided to invest in the still largely uncut woodlands of the Northwest. When his St. Paul neighbor, the railroad builder Jim Hill, offered him 900,000 acres of federal land-grant forest in Washington, Weyerhaeuser bought it for $6 an acre. The company subsequently bought more land, traded land, built mills, operated whole company towns, and started the first American tree farm in 1942.

Its ivy-draped headquarters in Federal Way just north of Tacoma is the nerve center for an organization that owns more standing timber than any other private company in the world.

Nobody stops to visit the corporate offices themselves, but Weyerhaeuser's headquarters campus contains the Pacific Rim Bonsai Collection and the Rhododendron Species Foundation, which are open to the public all year. The rhododendron collection is the largest in the world. Call (206) 661-9377 for information.

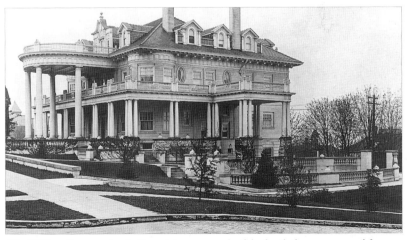

The William Rust mansion in Tacoma is one example of the family fortunes garnered from the city's industrial base. The Rusts' money came from the smelting business. (Washington State Historical Society, Tacoma)

Refuge. Walk through the refuge (reached from I-5 at exit 114) to the water's edge. To the north, beyond the sprays of purple daisies and the brown marsh grass beaten flat by high water, the gray-green Nisqually River flows toward Puget Sound. Mallards, bucking the wind, skim the surface of the river. Upstream, water originating from Nisqually Glacier above Paradise in Mount Rainier National Park glitters in the sunlight.

■ OLYMPIA

Less than 10 miles down the road from the wildlife refuge, Olympia sits at the junction of I-5 and US 101, at the narrow extremity of Budd Inlet—a fat finger of Puget Sound—where the fresh water of the Deschutes River mixes with the salt of the sea. Founded in 1850 and named for the majestic mountains that loom northwest of the city on clear days, Olympia has been Washington's capital since Washington Territory was severed from Oregon in 1853.

The first territorial legislature met here in 1854 in a room above the Gold Bar Store and Restaurant, when a few dozen houses and log cabins scattered on a broad patch of stump land above a muddy bay comprised the town. The massive, domed marble capitol that squats on its white stone haunches above the modern city wasn't completed until 1928. In the 74 years before that, legislators met in the Masonic Temple, a humble wooden hall, and finally in the old Thurston County Courthouse (currently known as the Old Capitol).

You can see the current capitol dome from the freeway, rising above the trees. Up close, it's an unusually handsome building set in a nicely landscaped campus—quite beautiful in spring, when the trees are in bloom. Down the hill from the capitol and the state office buildings east of Capitol Way lies downtown Olympia and the old center of political gravity at **Sylvester Park**. The turreted stone mass of the **Old Capitol** building, between Franklin and Washington streets, overlooks the park from the east. On the north stands the former Olympian Hotel, where generations of lobbyists bought politicians lavish meals, deals were made, big-time legislators set up housekeeping, and old pols hung out in the lobby. A lot of the state's real business was conducted at the Olympian until the late 1950s, when lobbyists and legislators moved to the new Tyee Motel south of town.

Olympia's downtown is low-key but interesting, replete with used book shops, cafes,

(previous pages) Mount Rainier forms a dramatic backdrop to the port of Tacoma.

and record stores. Interesting old brick buildings—many a bit rundown, some stripped of their cornices by a fierce earthquake in 1949—line the streets. The town's vitality shines in the scruffy bars where the worlds of middle-aged working stiffs and college kids with green hair overlap. Even around its dilapidated edges, Olympia is never threatening. The bicycle cop reading the yellowed newspaper taped to the window of a vacant storefront looks bored.

Because the small, nationally respected, aggressively non-traditional Evergreen State College stands near by, Olympia is something of an "alternative" culture center. The town hosts independent film festivals and supports a vigorous music scene— locals claim that Nirvana, the quintessential "Seattle band," got its start here. But if much of the crowd drinking in downtown pubs seems young and hip, they're also quite friendly. Shoot a game of pool at the Eastside Tavern—a gathering place for students, locals, and government types alike—and you're sure to meet an Olympian or two.

Timber dollars fed this area from the time its first settlers built a sawmill at Tumwater Falls, in 1845, until the middle of this century. Before World War II, when government was still relatively small, Olympia was primarily a Puget Sound port and mill town. In 1941, it contained 15 lumber, shingle, plywood, and furniture mills and 10 dairy and poultry processing plants. Even after the war, the port was busy loading lumber and plywood for the East Coast and the mills near the waterfront ran all night. Now, there is a pleasant pedestrian walk and lookout tower along part of the **waterfront**, and a busy public marina. Contemporary Olympia is essentially a government town. In fact, state and local government provide more than half the jobs in all of Thurston County. But you can get some sense of the way things used to be from the wonderful black-and-white photographs of huge trees and old-time loggers that adorn the walls of the Spar Restaurant on East Fourth Street, a historic watering hole of local mill workers and deal makers.

■ TUMWATER

The **Olympia Brewery** that stands beside the freeway right after the exits for downtown Olympia lets you know you're in Tumwater. Just south of Olympia (and essentially its suburb), Tumwater was established in 1845 as the first American settlement north of the Columbia River, and helped the United States build its claim to the land that is now Washington—an area that was dominated by the British until the boundary settlement of 1846.

State policemen keep a watchful eye in the lobby of the capitol building.

When built in the 1920s, the capitol dome was the fourth highest in the world.

Tumwater was founded by a party of Missourians led by Michael Simmons and George Bush, a black man who had fought with Andrew Jackson at the Battle of New Orleans and traveled to the Pacific Northwest as a Hudson's Bay Company employee in the 1820s. Bush's popularity exempted him from the Missouri law barring free blacks from residence there, but when the Simmons party asked him to go west, he went. Like most settlers bound for the Oregon Country, the party planned to settle in Oregon's Willamette Valley.

Michael Simmons was one of the state's earliest settlers. He and the party he led from Missouri established the town of Tumwater in 1845. (Washington State Historical Society, Tacoma)

Many of the Willamette's first American settlers came west from the border states, often fleeing the violent tensions building toward civil war. In an effort to obviate a crisis over slavery and racial issues in Oregon, the 1844 territorial legislature simultaneously outlawed slavery and required all blacks to leave the territory within three years; any black who stayed longer would be flogged every six months.

Though this law was seldom enforced, blacks could not own land or vote in Oregon, and on learning this, Bush and the Simmons party headed north of the Columbia, for land then claimed by the British, who were relative racial progressives.

The Simmons party settled at the mouth of the Deschutes River, where the pioneers built a gristmill and a sawmill at the base of Tumwater Falls. Among the people who came west to join the thriving community in its early years were a number of Crosbys, whose descendant, Bing—born in Spokane just half a century later—sang the original version of "White Christmas" and starred with Bob Hope in the classic "Road" pictures.

When Great Britain and the United States drew the international boundary at the 49th parallel in 1846, Tumwater officially became an American settlement. When Washington's first territorial legislature met in 1854, it approved a petition to grant George Bush title to his land, overriding the terms of the Donation Land Law of 1850 that allowed only "white citizens and half breeds" to file claims. Despite this victory, Bush was never allowed to vote and was never granted citizenship.

Beyond Tumwater lie the **Mima mounds**—symmetrical, dome-shaped hills 6 to 8 feet high and 20 to 30 feet in diameter. Rising one after another in all directions, they once covered the prairies in much of Thurston and Lewis counties. Only a few pockets of mound prairie remain, and they are mostly covered with small trees and scotch broom, the result of fire suppression begun at the turn of the century. The state is now trying to restore the remaining mound areas to their natural state by cutting, clearing, and burning the brush.

The origin of these strange formations, found scattered throughout Washington and other western states from Nebraska and Texas to California, remains a mystery. In 1841, explorer Charles Wilkes and his men dug up a few mounds in this area, thinking they were the graves of some early Indian people. Inside the mounds, they found no treasure, no artifacts, no bones—nothing but gravelly soil.

Conflicting explanations hold that the mounds were built by prehistoric fish as spawning nests when seas covered the continent, or that they are monuments of some vanished race, or that they were formed by the freezing and thawing that occurred as the Puget Glacier retreated. The glacier theory would sound plausible—except that the Mima mounds occur in areas never glaciated. Currently, the accepted theory is that the mounds were built by generations of pocket gophers—small but prodigious earth movers. The regular spacing of the mounds coincides with the gophers' territorial habits. To see the Mima mounds, take exit 95 off I-5, 10 miles south of Olympia, and head west to Littlerock. Follow the signs from there.

■ MOUNT RAINIER

Mount Rainier National Park lies less than an hour's drive southeast of Tacoma. Climbing the slopes of the 14,410-foot volcano itself, the park embraces broad tracts of old-growth forest, waterfalls, glaciers, and meadows smothered in summertime wildflowers. Lodges, campgrounds, hundreds of miles of hiking trails, and cross-country skiing at Paradise Lodge draw people year-round, although some of the

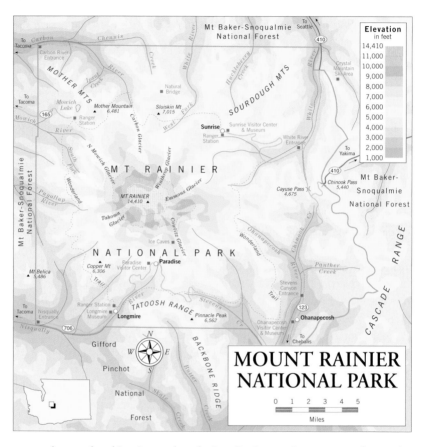

Mt Baker-Snoqualmie National Forest
To Seattle

Elevation
in feet

14,410
11,000
10,000
9,000
8,000
7,000
6,000
5,000
4,000
3,000
2,000
1,000

MOUNT RAINIER
NATIONAL PARK

0 1 2 3 4 5

Miles

approaches are closed in winter, when the Paradise Ranger Station, 5,500 feet up the south side of the mountain, once recorded 1,224 inches of snow in a year, a world record.

Visible all over central Puget Sound, the mountain has drawn climbers since at least the 1830s, when a Hudson's Bay Company doctor stationed at nearby Fort Nisqually made it part way up. In 1870, Gen. Hazard Stevens (the son of Washington Territory's first governor, Isaac Stevens) and Philemon Van Trump actually made it to the top. They spent the night on the summit, where a volcanic steam cave saved them from freezing to death. Twenty years later, a young teacher named Fay Fuller became the first woman to climb Rainier. Today, some 2,500 people make the climb every year.

Wildflowers blanket meadows in Mount Rainier National Park during the summer.

Complete novices can get a day of training from Rainier Mountaineering, which will then—weather permitting—lead them to the top. Very old people, very young people, and people with severe disabilities have all climbed Rainier in recent years. Nevertheless, Rainier challenges even the best climbers. The first American to scale Mount Everest, Jim Whittaker, learned to climb here and other climbers have trained on Rainier for a sense of Everest and Denali. But each year less fortunate climbers suffer illness, injury, or worse: they get altitude sickness, get caught in whiteouts, get trapped by winter storms. Sometimes, they fall from great heights. Sometimes, avalanches bury them or sweep them away. Willi Unsoeld, a world-class climber who taught philosophy at Evergreen State College, was killed by an avalanche while leading a group of college students up Rainier.

The hazards don't scare climbers away and the park gives non-climbers a lot to choose from. Roads lead to vantage points on all sides of the mountain, each with its own celebrated views, amenities, and summertime hiking trails. Of course, driving to a viewpoint doesn't guarantee anyone a view of the glaciers or summit: clouds frequently hide Mount Rainier from sight, even in the summer.

Park headquarters, including a visitors center and inn, are located in the southwest corner at **Longmire,** 2,761 feet above sea level. From there, the road climbs 13 miles to **Paradise,** at 5,400 feet.

You can drive through huge trees to the old **Paradise Lodge** at any time of year. From Paradise, which offers spectacular views of the mountain, you can walk through steep flower meadows on paved trails, hike into rough open country sliced by ravines, or start up toward the climbers' 10,000-foot base camp at Camp Muir. The summit that you see from Paradise stays white all year long. The mountain, 35 square miles of glaciers, trap 156 billion cubic feet of water and make up the largest single-peak glacier system in the nation. Five thousand years ago, an eruption melted the glacier, creating a huge mud flow that swept all the way to Puget Sound.

At 6,400 feet, **Sunrise** is the highest point in the park that can be reached by road. From the visitor center, a trail up Burroughs Mountain climbs 1,400 feet in slightly more than three miles to exquisite views of Emmons and Winthrop glaciers.

Ambitious backpackers can launch out on the 93-mile circumnavigation of the mountain on the **Wonderland Trail.** But you don't have to walk far to enjoy Rainier's wild beauty: even near a much-traveled entrance road, a brief uphill walk from the pavement can leave you standing all alone on a dusty trail, contemplating the sharp outline of a bear's fresh pawprint in the dirt.

Mountain climbers in the 1920s negotiate an ice formation high on Mount Rainier. (Underwood Archives, San Francisco)

WILDFLOWERS

Like people, wildflowers need lots of sunshine to be happy. Which is why the greatest floral displays are found in the sunnier parts of the state.

■ WEST OF THE CASCADES

West of the Cascades look for wildflowers in the San Juans. The small, rocky islands, accessible only by boat, seem to have the greatest variety of colors.

Wild tiger lilies along a foot trail on Mount Walker on the Olympic Peninsula.

Whidbey Island, stretched out in the rain shadow of the Olympics, also puts on spectacular displays. Look for **wild lily-of-the-valley** and **Venus-slipper orchids** in the shade of the woods, for **blue iris** at the head of Penn Cove, and admire the **rhododendrons** at Point Partridge. If you time it right (any time in June), you can admire **blue camas** growing in the diminutive meadows tucked beneath rocky outcroppings at Deception Pass. **Oxeye daisies** will soon whiten roadsides throughout western Washington, just before **fireweed** and **foxglove** paint them pink.

■ SOUTHEAST

East of the Cascades, few places can match the Yakima River Canyon for sheer scenic beauty, where the river breaks through the basalt flows of Manastash and Umtanum ridges in a series of steep-sided cliffs. In spring, the precipitous slopes are covered with wildflowers, but you can see an even more spectacular display of flowers at the Wenas State Game Range, along the old stage road which runs from Ellensburg to Selah via the Wenas Valley. Look for **lavender mariposa lilies** and **yellow columbines** among the brightly colored mounds of **pink phlox, purple sage,** and **blue lupine.** If you're lucky, you'll see meadows covered with **gold stars.** In spring and summer, before the start of the hunting season, the game range is also a great place to watch birds. Look for such uncommon species as bluebirds, tanagers, orioles, and wild turkeys.

In the Palouse, drive to the top of Steptoe Butte, where the green of the flowering meadows and the golden-brown of the soil lie half-hidden beneath a sea of pink, yellow, and blue flowers. **Wild roses,** low and spreading, dominate the pattern of the floral carpet, as they pour down the slopes of Steptoe Butte into an abandoned orchard. Their fragrance fills the air.

■ OKANOGAN

The rolling meadows of the Okanogan highlands are also bedecked with wildflowers in spring and early summer. This forgotten nook is so peaceful you can hear the birds sing as you drive along State Highway 155 which runs north from Grand Coulee Dam through the Colville Indian Reservation to Omak. For much of the summer, roadsides will be lined with bands of **scarlet skyrocket gilia** and **deeply blue larkspur.** But look for **asters, sunflowers,** and **blazing stars** as well.

—John Doerper

If you approach Rainier from its northwestern side via State Highway 165, you'll find the road climbs through the old coal-mining towns of Wilkeson and Carbonado to the **Carbon River entrance,** near Ipsut Creek. From the Ipsut Creek campground, a relatively short trail takes you to the **Carbon River Glacier.** The glacier isn't way up the mountain, it's just off in the woods, across a swaying suspension bridge. After climbing a slope that runs along the riverbank, get as close to the dense ice as you like—but don't stand at the base of the ice wall or even very near it, because boulders fall intermittently from the glacier's sheer face.

South of Ipsut Creek is Mowich Lake, with a trail leading to **Spray Park.** Here, in the bloom of the high country's late-summer "spring," you can look across acres of flowers to the snowcapped peak, so close it fills your field of view. Small streams run through the flower meadows. Clouds of insects wait to devour you along their banks.

■ CENTRALIA

Seen from I-5, Centralia looks like a typical freeway development— a strip of gas stations, fast food franchises, and factory outlet stores, thoughtlessly scattered a few blocks deep on either side of he highway. Off the freeway, though, the old face of Centralia remains remarkably intact. The town's commercial district along Tower Avenue is still dominated by stylish, beautifully maintained, two-story buildings of brick and stone, most of which date back to the 1890s and early 1900s. With the decline of the timber industry in recent years, Centralia has tried to cash in on its historical aspect. Antique stores stand on every block.

George Washington founded Centralia in 1852.
(University of Washington Libraries)

The fabulous Olympic Club at 112 North Tower is a saloon/tobacco store appointed in swank turn-of-the-century style. Its colored glass chandeliers, tiled floors, stenciled ceilings, and ancient, ornate cash register stand as monuments to the golden age of public drinking.

Centralia was founded in 1852 by George Washington, the son of a Missouri slave. Washington was raised by a white couple, the Cochrans, and the three came west together, fleeing the violent climate of the antebellum border states.

Although Oregon's territorial laws barred blacks from holding land, the territorial legislature granted George Washington an exemption—two months before the land north of the Columbia River became a separate territory, no longer governed by Oregon law. George Washington's exemption did not apply under Washington Territory law, and the Cochrans filed a claim for his land, which they deeded to him when the law was repealed in 1857.

The park at the corner of Main and Pearl, where the old **Carnegie library** stands, was part of George Washington's original land claim. The sentinel statue standing guard before the library is a monument to the four American Legionnaires slain by radical loggers in the Centralia Massacre of 1919.

■ MOUNT ST. HELENS

South of Centralia come the turnoffs for Mount St. Helens. Until 1980, Mount St. Helens was a particularly serene-looking 9,677-foot volcano, younger, slightly smaller, and easier to climb than the Cascades' other landmark peaks. Visitors to nearby Spirit Lake enjoyed the reflection of the perfectly symmetrical cone in the lake's blue water—although other folks had long noticed steam coming out of the mountain's vents. Then, geologists noticed some ominous rumblings, and warned that St. Helens was about to erupt. No living person had ever seen one of the Cascade volcanoes go up in smoke. Nevertheless, scientists, photographers, and the merely curious started watching St. Helens around the clock.

No one was really prepared for what happened. On the morning of May 18, 1980, the mountain exploded. More than 1,300 feet of its top simply disappeared. Instead of going straight up, the blast went north, destroying everything in its path. Old-growth forests were vaporized. Big trees a little farther from the blast were scattered across the hillsides like straw or simply killed where they stood. Soil was incinerated, too, and nearby slopes were scoured down to bedrock. Volcanic ash fell

on 22,000 square miles of land, including much of eastern Washington. The sky in many eastern Washington communities darkened at midday, and ash piled up like drifted snow on the streets and sidewalks. Real snow and glacial ice melted by the blast poured down the mountain, creating rivers of mud that swelled the Toutle River, which rose 66 feet above its normal level, taking out homes and bridges. Mud flowed down to the Cowlitz and Columbia, where millions of tons had to be dredged from the shipping channel. And 57 people died. A *National Geographic* photographer watching the mountain from what seemed to be a safe distance was killed. A geologist watching it from what seemed to be a safe distance simply disappeared.

The devastation appeared complete. But pocket gophers living underground survived the blast, and fireweed and other plants started recolonizing some of the blast area within a year. Much of the area remains a moonscape, but life is returning—as it has after volcanic eruptions in the Cascades for millions of years. Weyerhaeuser, which owned most of the land in the path of the blast, traded some to the federal government, which included it in a new Mount St. Helens Volcano National Monument. On the land it kept, the company has planted millions of new trees.

Even years after the blast, the landscape remains surreal: forests of dead trees, thousands of gray logs jackstrawed across the ground, ridges burnt down to bedrock where forests once stood. In the track of the mudflow, the Toutle River flows through a gray moonscape—with whole herds of huge, brown elk wandering comfortably across the mud and the ridges above. From a helicopter at the crater's rim, you look into an amphitheater of sheer gray cliffs and see a lava dome steaming in the shadows.

Before making the long drive to the mountain along State Highway 504, stop at the **National Park Service Visitors Center** at Silver Lake, where you can walk through a giant model of the volcano and pick up maps and information for touring. It is also possible to hire guides to lead you into the volcano's blast zone for overnight camping.

■ VANCOUVER

On the north shore of the Columbia River, where I-5 crosses to Oregon, Vancouver lies more in the economic orbit of Portland, Oregon, than of any place in Washington State. Vancouver's downtown rarely rises above two stories, and its tallest building resembles a sawed-off corncob. The city never quite condenses; you don't feel like you can find the center of things.

Vancouver boasts a handful of beautiful art deco buildings built during the 1930s.

(previous pages) Moments after Mount St. Helens exploded on the morning of May 18, 1980, a photographer captured the event near the town of Toledo some 30 miles west of the mountain. (Photo by Rocky Kolberg)

The elaborate brick and terra-cotta styling of the Telephone Exchange building is one of the city's architectural highlights, along with the beautiful Elks building—a three-story brick masterpiece with wrought-iron balconies and marble inlays. The old Municipal Building on Washington Street, with its busted windows and "For Sale" signs, housed city offices and the police department after it was built in 1930, and was later taken over by the now-defunct brewery where Lucky Lager was made.

While Vancouver doesn't have much to recommend it as a place, the people who live there are friendly, and the city demonstrates an ethnic diversity uncommon for southwestern Washington. If you like pawn shops, you'll love Vancouver. There must be more hock shops per capita here than anywhere else in the state.

Short though it may be on modern attractions, Vancouver has plenty of history. It developed on the site of the Hudson's Bay Company's **Fort Vancouver,** which in the early nineteenth century served as the administrative and social center of the Anglo-American Pacific Northwest.

The Hudson's Bay Company (or H.B.C. as it's better known in Canada) was originally a British fur trading monopoly that established a network of forts, farms, and way stations, and served as an arm of Her Majesty's government in the Oregon Country. The company built Fort Vancouver on the river's flat north bank in 1824. After the British left, the fort was taken over by the U.S. Army. During World War I, it served as headquarters for the army's Spruce Production Division, and a mill on the site cut Sitka spruce into lumber for wood-and-fabric military aircraft. Army barracks built in 1849 adjoin the Fort Vancouver National Historic Site and are still in use. And the Hudson's Bay Company is still in business, making its famous point blankets and maintaining stores in shopping malls throughout Canada.

The last of the original fort burned to the ground in 1866, but since the mid-1960s, most of its (hypothetical) buildings have been reconstructed of heavy, rough-milled timbers inside a stockade of pointed logs, on the fort's original site (just east of I-5, on exit 1-C). While old Fort Vancouver stood at the edge of the Columbia River, a more modern avenue of commerce—State Highway 14—now runs between the reconstructed fort and the river.

Outside the stockade stands an apple orchard and a large, orderly garden full of flower and vegetable species—everything from Japanese lanterns to artichokes—that were cultivated by the fort's inhabitants 150 years ago. Inside the stockade, park rangers dressed in period costume offer demonstrations in the bakery and the smithy.

The original fort owed its importance to early nineteenth-century geopolitics.

After the War of 1812, Great Britain and the United States set the U.S.–Canada border east of the Rocky Mountains at the 49th parallel, but failed to agree on a border west of the Great Divide. The two countries agreed to a joint occupation of the disputed Oregon Country—a great wilderness stretching from the Alaska panhandle (then Russian America) to California (then part of Mexico), and bounded east and west by the Rockies and the Pacific Ocean.

In the early years of joint occupation, Fort Vancouver was the vast territory's sole bastion of Anglo civilization, and orders from the H.B.C were law. The H.B.C strove for self-sufficiency, building farms, sawmills, and smithies to supply its forts and outposts. It guaranteed protection to anyone (white or Indian) traveling to or from its forts with furs, forbade its employees to trade liquor to the Indians (who did most of the trapping), and kept out of native peoples' affairs, unless a white man was involved.

Northwest historian Carlos Schwantes writes that within its 20-foot stockade "Fort Vancouver constituted a small, almost self-sufficient European community that included...30 to 50 small houses where employees (engages) lived with their

An illustration of Fort Vancouver from the journal of the Stevens expedition.
(Washington State Historical Society, Tacoma)

WHO LIVED HERE IN 1828?

*W*hen I descended the Cowlitz in 1828… our bateau carried as curious a muster of races and languages as perhaps had ever been congregated within the same compass in any part of the world. Our crew of ten men contained Iroquois, who spoke their own tongue; a Cree half-breed of French origin, who appeared to have borrowed his dialect from both his parents; a North Briton, who understood only the Gaelic of his native hills; Canadians, who, of course, knew French; and Sandwich Islanders, who jabbered a medley of Chinook, English and their own vernacular jargon. Add to all this that the passengers were natives of England, Scotland, Russia, Canada and the Hudson's Bay Company's territories, and you have the prettiest congress of nations, the nicest confusion of tongues, that has ever taken place since the days of the Tower of Babel.

—Sir George Simpson, *Overland Journey Around the World*

Indian wives." The fort also housed a hospital, storehouses, workshops, mills, a shipyard, a dairy, orchards, and a farm of several hundred acres. Bells rang to signal changes of shifts and activities. "Ships from distant ports called at Fort Vancouver bringing news, books, and periodicals to stock the post's library."

Schwantes adds that:

. . . *A*n unusually cosmopolitan population collected around Fort Vancouver: Delaware and Iroquois Indians from the East, local Chinooks, Hawaiians, mixed-blood Métis from the prairies, French Canadians, and Scotsmen, and presiding over them all was the imperious John McLoughlin [the Hudson's Bay Company's chief factor for the Columbia district], harsh, brooding, and given to occasional temperamental outbursts. More than profit and loss were involved in a Hudson's Bay post: Each enclave was a visible link in a truly imperial system joining London with the vast hinterlands of the Pacific Northwest.

John McLoughlin ran the fort on the Columbia in a truly imperial manner. "Nightly," writes Peter C. Newman in a history of the Hudson's Bay Company, "the Company's traders and visiting dignitaries…gathered at the…officers' mess to trade tall tales in the warm light of candelabra, lolling at tables laden with crested cutlery, crystal glasses and blue earthenware dishes…with McLoughlin leading spirited exchanges of ideas that spun on long into the convivial nights." McLoughlin's virtues as a host did not mean that he was soft on the people who worked for him or on anyone else who strayed into the Company's sphere of influence. "What impressed the Indian chiefs who came to call was McLoughlin's sense of justice," Newman writes. "Anyone—white or Indian—caught breaking the Chief Factor's concept of permissible behavior was sentenced to be lashed while tied to the fort's cannon."

Nevertheless, McLoughlin fed American trappers who showed up hungry on his doorstep, and he gave supplies on credit to American settlers who came over the Oregon Trail—despite company policy against helping the Americans and despite the fact that few settlers paid him or the company back. Although McLoughlin was later called "the Father of Oregon," he died in Oregon Territory unappreciated and bitter.

By that time, Vancouver was part of the United States. Hudson's Bay Company governor George Simpson had foreseen the outcome of the boundary struggle between the United States and Great Britain and had relocated Company headquarters to Vancouver Island in 1843. Three years later, Britain gave up all claim to what is now Washington and Oregon.

And only 10 years after that, five Canadian nuns—Sisters of Providence—made a 6,000-mile sea journey to Vancouver from the cosmopolitan French-Canadian city of Montreal. Their leader was Mother Joseph, a rangy 23-year-old with a thin-lipped mouth and a stubborn chin jutting beneath her nun's cowl. She had learned carpentry and design as a girl from her father, a Quebec carriage maker.

Finding no home prepared for their arrival, the Sisters set to work remodeling an abandoned Hudson's Bay Company building, and made their home there. In her first years in Vancouver, Mother Joseph planned and oversaw the construction of a school, a hospital, a lunatic asylum, and an old folks' home. Her building crews respected her as a fine carpenter, although her habit of praying aloud as she labored with hammer and saw, or hitching up her skirts and crawling beneath a building to inspect its foundation, may have disconcerted some of the workers.

In the last four decades of the nineteenth century, the Sisters of Providence built more than two dozen hospitals, schools, and orphanages throughout the Pacific Northwest. To finance their many good works, the sisters made heroic begging tours of Washington Territory's remote mining camps by horseback and canoe, navigating wild rivers, rugged highlands, and vast, arid plains.

Mother Joseph herself survived into the twentieth century. The American Institute of Architects later named her "the First Architect of the Pacific Northwest." Statues of her stand in the Washington State Capitol and the United States Capitol's Statuary Hall.

The Sisters of Providence toured mining camps in the late 1800s to collect donations in gold and coin to fund schools, hospitals, and Indian missions. (Courtesy Sisters of Providence Archives, Seattle)

When Mother Joseph and her fellow Sisters of Providence completed Vancouver's Providence Academy in 1874, it was the largest building west of the Rockies and north of San Francisco. Mother Joseph was the Academy's architect and contractor, and carved its elaborate wooden altars and benches herself. The big colonial brick building, since converted into an office mall, still stands at the edge of downtown Vancouver.

■ COLUMBIA RIVER GORGE

The Columbia River Gorge marks the spot at which the river flows west through the Cascades between basalt cliffs that are older than the mountains themselves. US Highway 14 follows the north bank of the river all the way through the Gorge, although most visitors follow the freeway on the Oregon side.

When Lewis and Clark followed the Columbia through the Gorge in 1805, the Indian groups they found along its banks had been fishing here for perhaps 9,000 years.

The Indians fished at rapids and falls where salmon leapt upstream and, breaking the surface of the water, could be speared. Those same rapids and falls formed impassible barriers to navigation. Lewis and Clark portaged around them, and even at the turn of the century, wheat shipped downriver by steamboat from the Palouse Hills had to be unloaded, hauled around the rapids by rail, and loaded onto another boat in the calmer water below. Now, railroads and highways follow both banks of the river, and a system of dams and locks enables boats to go all the way to Idaho.

The road along the Washington shore provides more dramatic views but slower driving than the freeway on the Oregon side. (The Columbia Gorge Scenic Highway on the Oregon side is also slow but spectacular. Built with the help of Italian stonemasons and finished in 1916, the highway leads to 620-foot Multnomah Falls, Bridal Veil Falls, Horsetail Falls, the Oneonta Gorge, and a series of state parks.) It winds around rock walls and bores through the rock in short tunnels, passing fruit warehouses, small sawmills, and outcroppings softened by moss. On the opposite shore, you can see the mountains plunging straight to the river, appearing and disappearing in the mist, their forested slopes split by ravines. In winter, snow dusts the upper slopes.

For a long view up and down the river, you can climb a series of ramps and steps up 848-foot-tall **Beacon Rock**. Beacon Rock State Park offers campsites and chance to swim in the Columbia. East of Beacon Rock, near the Hood River, you'll probably see the countless colorful sails of windsurfers taking advantage of the Gorge's world-class windsurfing conditions.

Bonneville Dam was the first of the great federal dams built across the Columbia, the irreversible step toward transforming the river and much of the region with millions of tons of concrete. Now, in addition to the dam itself, you can see the locks, where barges and tugs wait for rising or falling water to lift them up or let them down to the river level on the other side of the dam. When salmon are migrating upstream, you may be able to spot them through underwater viewing windows.

Before Bonneville Dam was built, this spot was known for its dangerous rapids. On November 1, 1805, Lewis and Clark "Set about takeing our Small canoe and all the baggage by land 940 yeards of bad slippery and rockey way" to avoid them. They saw "Great numbers of Sea Otters" and "got the 4 large canoes over by slipping them over the rocks on poles placed across from one rock to another." This was their last portage. Less than a week later, when the river mouth widened, they thought they saw the ocean. They were wrong, but only a couple of weeks after dragging their canoes around the rapids, they were walking beside the Pacific.

A view down the Columbia River Gorge towards the Cascade Locks and Bonneville Dam.

Where The Dalles Dam has flooded the ancient Indian fishing site at Celilo Falls, a steep road leads downhill to the town of **Wishram**, which once stood near the north end of the falls. Long lines of freight cars wait in the railroad marshalling yards. Kids play in the narrow streets, and people take good care of their small lawns. Behind the town, a line of sheer, craggy cliffs reaches out toward the river. That is the only sign that the natural river might once have dropped over a falls. But drop it did, and Indians gathered here to spear or net salmon for perhaps eight millennia. Celilo Falls was one of the great fishing spots in North America.

Sam Hill, who built the first highway on the Oregon side of the Gorge, chose the Washington side to build his grand, out-of-the-way home, now the **Maryhill Museum**. Peacocks stroll the landscaped grounds. Signs warn human strollers to watch out for rattlesnakes. From the grounds, you can see barges on the river and the basalt cliffs and rolling wheat land of the Oregon shore.

Hill originally planned to live here in the midst of a utopian Quaker farming colony, but changed his mind and completed the mansion instead as a museum. The collection reflects his eclectic interests and personal relationships. It includes a large number of Indian baskets, Russian icons, a Charles Russell painting of an Indian hunter on horseback being charged by a buffalo bull, and a lot of mostly small Rodins. Hill knew the American dancer Loie Fuller, and there are various mementos of her career, including a small statue of her dancing, with veils swinging out all around. Wrote William Butler Yeats in "Nineteen Hundred and Nineteen":

> *W*hen Loie Fuller's Chinese dancers enwound
> A shining web, a floating ribbon of cloth,
> It seemed that a dragon of air
> Had fallen among dancers, had whirled them round
> Or hurried them off on its own furious path...

Hill was friendly with Queen Marie of Romania, too, and the museum contains a lot of objects that once belonged to her, including a collection of gilt furniture and the long, rhinestone-studded brocade gown in which she attended the coronation of Czar Nicholas II.

On a high cliff overlooking the river, Sam Hill built another improbable monument: **Stonehenge;** not quite the Stonehenge you see on England's Salisbury Plain, but a slightly scaled-down model with all the stones in their original places, the circle unbroken. It is a memorial to the soldiers who died in World War I.

N O R T H E A S T

CLOUDS BLOWING INLAND FROM THE PACIFIC rise and drop most of their moisture before they make it across the Cascade Mountains; consequently, the Cascades' eastern slope is considerably drier than the west, and the plateau farther east is drier still. Instead of Douglas fir and hemlock, you see ponderosa and lodgepole pine. Before you've gone very far east, you encounter sagebrush. Most of the state's people live on the west side. Most of the state's agriculture takes place on the east. The political climate changes at the mountain crest, too. Eastern Washington has long been the more conservative part of the state.

Northeastern Washington follows the Canadian border from the Cascade mountain crest to the Idaho panhandle. Wilderness areas along the border connect with wild country on the Canadian side, and they support mammal species that are rare in most of the United States. The Columbia River flows south from Canada here, and the nation's largest dam, Grand Coulee, backs its waters up into 151-mile-long Franklin D. Roosevelt Lake. On benches above the river, orchards grow many of the apples that make Washington the preeminent apple-producing region in the world. On the arid plateaus, farmers grow miles of winter wheat. The region's economic hub is the mid-sized city of Spokane.

■ LEAVENWORTH

If you cross the mountains at Stevens Pass—where, in fall, the rocky slopes are dappled with the rust, yellow, and scarlet of autumn foliage—you may think more than the climate or the politics has changed: Leavenworth, on the east side of the pass, has transformed itself into a faux Bavarian village. In the 1960s, as a railroad and sawmill town that had long since lost its railroad and sawmill, the community decided to go for the tourist trade by giving the whole town a German Alpine look. The economic gamble paid off. Now, people stop in Leavenworth to eat and shop and spend the night and buy gas. And why not? The location is spectacular.

Near Leavenworth, the Icicle Creek Road leads to trailheads for hikes to a number of alpine lakes, including the **Enchantments**—a justly famous, overused, and now-restricted hiking destination. A dusty trail leads past the yellowed bark of ponderosa pine, but soon you walk in the shade of pine and fir in a valley loud

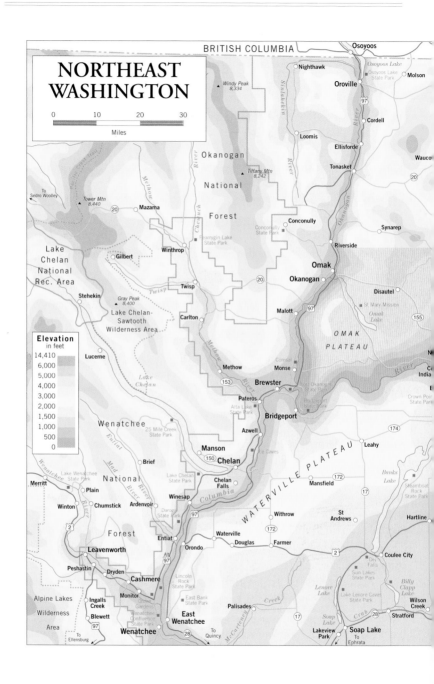

NORTHEAST WASHINGTON

0   10   20   30

Miles

BRITISH COLUMBIA

Osoyoos

Nighthawk

Osoyoos Lake
Osoyoos Lake
State Park

Molson

Windy Peak
8,334

Oroville

97

Cordell

Loomis

Ellisforde

Wauco

Okanogan

Tiffany Mtn
8,242

Tonasket

20

National

To
Sedro Woolley

Tower Mtn
8,440

20

Mazama

Forest

Conconully

Synarep

Conconully
State Park

Bearrygin Lake
State Park

Winthrop

Riverside

Lake
Chelan
National
Rec. Area

Gilbert

Omak

20

Okanogan

Twisp

Disautel

Stehekin

Gray Peak
8,400

Twisp

Carlton

Malott

97

St Mary Mission

Omak
Lake

155

Lake Chelan-
Sawtooth
Wilderness Area

OMAK
PLATEAU

Elevation
in feet

14,410
6,000
5,000
4,000
3,000
2,000
1,500
1,000
500
0

Lucerne

Comsal

Methow

Monse

Co
India

153

River

Brewster

Lake
Chelan

Pateros

Crown Poi
State Park

Alta Lake
State Park

Bridgeport

Bridgeport
State Park

Okanogan
State Park

Wenatchee

Azwell

174

25 Mile Creek
State Park

Manson

Le Caves

Leahy

Brief

150

Chelan

WATERVILLE PLATEAU

Banks
Lake

Merritt

Lake Wenatchee
State Park

National

Lake Chelan
State Park

Chelan
Falls

Mansfield

172

Steamboat
Rock
State Park

Plain

17

Winton

Chumstick

Ardenvoir

Winesap

Columbia

Withrow

St
Andrews

Hartline

2

Darcy
State Park

97

172

Forest

Entiat

Waterville

Douglas

Farmer

2

Dry
Falls

Coulee City

Leavenworth

Orondo

Sun Lakes
State Park

Billy
Clapp
Lake

Peshastin

Dryden

Cashmere

Lincoln
Rock
State Park

Lenore
Lake

Lake Lenore Caves
State Park

Wilson
Creek

Alpine Lakes

Monitor

East Bank
State Park

Palisades

Creek

17

Soap
Lake

28

Stratford

Wilderness

Ingalls
Creek

Ohme
Gardens

Area

Blewett

97

Wenatchee
Confluence
State Park

East
Wenatchee

Lakeview
Park

Soap Lake

To
Ellensburg

Wenatchee

28

To
Quincy

McCarteney

To
Ephrata

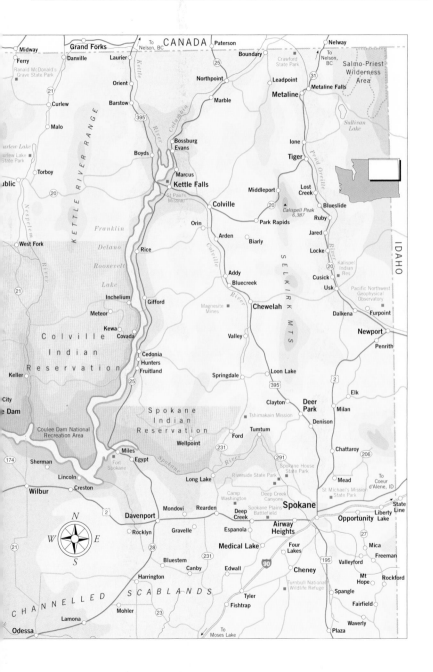

with rushing water. The trail is damp as it passes the heavy, ridged bark of Douglas fir and the feathery, Asian-roofline dip of cedar branches. Water flows green and placid under the cedars, and boils through a race of lichened stone. The trail climbs and climbs some more, making its last real ascent over steep sheets of solid granite and winds down to the lake. Trails leading to **Klonqua Lake** are less populated and run beside cascading creeks most of the way. From the end of Icicle Creek Road take Icicle Creek Trail until you reach French Creek Trail. It intersects with Klonqua Creek Trail, which ends at the lake.

East of Leavenworth, mountains and forests give way to orchards. **Wenatchee,** on the west bank of the Columbia River, is considered the capital of Washington apple country, which makes it, arguably, the apple capital of the world. It holds an apple blossom festival every spring, and as early as 1905, it was billing itself as "the home of the big red apple." Apples grow along the Columbia River here, on the hillsides overlooking Lake Chelan, up the Methow and Okanogan valleys. Once upon a time, whole orchards on the slopes above Chelan grew Rome apples for the Great Northern Railway, which served them, baked, in its dining cars.

■ UP THE COLUMBIA RIVER

North along the river from East Wenatchee, thick irrigation pipes carry water up the banks to the arid benches, where people have been planting apple trees for most of this century. At pruning time, when there is snow on the hills, big, widely spaced apple trees in the old orchards stand gray and bare. Smoke rises from piles of cut branches. Men wearing checkered woolen jackets over sweatshirts with the hoods pulled up stand on tall aluminum ladders and whack branches off acres of trees, one by one. In the spring, the trees are covered with pink blossoms, and the air is heavy with the scent of blooms. In the summer, the branches of the old apple trees create caverns of shade, and one thinks of Dylan Thomas' line, "Now as I was young and easy under the apple boughs." At harvesttime—when the apple trees are loaded with fruit, the effect is lapidary—the fruit jewel-like, the orchards like enamelwork by Fabergé.

In newer orchards, trees are short enough to prune from six-foot ladders, and are pruned to form single "central leaders." (In some very new orchards, trees are supported by huge trellises.) "These trees aren't as pretty as the old ones," says one grower. "If you want to be in an orchard and sit in the shade you can't do it with

The apple of someone's eye. (University of Washington Libraries)

this tree. This is an apple machine."

Near **Orondo,** you pass the orchards in which Grady Auvil has grown apples since the 1920s, when the river down below flowed freely and growers still hauled their fruit to the railroads with wagons and teams. Auvil grew Red Delicious apples back when Babe Ruth was playing for the Yankees. He subsequently became known as the prophet of the Granny Smith, an apple first grown in New Zealand.

From Orondo, a short ascent through dry canyons on US 2 takes you in minutes from apples to wheat. Up a steep two-lane road, you pass through Easter Island–like rock outcroppings, hillsides quilted with bunchgrass, dark clumps of pine. On top, suddenly, the land flattens out and you're driving through brilliant green wheat fields. Wheat has been planted to the rim of the canyon, to the edge of the blacktop. The nearby town of **Waterville** has a great turn-of-the-century downtown. Beyond it, you can drive for mile after mile through the wheat.

■ LAKE CHELAN

Lake Chelan itself is known more for its scenery than for its apples. The lake's narrow basin—gouged by ice-age glaciers between the jagged, barren ridges of the Sawtooth divide and the Chelan Mountains—snakes 55 miles from the rolling semi-desert above the Columbia River to the North Cascades. The Stehekin River feeds the lake on Cascade glacier melt, and a dam at the lake's southeast end, built in 1927, keeps the water level high. Unlike Ross Lake to the west, Chelan is a natural lake, but without the dam, its water level would fluctuate, rising when the Cascade snows melted in the late spring and summer, and falling later in the year.

Chelan's waters retain the ice-blue cast of their glacial sources, a cobalt transparency that combines with the dry climate of eastern Washington and the blazing heat of summer to give it a Mediterranean aura. But unlike the Mediterranean Sea, the waters of Lake Chelan retain a glacial chill, and remain frigid a foot below the surface even on 90-degree July afternoons.

Lakeview condos and three-story, glass-fronted houses crowd the lake's south end, spreading out from the congested tourist town of **Chelan,** at its southern tip. The town is a rather charmless collection of low, mostly modern buildings, shadowed by high, rounded hills at the southern tip of the lake. You'll find bland motels, condos, college kids cruising the evening streets in open jeeps, grassy waterfront

Snow blankets apple orchards near the town of Chelan.

HIDDEN CENTER: MAGICAL VIEWS

I'm standing on the southern bank of the Columbia River—here called **Lake Roosevelt** because it has been dammed up behind Grand Coulee Dam. But it doesn't look much like a lake, more like a placid river, since it is confined in the rocky coulee carved from the river over the millennia. I have time to think about this sort of thing, because I just missed the ferry to the north shore, the ferry which ties the two loose ends of State Route 21 together where the river-lake snaps them in two. The ferry will be back soon, since the "lake" isn't wide—a mere 15 minutes or so. (The ferry runs from 6:00 A.M. to 11:30 P.M., and it's free.)

I take the time to look around. Cirro-cumulus clouds drift overhead, dropping a quilted camouflage pattern over the landscape, highlighting trees, smoothing out hollows, creating the illusion of precipices where there are none. Ahead, on the other shore of the gray water, dark cliffs loom, rugged and topped with tall trees, quite unlike the gentle grassy shore I'm standing on. Behind me the road runs in a series of switchbacks through the folds of a dry creek valley to the top of the coulee. Here and there a touch of fall color enlivens the landscape, and an occasional aspen is highlighted in full golden glory. South of that lie the rolling wheatlands of the Waterville plateau and the steep canyons and blue lakes of the Grand Coulee country. A prairie falcon circles overhead, tail feathers spread to the wind. In a flash the feathers fold up like a fan, the raptor plunges down the grassy slope. One more field mouse has taken its natural place in the food chain.

There are no switchbacks on the north shore. The road follows a deeply glaciated valley (Lake Roosevelt is about as far as the continental glaciers pushed south during the last ice age in this neck of the woods). Steep cliffs hem in the trees. The **Sanpoil River,** a smallish stream, sparkles as it purls in its rocky bed. The light changes constantly. Just as I make up my mind that the scenery reminds me of a Ma Yuan painting, with its tortured rocks, twisted trees and misty skies, the sun breaks through some unseen mountain cleft and lights up trees, shrubs, and grasses with chiaroscuro effects worthy of Claude Lorrain. A ruffed grouse waddles across the road, slowly and deliberately as though there were no speeding cars. Looking at the greenery around me, I wonder why the natives called them themselves "Sanpoil," which translates as "people of the gray country." Green, red, and golden certainly, but there's not much gray here, except for the misty tops of the cliffs. The names of former Indian villages give a better feel of the land: "Cold Water," "Rugged Gulch," "Grass Growing Along Creek," "Potholes in Ground." "River Enters Basin Causing Eddy" must have been a wealthy place in the old days, for big salmon were plentiful in these waters, until Grand Coulee Dam cut off the flow.

In this remote corner of the state, things haven't changed much. **Curlew** looks still pretty much the way it did years ago: small, picturesque, and a touch decayed. I cross the one-lane log bridge over the Kettle River and cruise the one-block business district. The dog sleeping in the middle of the road doesn't even look up as I drive around him. I've picked the wrong day, and the Riverside Cafe and Lounge are closed. Which means I don't get to sit on the deck and watch the river swirl by.

The **Kettle River** is one of this region's great assets. Like the Sanpoil, it flows on the broad floor of a glaciated valley, but it's broader and stays in the open for much of its course, meandering through meadows or golden-leafed cottonwoods. There are few cliffs along the valley's flanks—the glaciers have ground and polished and scoured and rounded the granite into gentle highland slopes. As I take the back road to Wauconda, along Toroda Creek, I am reminded of a drive through the Scottish highlands. Except here I don't encounter mad sheep dashing down the center of the road, and the cottages and barns are built from square logs instead of whitewashed fieldstone.

I push on, west along State Highway 20 and south on US 97. Just before dark, I cross the Okanogan River at Omak. To my right I can barely make out the cliff down which Indian horsemen will plunge later on this month, in the mad annual suicide race.

—John Doerper

parks—one of which hosts a summer Bach festival—and a few interesting old buildings.

Roads and development follow both shores of the lake northwest from Chelan until national forest land begins and the mountains close in. North of the campground at **25 Mile Creek,** on the western shore, the roads end, and the only vehicles that travel farther up the lake are boats and sea planes. Two scheduled boats make the 110-mile round trip from Chelan each day, carrying passengers, mail, and supplies to and from Stehekin, at the north end of the lake. Privately owned power boats and the occasional kayak or canoe ply the lake's winding corridor from end to end. Strong north winds blow down the gorge, rising suddenly, then falling still. Even in summer, fierce storms come out of nowhere, and 70-mile-an-hour winds peel six-foot waves off the lake surface.

The isolated waterfront homes you see on the upper reaches of Lake Chelan occupy the sites of old homesteads, grandfathered onto public land. Here and there, abandoned orchards and ruined cabins remind you of the lake's pioneer days, when dairy farms and fruit trees stood on its northern shores, and miners

The Methow Valley in fog near Winthrop (above). Washington cherries grow best in the Yakima Valley region, although these thrive in the Wenatchee area (right).

and trappers worked the creeks and drainages of the surrounding mountains.

About 10 miles south of Stehekin, on the western shore, a boat dock and a few small houses stand at the mouth of Railroad Creek. This is **Lucerne,** once the jumping-off point for prospectors bound up the creek. It later became a settlement of dairy farmers, whose land was subsequently planted in apple orchards and finally abandoned.

A steep, 11-mile trail leads up Railroad Creek from Lucerne to **Holden Village,** formerly the Howe Sound gold and copper mine. The mine ran from 1938 until 1957, and at its peak, 450 people lived in Holden Village. Children attended the schoolhouse, and miners spent their paychecks at the company store. When some got feeling cooped up, they hired private planes to fly them into town for sprees.

The mine folded when copper prices dropped in 1957. A few years later, the site was donated lock, stock, and barrel to the Lutheran church, and today, Holden Village is a church camp.

The town of **Stehekin** sits at the north end of Lake Chelan, near the mouth of the Stehekin River, in the shadow of the North Cascades. Regular boat service from Chelan makes Stehekin a popular day trip, and a few pricey restaurants and shops near the ferry landing do a brisk summer business. Stehekin is a popular point of departure for climbers and hikers, and a shuttle bus runs up a steep mountain road to the Pacific Crest Trail.

From the 1880s to the 1950s, Stehekin was an isolated community whose 50 or 60 residents worked small farms and orchards and sustained a self-contained barter economy. Apples, peaches, and apricots thrive in the lake's moist air and long, hot summers. Prospectors and trappers worked out of Stehekin, and horse packers led hunting and fishing parties (who stayed in the town's one hotel) into the mountains for cash income.

Then, as now, the *Lady of the Lake* (in a prior incarnation) was the town's line to the outside world, bringing Stehekin mail, supplies, visitors, and news each day.

When the **Lake Chelan National Recreation Area** was established in 1968—at the behest of Seattle citizens' groups, not locals—the land around Stehekin passed from the laissez-faire hands of the Forest Service to Park Service control: no more trap lines or hunting trips, no more gold mines. The lake's old-timers still resent the way the Park Service cramped their frontier style, and few residents support the current effort to keep Stehekin from growing. Already, all land not privately owned is supposed to be managed as wilderness. Environmentalists want human activity in the Stehekin Valley held to its current level and in some cases reduced by closing the road to the upper valley, closing the airstrip, and having the Park Service continue to buy some private property.

■ METHOW VALLEY

Winthrop, at the eastern end of the North Cascades Highway in the Okanogan National Forest, has become a Wild West town in much the same fashion that Leavenworth has become a Bavarian village.

One can reach Winthrop by driving north from Chelan, following the Methow River north along State Highway 153 and taking State Highway 20 west, or simply by following the North Cascades Scenic Highway east across the mountains. People who want to hike in the North Cascades National Park, ride mountain bikes through the Okanogan forest, or simply drive across the North Cascades Highway keep Winthrop hotels and restaurants busy all summer long. In winter, others come to cross-country ski. In fall, a third clientele arrives to hunt in the national forest.

Trails into the southern part of the **Pasayten Wilderness** start nearby. The Pasayten covers 520,000 acres of wild and varied terrain east of the Cascade crest and south of the Canadian border. It is the most remote stateside corner of a huge wilderness tract that includes Manning and Cathedral provincial parks in Canada, and the North Cascades Complex (which includes the half-million-acre North Cascades National Park, the Glacier Peak Wilderness, and the Ross Lake and Lake Chelan recreation areas). A long drive from Puget Sound cities, the Pasayten is relatively little traveled, and is still home to wolf and grizzly bear—animals suited to the grand scale of this wild land.

Drier than most of North Cascades National Park, the Pasayten landscape runs the gamut from the open, rolling meadows of Horseshoe Basin, west of Nighthawk, to high, rounded hills and steep ravines, thickly forested with pine and larch, to massive escarpments trailing talus skirts, thrust from the ground near the Canadian border. A few sharp, snowy peaks stand out from the bare, wind-bitten ridges.

The vastness and unmanaged quality of the area are striking. Although major trails are well traveled in summer months and the area is popular with horse packers, if one strays from the trail one can wander these meadows and forests and ridges for days and see nary a boot print—just the tracks of white-tailed deer and coyotes.

It's hard to imagine cattle grazing on the summer grass of Horseshoe Basin, as they did 60 years ago, or that the ghostly tungsten mine abandoned on the trail to Cathedral Lakes once echoed with shouts, the rasp of steel on stone, and the creaking harnesses and braying of ore-laden mules trudging out of the hills. But merely one lifetime ago, most of the state was wilderness like this, and men lived day-to-day in it, hunting, trapping, running cattle, mining, logging, and home-steading.

Summer is long and fair here, but in the uplands, weather is unpredictable, and violent summer storms may strike as suddenly as the lightning that flashes from their clouds. Even in the best of weather, the lakes and meadow swamps breed a plague of mosquitoes from which there is no escape, save the confines of a nylon tent or the icy winds that blow above tree line.

Fort Okanogan was established by the Pacific Fur Company in 1811, then changed hands several times before coming into ownership by the Hudson's Bay Company in 1821. (University of Washington Libraries)

This early miners' supply and way station near Omak was one of the area's first permanent structures. (University of Washington Libraries)

■ THE OKANOGAN

Many people who hike the Pasayten start not at Winthrop but west of **Tonasket**, which lies far up the Okanogan Valley. The Okanogan follows the Columbia just above the town of Brewster. There, US 97 picks up the path of the old **Cariboo Trail**, which was first traveled by local Indians, and later by Hudson's Bay Company fur brigades carrying pelts downriver to Fort Vancouver. On a point of land where the Okanogan River meets the Columbia, now drowned in the reservoir behind Wells Dam, Fort Okanogan was built by the Pacific Fur Company in 1811. The Hudson's Bay Company took control of the fort in 1821, and ran it as a way station and supply post until the British abandoned the Oregon Country in 1846. By then, the local beaver had been trapped nearly to extinction, and most of the native trappers were dead of diseases brought by settlers from the east. This era is now memorialized in **Fort Okanogan State Park.**

The parched sagebrush steppes of the Columbia Basin extend up the Okanogan Valley, and rattlesnakes thrive in the hills outside the river's irrigation range. The valley landscape is starkly beautiful. The treeless, rolling hills that rise on both sides of the river lie four months under snow, turn briefly, beautifully green in late spring, and soon settle under the bleached straw blanket of summer.

Noon's naked heat beats down on the valley floor, and bakes it to dust. The sun hangs small and pale on a gray-white sky; no breeze stirs. In this heat, the brown hills, mottled with gray-green sagebrush and broken by rocky outcrops, feel downright inhospitable. At 60 miles an hour, the wind is like a blow-drier in your face. The river flows slowly between its many dams, and Rainbird sprinklers tick in the pastoral geometry of orchard rows. Cottonwood and willow grow along the Okanogan's banks, and farm houses scattered on exposed, low hills are shielded by windbreaks of soldierly poplars, planted 80 years ago.

Gold strikes on Colville Indian land in 1855 and in British Columbia's Fraser River country in 1858 brought new waves of traffic over the Cariboo Trail. In the 1860s and 70s, Oregon cattle baron Ben Snipes made a fortune running beef up the trail to mining camps in British Columbia. Snipes fattened his herds on Okanogan grass, and left behind a legacy of rodeos and Indian cowboys. For 50 years, cattle dominated the regional economy.

About four miles southwest of Okanogan, where State Highway 20 follows the hillside above the river's west bank, the site of the Curtis Sheep Slaughter recalls the hostility that existed all over the West between cattlemen and sheepherders. A herder named Curtis awoke one morning in 1903, after numerous threats from local cowboys, to find hundreds of his fleecy friends bludgeoned to death. For years the hillside was strewn with their bones.

Long after the range wars ended when the federal government started building massive hydroelectric dams along the Columbia and its tributaries in the 1930s, eastern Washington became a battleground between public and private utility companies. By now, those battles may seem as archaic as the ones between sheep men and cattlemen, but they are not entirely forgotten. Okanogan, for example, still proclaims itself a "Public Power Community," and its sidewalk clocks bear the motto "Live Better Electrically." The stucco, Spanish-style **Okanogan County Courthouse,** built in 1915, is a grand building, and the **Methodist church,** built of uncut rock, isn't bad either. Okanogan has a couple of pleasant cafes, and a Saturday farmers' market on the library lawn.

Okanogan County depends on agriculture for nearly a third of its jobs, and while apples wear the crown in this valley, the Okanogan remains cow country. Most of the roads that branch off US 97 cross open range land, and the steel grates of cattle guards bisect gravel and blacktop. (Drive with caution: if a cow jumps in front of your car on open range land and you hit it, you pay for it.)

Cattle dominated the valley until federal irrigation projects in the early twentieth century brought the fruit orchards: cherry, peach, and apricot, but chiefly apple. These orchards now line the Okanogan Valley. Huge quonset hut apple sheds and mountains of wooden fruit crates stand on the river banks, and small trees, their pregnant branches propped with wooden stakes, grow row upon evenly spaced row along the road. In summer, trees are hung with ribbons of brightly colored plastic. In winter, like trees from the Snow Queen's garden, some are coated with a thin gloss of ice to insulate the branches against sub-freezing cold.

Along the edges of orchards stand shacks where migrant workers sleep. The apple industry depends on cheap seasonal labor, often provided by migrant workers from Mexico. By now, nearly 10 percent of Okanogan County's population is of Hispanic descent, and towns throughout the valley stock tomatillos and green chile sauce in their supermarkets and host occasional curbside taco vendors. Most of the signs on **Brewster's** one-blink commercial strip are in Spanish—a tortilleria, a Mexican video store—and in the noisy cantina near the bus stop in Okanogan town, campesinos in white T-shirts and straw cowboy hats shoot pool while the jukebox plays Flaco Jiménez.

An Okanogan cash crop more recent than apples is baby's breath. In summer, plastic hoop sheds are hung with drying bouquets of the tiny white flowers. Paid by the pound, pickers are said to make as much as $100 a day harvesting the weightless stuff.

Five miles northeast of Okanogan, on the river's west bank, the big town of **Omak** draws thousands of people every August to its annual Stampede and Suicide Race (see "Omak Stampede" in this chapter).

One of the Northwest's most famous Indian leaders, Chief Joseph, is buried just east of Omak. Chief Joseph led his people on their famous 1,000-mile odyssey from eastern Oregon through parts of Idaho, Wyoming, and Montana, fighting off the U.S. cavalry and trying to reach safety in Canada. When the cavalry caught them just short of the border, Chief Joseph made a great speech that ended, "I shall fight no more forever." He is buried on the Colville Indian Reservation at Nespelem, north of Grand Coulee Dam.

A beautiful drive north of the town of Omak is along Route 215 to Conconully. Between the towns of Omak and Tonasket, US 97 and State Highway 20 are one road, but at Tonasket they go their separate ways. From here, you can follow US 97 north to Canada, or take State Highway 20 east through the high pine

country to **Republic,** an 1896 gold rush boomtown where corporate miners are still finding gold. A gold-painted cube in the small, grassy city park announces that between 1941 and 1989 the Hecla mining company took two million ounces of gold from the ground here.

Gold isn't the only thing that people have found in the ground around Republic. Across from the park, the non-profit **Stonerose Interpretive Center** contains plant fossils and information about the fossil beds in Republic that have yielded more varieties of early Eocene temperate plant fossils than any other site known to science—over 200 species and still counting. "There's certainly no place like it in North America," a Smithsonian paleobotanist said in 1991, "and probably not in the world." The center continues to unearth fossils in nearby sites, and visitors are welcome to particpate in digging expeditions. Call (509) 775-2295 for more information.

■ PEND OREILLE AND COLVILLE RIVER VALLEYS

Two attractive rural river valleys lie east of Republic and north of Spokane. To the east of Metaline Falls, beyond Sullivan Lake, lies the **Salmo-Priest Wilderness.** Few people visit the Salmo-Priest, but grizzlies, wolves, mountain caribou, lynx, wolverines, and fishers all live in or pass through its remote forests. The wilderness itself is too small to support full-time populations of animals as large or as far-ranging as some of these, but it is linked to wild areas in Idaho and British Columbia, and the critters don't stop at the border.

The Colville River meets the Columbia near the town of **Kettle Falls.** Lodgepole pines darken the hills, while the brighter greens of hay field and pasture line the valley floor. Mills cut pine lumber in Colville and Chewelah. Log trucks rumble down the roads. A big mill dominates Kettle Falls. Near the bridge that crosses the Columbia, a power plant burns sawdust to produce electricity.

Until Grand Coulee Dam was built, the river was relatively narrow here. Early in the century, the widely scattered inhabitants of the region crossed it on small ferries. M. J. Lorraine wrote in 1924 that "What adds more life than anything else to the appearance of the Columbia River are the frequent ferries constantly plying from shore to shore. Every few miles a steel cable is seen stretched across, above the water over high towers erected on the banks, and trailing from which, with its guy wires, is the ferry-boat slowly but steadily being pushed by the current towards the desired shore."

(previous pages) The Cascades loom over the Wenatchee Valley at sunrise.

OMAK STAMPEDE

Look down from the ferris wheel: sunburnt families and packs of teenagers roam through the tents and painted plywood stands of the midway, trailing pink clouds of cotton candy and plush stuffed animals won at ring toss or darts. On a stage nearby, a family of born-again country-and-western singers is performing for a small, distracted audience, but you lose their voices in the shrieks and clatter of the carnival rides.

Down toward the river, hundreds of white canvas tepees, Travel-Eze motor homes, and nylon dome tents waver in the heat. This is the "genuine Indian encampment" where members of the Colville Confederated Tribes and other western Indian nations have gathered. In rows of booths by a huge, dusty, gravel parking lot, Indian vendors hawk everything from traditional jewelry and wind-dried salmon to cotton candy and feathered roach clips.

On stage beneath the giant umbrella of a surplus parachute, two dancers move with dizzying speed to the hypnotic, circular rhythm of skin drums. In the shade of a tepee, a young man in mirrored sunglasses and the feathers and fringe of a Fancy Dancer sits waiting.

The Indian encampment stretches as far as the Stampede Arena, where the August air is heavy with the barnyard smell of livestock holding pens behind the bleachers. Sweat stains the armpits of embroidered Western shirts, ruddy-faced men gulp beer from plastic cups, and women fan themselves with programs or try to tease a little life back into their lacquered bouffants.

Down in the chutes, a young man with a knee brace wound outside tight Wrangler jeans eases himself down onto the massive humped back of an agitated Brahma bull. Every muscle tenses as the announcer's voice drones its last and in a moment of rigid silence, the rider awaits the buzzer and the swing of the gate.

The rodeo's grand finale is the Suicide Race, in which 20 riders spur their horses over the sandy brink of Suicide Hill, skid dangerously down a long, steep slope to the Okanogan River, then gallop across the shallow river, up the far bank, and into the arena. Scores of spectators stand in the cooling river or wait on its shaded bank for the riders to crest the hill. So do animal rights activists protesting this treatment of horses.

The race's all-time champion was a Nespelem man named Alex Dick, who claimed his first victory in 1940 and remained undefeated for 16 years straight. A bull gouged out one of Dick's eyes early in his rodeo career, and he rode to most of his Suicide Race victories on a one-eyed horse named Brownie. During his long reign, regulars said that the race was always won by "a blind Indian riding a one-eyed horse."

West of the bridge, in what is now the front yard of a small motel, a gravestone marks the final resting place of a Colville chief.

East of the bridge, a turnoff takes you to one of the richest historical areas in Washington. Just upstream from the present highway bridge, the river once tumbled over Kettle Falls, where local tribes speared salmon for perhaps 8,000 years. After Grand Coulee was built, and Franklin D. Roosevelt Lake flooded the falls, they simply ceased to exist.

The old town of Kettle Falls, which used to stand beside the river also wound up under 30 feet of water. The inhabitants moved to higher ground.

Before the dam and the highways were built, people traveling up or down the river had to portage around the falls. Traditionally, they walked up over a pine-covered bench on the south shore, where Catholic missionaries built **St. Paul's Mission** in 1837. Signs now direct you to the St. Paul's Mission, where an interpretive center tells you about the history of the place. The mission building still stands, its squared-off log walls tight and plumb. It was rebuilt in 1939. Inside, you stand on wide, pegged floorboards and look up past heavy, hand-hewn cross-beams into the dim space above. When Lorraine portaged past the spot in 1924, he made note of the "former Jesuit mission, empty and with its doors and windows gone. It had been built in 1837 of the most evenly-sized and smoothly-hewn logs I ever saw, and although not a single nail held the structure together, the walls were still upright, sound and substantial."

Walk toward the water through the park-like woods of second-growth ponderosa pine. In late spring, the forest floor is sprinkled with wildflowers: blue larkspur, yellow and purple daisies, the bright red cups of low-growing rocket. In a fenced-off area, old headstones mark a spot in which traders, settlers, and Indians were buried.

At the edge of the bluff, you can look over the bay that covers the site of old Fort Colville, built and manned by the Hudson's Bay Company. Look up the river through dark, misty hills toward Canada. Right at the brink rests a long black boulder with a heavily scored surface. A sign tells you that this rock used to stand beside the river, and that the Indians who fished at Kettle Falls honed spear points on it.

At dusk, the mission interior is lost in shadows, the interpretive center is closed, and no one is around. Nothing moves among the pines. The water is still. The black boulder lies on the bluff with its weight of human history dating back, perhaps, eight millennia. The spot isn't really quiet—you can hear traffic whipping by on US 395—but it is serene.

(previous pages) The medicinal waters of Soap Lake near Ephrata draw people from around the state.

SASQUATCH

Everyone knows about the Sasquatch (or Bigfoot, to some)—that huge and hairy hominid some people swear they've glimpsed in the forests of the Pacific Northwest. Those enthusiastic few who've made Bigfoot their life's study point to British Columbia's Kwakiutl Indians, whose masks often depicted "Bukwas" (Wild Man of the Woods), a frightening human-like creature, and to the Salish Indians, who told tales of Sasquatch, the giant cannibal. In 1811, explorer David Thompson crossed the Rockies near Washington Territory and recorded the following in his journal.

(January 5) ...We are now entering the defiles of the Rocky Mountains by the Athabasca River...strange to say, here is a strong belief that the haunt of the Mammoth is about this defile...I questioned several (Indians), none could positively say they had seen him, but their belief I found firm and not to be shaken. I remarked to them, that such an enormous heavy animal must leave indelible marks of his feet, and his feeding. This they all acknowledged, and that they had never seen any marks of him, and therefore could show me none.

(January 7) Continuing our journey in the afternoon we came on the track of large animal , the snow about six inches deep on the ice; I measured it; four large toes each of four inches in length to each a short claw; the ball of the foot sunk three inches lower than the toes, the hinder part of the foot did not mark well, the length fourteen inches, by eight inches in breadth, walking from north to south, and having passed about six hours. We were in no humour to follow him; the men and Indians would have it to be a young Mammoth and I held it to be the track of a large old grizzled bear; yet the shortness of the nails, the ball of the foot, and its great size was not that of a bear, otherwise that of a very large old bear, his claws worn away; this the Indians would not allow...

Folks have been spotting Bigfoot ever since.

On the Colville side of Kettle Falls, a spacious bed-and-breakfast occupies the site that was once St. Agnes Convent, built in the 1860s. Out back is a little graveyard where nuns who died between the 1940s and the1960s are buried. Near the graveyard, behind a barbed wire fence, lies a pile of lumber. The pile of gray, hand-hewn beams, notched where they once fit together, are the remains of the convent building.

■ GRAND COULEE DAM

Across the dry, broken landscape that is known as "channeled scabland," a landscape of rock and sagebrush that was fissured by unimaginably great ice-age floods, stands Grand Coulee Dam.

Today, **Dry Falls** is a huge amphitheater of stone, a horseshoe of dark cliffs with pools of water at their bases, 400 feet below. Climb down a trail along the infinitely-fractured rock. Sunlight on the far cliffs, perhaps three miles away, brings out the rust and gold of lichen. There is a great stillness here. Down inside the amphitheater, you hear the songs and cries of many birds.

This was once the greatest waterfall in the world, perhaps the greatest waterfall in history, dwarfing Niagara, dwarfing Victoria Falls (which is slightly taller but less than one-third as wide). Ice dammed the Columbia, flooding much of Idaho and Montana. Then the ice dam broke, and the floodwaters rushed out, scoring the landscape, gouging out the coulees, pouring over what is now Dry Falls. Successive floods swept across the landscape and over these cliffs. A sign at the site tells you that at the peak of the great floods, the amount of water plunging over the falls may have equaled the combined flow of all the rivers in the world.

The most massive man-made structure in the world, Grand Coulee Dam couldn't hold back all the rivers of the world—but its four-fifths of a mile of concrete backs up the Columbia into a lake 151 miles long. Rising 550 feet above bedrock, the big dam fills the gorge for which it is named, the pale concrete L of the structure joining the pale rock of the coulee's sides below the pale earth of the dry hills above. You don't realize quite how tall the dam is until you drive across it and look far down at the trees and rooftops in the town of Grand Coulee, built originally to house construction workers.

From the north end of the dam, you can see the 12-foot pipes that carry irrigation water up the cliff on the south side, gleaming in the sun like a cluster of silver organ pipes. Up close, you can see that they're segmented like the stalks of some alien marsh grass. All the water that irrigates more than half a million acres in the Columbia Basin Project gets pumped up that cliff.

Outside the pump generator plant, you hear the hum of distant transformers. Inside, behind glass doors, you see a gallery of great pumps, a line of huge, institutional-green cylinders, each with a little metal cupola on top, running the length of a huge, empty room. A catwalk along one side runs past a bank of gauges

Giant power generators in the Grand Coulee Dam complex provide more energy than any other dam in the world, with the exception of Brazil's Guri Dam.

When under construction, the Grand Coulee Dam required more lumber for its framing forms than any other known project, resulting in the world's largest all-concrete structure. (Museum of History and Industry, Seattle)

and switches for each pump. A lone workman walks along the catwalk checking the gauges. The huge room is spotless and still. There is no dirt, no noise, no visible motion. This room—this whole place—can be considered a kind of hymn to the ideal of technological progress embraced during the first half of the twentieth century.

Grand Coulee was by far the largest of the dams that transformed much of the Northwest during the New Deal and the years that followed World War II. It has nearly one-third the generating capacity of the entire vast Columbia River hydro system, and more generating capacity than any two of the other dams. It remains the largest single producer of hydroelectricity on this continent. With hindsight, one can also consider Grand Coulee the greatest of the river's many fish killers, walling off 1,100 miles of salmon spawning streams. It was the only dam at which society had to make an explicit choice: at the other dams, people could build fish ladders which they thought might enable salmon to get upstream. (When the first fish ladders were built at Bonneville Dam, no one really knew whether or not they'd work. And no one even thought about the problems of moving young fish downstream.) Grand Coulee was considered too tall for fish ladders, and when it was built, people knew that they were trading electric lights and irrigation for fish that could swim 1,500 miles from the Pacific Ocean to interior British Columbia, for the "June hogs" that weighed 100 pounds apiece. The first fish runs that found the dam in their paths battered themselves to death against its concrete base.

On the other hand, irrigation water and electricity saved some people who had been battering themselves to death trying to wrest a living from an arid land. When Stewart Holbrook, author of *The Columbia,* drove through the area around Grand Coulee, he found:

> . . . *No* human being, though occasionally sighted a reminder that some poor soul had tried to live here until one desperate day when he could stand it no longer and walked away, leaving his house as it stood, or leaned, complete with a rusting cultivator in the yard, and a mile or so of barbed wire between pitiful posts supported by little piles of stones.

■ CRESTON AND WHEAT COUNTRY

Holbrook's description hangs in the air as you drive uphill through sage and rock on the road from Grand Coulee toward Wilbur. But it evaporates when you see

APPLES OF ENDLESS VARIETY

Washington State and apples are synonymous. No wonder, since apples grow almost everywhere, both east and west of the Cascade Mountains. Once known only for the much-maligned Red Delicious, the state's growers have branched out into multiple varieties during the last two decades. Larry's Market, a Seattle supermarket chain, holds an annual fall apple fest at its stores with as many as 20 different varieties to taste, including such rarities as Rhode Island Greening, Arkansas Black, and Bramling. The greatest variety can be found in the countryside, east and west. All over the state, farmers' markets, farm stands, and small-town markets sell such uncommon apples as the Braeburn, Cox Orange Pippin, Winter Banana, Russet, Criterion, Jonagold, Idared, Fuji, Mutsu, and Spitzenberg, besides the more widely commercially grown varieties like the Jonathan, Winesap, Rome Beauty, Newton Pippin, Golden Delicious, and Gravenstein. Of the latter two, the Golden Delicious is the ideal storage apple. When grown in orchards near Lake Chelan, it reaches an unequalled crispness and firmness, with a balance of sweetness and crispness matched only by the finest dessert wines. The Gravenstein is a cool climate apple and grows best west of the Cascades. Like the Golden Delicious it is best when grown near water, as it is in Skagit County, where orchards overhang the tideflats of Padilla Bay. It does not keep well, but must be eaten fresh, in season. It is inimitable in apple sauces and pies, however. Both of these golden apples are perfect with a well-aged, sharp Washington cheddar.

—John Doerper

A postcard announces the arrival of the National Apple Show in Chicago, sponsored by Washington State growers. (University of Washington Libraries)

Grain elevators rise above the green fields of the eastern region.

the brilliant green of irrigated winter wheat growing almost to the drainage ditch beside the road.

At Creston, a grain elevator stands by the railroad tracks and semis are parked in the unpaved lot outside the cafe and dance hall, but not much is happening. It's quiet on the main street, except when traffic goes by. A woman behind the cafe counter complains to a trucker about how much she just paid for a small lot in town. He says he paid more for a lot in his own hometown. Yes, she says, but "there's nothing here!" Actually, in a weedy lot, there is a faded wooden sign announcing that this was where the outlaw Harry Tracy met his death.

The name may evoke blank stares now, but in the early 1900s, Harry Tracy was a famous desperado. In 1902, he broke out of the Oregon state penitentiary in Salem and made his way to Olympia, Seattle, and finally eastern Washington, eluding police and state militiamen and killing seven people on the way. A small group of well-armed locals surrounded him in a wheat field just outside Creston. After a brief shootout, night fell, and they watched the wheat field all night. In the morning, they found that Tracy, wounded in the shootout, had killed himself with his own gun. Tracy's death was big news all across the country. "The first piece of business after discovery of the body," Holbrook writes, "was to pose the dead thug on his left side, gun in hand, finger on trigger, with the tall wheat as background, to make a picture that was to sell in postcard size by the hundred thousand."

The posse that surrounded Tracy had been part of a group discussing the outlaw that morning in the local barbershop. Today, it is as hard to imagine a barbershop posse in one of these small towns as it is to imagine a famous bad man hiding out in the wheat fields.

If the area's small agricultural towns are somewhat depressed economically, people still find satisfaction in the farms and orchards, and in the spaciousness of a huge landscape, far from the cities. One evening not long ago, a man and woman who farmed 2,000 acres of dryland wheat southwest of Creston were saying that they were in it for the way of life, and they wanted to see the way of life continue. The man had been sitting by the living room window, looking out over a field that sometimes was bright green with new wheat and sometimes was covered with blowing dust right after plowing; today, it was unplowed and unplanted, and he had been sitting there with two calculators trying to figure out whether it would be more profitable to plant wheat there this year or to let the land lie fallow. He and his wife couldn't have afforded this place if his father hadn't more or less given it to them years ago. They hadn't had an easy time of it. In addition to the long days of plowing and planting and harvest, they had battled federal bureaucrats. One day, cleaning out a moving combine, the man had lost an arm. Still, they liked the life, and they hoped, *really* hoped, that they could pass it along to one of their kids. After all, the man said, "that's what it's all about."

■ SPOKANE

For generations, Spokane has billed itself as the capital of the "Inland Empire" of Washington and Idaho. Hardly a metropolis by coastal standards, Spokane is nevertheless the largest city between Seattle and Minneapolis. The railroads made it a regional center in the late nineteenth century, and it remains a source of supplies and financing for a large hinterland. The local economy also depends heavily on jobs at Fairchild Air Force Base—where B-52 bombers armed with nuclear warheads stood ready for decades to attack the Soviet Union.

For a good deal of the country, Spokane's 1974 world's fair put the city on the map, much as the 1962 fair put Seattle on the map. Never as big a deal as Seattle's extravaganza, the Spokane fair nevertheless enabled the city to properly install a great park on the Spokane River. Early in the city's history, the Olmsted brothers, who also designed Spokane's curving Riverside Avenue, conceived of a park that would let people walk along both banks of the river. The railroads weren't about to give up their access to the water, though, and for generations, most of the park was covered by railyards. But with the world's fair immenent an extensive citywide clean-up began, and **Riverfront Park** was laid out in full, covering 100 acres of land, river, and two river islets. With the park as its centerpiece (especially in summer), Spokane is much closer to its river than, say, New York is to the Hudson or, really, than downtown Seattle is to Puget Sound.

Downtown Spokane, circa 1900. (University of Washington Libraries)

The big windows of the new downtown library, which opened in 1994, provide spectacular views of water cascading over gray bedrock. On the south bank, parents with young children head for a 1909 carousel with carved horses in full gallop, elaborate woodwork, light bulbs gleaming off mirrored backdrops. Loud organ music drifts through the open doors. On a nearby island, the old brick Great Northern Railway station clock tower rises above the weeping willows at its base.

A string of twenty-odd cast-steel runners are caught mid-stride along the southern edge of the park, monuments to the city's annual Bloomsday Run. These slightly larger-than-life sculptures were created by Spokane-area artist David Govedare (the artist who installed cast-steel horses in the hills near Vantage). The Bloomsday Run, which draws more than 50,000 runners every May, is part of the Spokane Lilac Festival, several days of exhibits, flower shows, and concerts.

The river has always been the heart of the city. At first called "Spokane Falls," the community started on the south side of the river, right by the falls where Indians had speared salmon; the first people who settled on the north side had to row

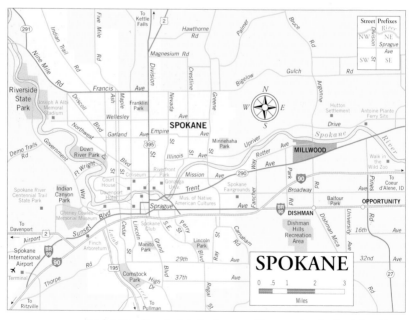

(right) Riverfront Park in Spokane provides recreation for the city's residents.

WOBBLIES

In the early twentieth century, loggers, miners, field hands, and other workers were frequently ill-paid and ill-housed, doing hard, dangerous work under often despotic management. Northwestern workers were particularly receptive to the ideas of the Industrial Workers of the World, the IWW or Wobblies, founded in 1905, which called for all workers to join in one big industrial union and ultimately take over the capitalist means of production. "At first people did not pay much attention to IWW slogans painted on stumps," Archie Binns recalled in a 1942 memoir entitled *The Roaring Land,* "and then sometimes on weekdays in good logging weather, towns would be dark and faintly ominous with striking men in stag shirts and overalls." In 1909, Wobblies went to Spokane to speak on the street corners against the employment agencies that controlled jobs in the logging camps. The city passed an ordinance against speaking on corners. Every time a Wobbly spoke, he—or she—was arrested. But as fast as IWW speakers were arrested, more Wobblies poured into the city—many

Labor unrest resulted in violence throughout the state in the 1920s and '30s, as this scene in Seattle illustrates. (Underwood Archives, San Francisco)

riding freight cars with the hobos—to take their places. Eventually, more than 500 Wobblies filled the jails, and when the city got tired of feeding them, it repealed the ordinance. Other cities didn't worry about where to put Wobblies. IWW organizers were beaten, shot, run out of town. For a decade or so, the Wobblies inspired a fear in some employers and civic leaders out of all proportion to their numbers.

World War I and the Red Scare that followed it marked the end of the IWW as an organization that many people feared—or hoped—would lead a revolution. By organizing strikes and slowdowns in the woods during wartime, the Wobblies stirred up even more antagonism than usual, and Colonel Brice Disque, who was in charge of producing spruce for military aircraft frames, organized a competing labor group, the Loyal Legion of Loggers and Lumbermen. Disque took away one of the Wobblies' main issues by forcing employers to give the loggers an eight-hour day.

across. Individual citizens pledged money to build the first bridge in 1881. Only four years later, the first hydroelectric plant in the state was built beside the falls. Today, a blocky, pastel 1922 powerhouse still generates electricity on the river's south bank. Peek inside and you see the top of a single big generator in a huge, empty room. Stand near the building, and you can hear it hum.

Downtown Spokane has an unusually fine collection of old commercial buildings, some grander versions of the brick commercial blocks that line main streets in market towns all over eastern Washington, and some far more ornate. The old **Davenport Hotel**, once the grandest hostelry in eastern Washington and now in the process of restoration, is a Moorish fantasy. The **Paulson Center** includes two early twentieth-century office towers with patterned white facades, while the fancy brickwork of the Spokane Club, by the river, complements the exterior of the nearby Our Lady of Lourdes Cathedral. The brick face of the *Spokesman-Review* building curves along West Riverside Avenue. The Spokane County Courthouse, built in seventeenth-century French chateau style, sports turrets at the corners, more turrets surrounding a central tower, and windows topped with ogee arches and masonry scallop shells.

All this suggests a city that once upon a time had a rather grandiose view of its future, very much in the Old West tradition. Today, Spokane isn't and doesn't want to be a modern metropolis in the manner of Seattle. It likes to think of itself as a community of neighborhoods and friendly people.

S O U T H E A S T

EAST OF THE SOUTHERN CASCADES, the Yakima Valley produces most of the country's hops and spearmint, much of its apples and asparagus, some of its best wine grapes. At the Big Bend of the Columbia, where the Yakima and Snake rivers meet the River of the West, stand the Tri Cities of Richland, Pasco, and Kennewick and the Hanford nuclear reservation. Beyond the Columbia, you find the city of Walla Walla, the college town of Pullman, the northern end of Hell's Canyon and, above all, the rolling hills and dry plateaus of wheat country. The Palouse Hills get more moisture than the central part of the state and produce some of the highest wheat yields per acre in the world. The drier regions, where farmers have to let a field stand fallow every other year to build up moisture, raise a lot of wheat, too, and some farmers there have increased their yields by irrigating from deep wells or from the federal Columbia Basin Project.

HAS SHE NOT REASON TO BE THANKFUL ?

A fanciful ideal of life in the state of Washington. (above)
(right) The rolling hills of the Palouse region.

■ FROM ROSLYN TO GEORGE

Heading east from Snoqualmie Pass you'll pass the old coal towns of Roslyn and Cle Elum. **Roslyn** has recently become a destination in itself for visitors interested in seeing the set of television's "Northern Exposure." Watching scenes filmed along the town's main street oftens draws a crowd but other sites deserving attention are the town's 23 cemeteries—one for each nationality of coal-miners who ended up in Roslyn. Farther east you'll pass through the university and rodeo town of Ellensburg, one of many eastern Washington communities with historic, turn-of-the-century downtown commercial blocks. Its Labor Day weekend rodeo was first held in 1923, and is one of the largest in the Northwest. But Central Washington University's presence has made cafes and bookstores big draws as well. Off I-90 as it heads east toward Vantage, stone columns of petrified tree trunks lie in the sagebrush of Gingko and Wanapum state parks. A bridge spans the Columbia River, blue beneath the basalt cliffs, the road beyond climbing toward George—George, Washington; get it?—where thousands of people go to hear rock and blues concerts every summer at a natural amphitheater. On the way, a turnout to the right takes you to the wild horses. Rust brown, silhouetted against the sky, manes and tails flying in the wind, the horses race along a flat ridgetop overlooking the river. The lead horse rears at the brink of the ridge. Eventually, if funds materialize, these life-sized horse statues—sculpted by David Govedare—will seem to be spilling from a huge Indian basket, a Native American legend turned into enduring steel.

■ YAKIMA VALLEY

The high ridges on the way to Yakima are dry, rugged, sagebrush-covered rangeland. On an overcast day, the misty folds of the hills stand out clearly in patterns of light and dark, like the colors in a Cézanne painting.

As you descend into the Yakima Valley, the transition from wasteland to cornucopia is abrupt. One minute, you're in the sagebrush and the next, you're driving through orchards and vineyards, past the tall support posts with overhead wires and angled braces of hop fields, past warehouses with huge wooden fruit boxes stacked outside.

The Yakima Valley produces many of the state's apples, most of its cherries and

Migrant workers have been harvesting Washington apples for almost a century. This scene dates from the early 1900s. (University of Washington Libraries)

other soft fruits, and most of its winegrapes. The valley and the nearby Columbia Basin also produce more asparagus than any state but California, most of the nation's spearmint, and most of its hops. All in all, the valley produces more than 70 different crops. Stop by the Chamber of Commerce at 503 First Avenue in the town of Zillah where you will find a map of the Yakima Valley Wine Tour and Fruit Loop, directing you to wineries and orchards.

To become a center of fruit growing, eastern Washington needed at least three things: irrigation, cold storage, and a railroad. Before the nineteenth century ended, the Yakima Valley had all three. The first apple trees were planted in 1870. The valley shipped its first carload of apples in 1894. It has been shipping fruit and other crops ever since.

Harvesting the valley's crops has always required large numbers of seasonal pickers. Originally, here and in other parts of Washington and the West, a lot of the pickers were Indians. Later, thousands of non-Indian pickers would stream into the valley at harvesttime and live in tents along the irrigation ditches. Before World War II, at the peak of the harvest, the valley's fields and orchards employed 35,000 pickers.

During the Depression, a lot of the migrant pickers were people from Oklahoma and Arkansas, displaced by the Dust Bowl and the dismal economics of

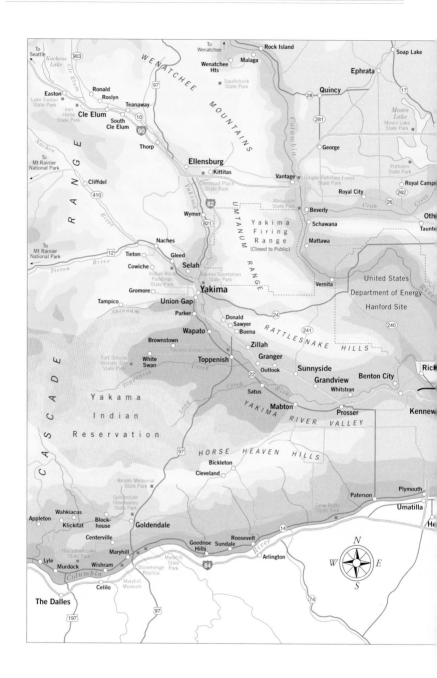

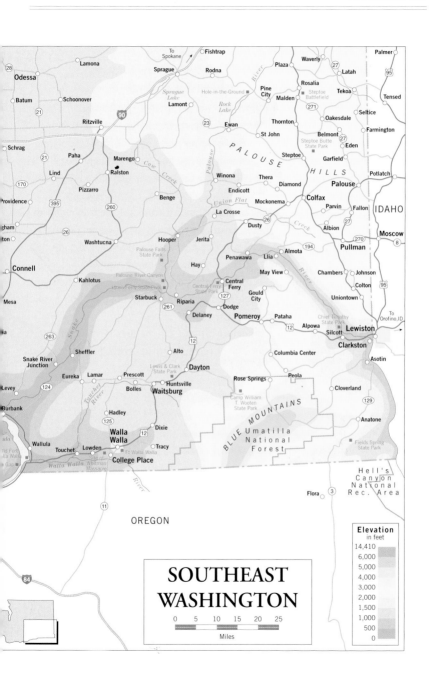

SOUTHEAST WASHINGTON

0   5   10   15   20   25
Miles

Elevation
in feet

14,410
6,000
5,000
4,000
3,000
2,000
1,500
1,000
500
0

farming in hard times. After the war, they started settling down in Yakima and other fruit-growing communities. Some of their families have since become pillars of the local establishment.

Hispanic workers have gone through much the same process here. During World War II, when labor was scarce, the federal government started bringing in Mexican workers for the harvest. These "braceros" kept coming for decades. Some settled legally in Washington's fruit-growing areas. Some worked here illegally. By the 1980s, fruit growers said that without illegal workers, they couldn't possibly harvest their crops.

After the federal government declared an amnesty on illegal aliens living in this country, a lot of previously migratory farmworkers put down roots in Yakima and other eastern Washington communities. But Hispanic families had already been living in Yakima for generations, and the Hispanic community now includes business owners, bank presidents, professionals, and people who own their own orchards. Most of the Hispanic population has Mexican origins, but a small percentage came from other Latin countries.

There have also been Asian populations in the Yakima area for generations. A sizable Japanese-American population lived here until 1942, but after Japan

The advent of the railway was a boon to the development of southeastern Washington, as it enabled farmers to get their produce to markets in Seattle. (Underwood Archives, San Francisco)

bombed Pearl Harbor everyone of Japanese origin was sent to Utah until the end of World War II. Many of the families "interned" during the war didn't bother coming back.

Yakima was the boyhood home of one of the United States' most controversial Supreme Court justices, William O. Douglas, who served on the court from 1939 until 1975.

In the early years of the century, the Yakima Valley was a treeless plain and Douglas recalled that "the land around town was mostly bleak sagebrush, occupied only by jackrabbits and rattlesnakes" when his family moved there. Orchards and shade trees were just starting to grow, and he relished the unobstructed view of the mountains. "With no trees to block the view, we could look west from our front porch on the outskirts of town and see thousands of sunsets over the Cascades—sunsets which tinged the dominant glaciers of [Mounts] Adams and Rainier with reds and golds."

In 1917, when he was 19 years old, Douglas watched a train come through town carrying Wobblies (IWW labor organizers) who'd been indicted by a federal court for conspiring to obstruct the war effort and were traveling under escort to Chicago to stand trial. "These were sealed boxcars carrying human beings, 30 to 40 in each car,"

Irrigation, made possible by the reservoirs along the Columbia and the advent of electric pumps, enabled the arid region to sustain major crop cultivation. (University of Washington Libraries)

Douglas recalled years later. "The authorities were taking outcasts through our city. There were no toilets, no food, no water, just sealed boxcars with these poor bastards inside. I walked home with tears in my eyes."

During Douglas's many years in Washington, D.C., he returned every summer to a home at nearby Goose Prairie, at the edge of what is now the **William O. Douglas Wilderness.** Douglas became a champion of Northwestern environmental causes.

The nearby **Yakama Indian Reservation,** the largest in Washington, includes irrigated orchards and fields, open range, miles of commercial forest, a cultural heritage center open to the public, and much of 12,276-foot Mount Adams, the state's second-highest peak. The tribal government is in Toppenish. The name was written "Yakima" until 1994, when it was changed to better reflect actual pronunciation. The tribe also has treaty rights to salmon in the Yakima and Columbia rivers. The Yakima no longer contains enough water year-round to irrigate all the valley's farms

During the 1890s, Mr. Thomas Oaks of Massachusetts was chief engineer of the Great Northern Pacific Railway, and was in charge of laying out the tracks across the state of Washington. A friend in the area took him and his daughter, Zillah (pictured above) for a drive in a wagon to survey potential sites for laying the tracks. As they crossed a creek, the wagon hit a rock and Zillah was tossed into the water. They pulled her out and Mr. Oaks's companion said the spot would make a good place for a town along the railway. They would name it Zillah. Today, Zillah is in the heart of Yakima Valley wine country, and one winery even features the lovely Zillah on its label. (Story and photo courtesy Zillah's granddaughter, Margaret C. Burt)

and orchards and still assure the survival of the fish. The highlight for visitors to the reservation is the museum at the **Yakama Cultural Heritage Center** on State Highway 97 (or off exit 50 from Interstate 82). The museum is one of the best Native American archives in the state. **Toppenish,** off US 97, is a Western-style town best known for the many outdoor murals which adorn over 30 historic brick and masonry buildings. Every year the towns hosts a "Mural in a Day" festival: artists gather in the downtown Pioneer Park to create a painting, which is then moved to a building wall.

■ PROSSER AND HORSE HEAVEN HILLS

Prosser is a center not only of cherry and other orchards, but of vineyards. While not long ago the idea would have seemed startling, people now come here for wine country tours. Originally, it was a wheat town, with a mill that used the power of a small waterfall. East of Prosser between the Big Bend of the Columbia and the Yakima River is a region known as the Horse Heaven Hills. When *Washington: A Guide to the Evergreen State* was written fifty years ago, the hills were described as:

Teapot Dome, near Zillah, is listed as the nation's first and oldest gas station.

. . . *A* great natural grazing area where roving bands of wild horses feed on the abundant grass. A fat, sleek bay occasionally gallops over broken terrain, without halter, saddle or shoes, his luxurious mane and tail flowing in the breeze. Smaller pintos, more nervous and less majestic, are easily agitated by an approaching automobile. Perky colts worry their mothers by wandering toward the road to investigate the queer, shiny vehicles that raise so much roar and dirt.

Travelers driving through the Horse Heaven Hills, also reported strange sights: "At night, will-o-the-wisps are frequent along this bleak and lonely road. Flame-colored, and about three feet above the ground, they are often mistaken by motorists for a single vehicular light. Sternly realistic farmers, their hands still smarting from the handle of a plow have reported 'balls of fire' coming down the road at the speed of an automobile."

No Place Like Home

*W*hen you mention home to a man from Washington there is no telling what he may be thinking of . . . .

He could be thinking of the Horse Heaven Hills, caught snug in the sharp bend of the Columbia, and could be hearing the creak of his saddle and the light music of the bit-rings. He could be remembering himself at the wheel of a fishing boat in waters off Point Roberts . . . . or it could be down by Dungeness, watching the stern rise and fall in the swell that is rolling up old de Fuca from the greatest of the oceans . . . .

Yet "home" need not mean the waterfront at all. A Washingtonian may never have gazed at the sea, and he may die east of the Cascades without seeing Puget Sound or the San Juans or the Queen City whose towers were built on more than seven hills. Mention home to him, and he may think only of the rolling fields of wheat or rye grass and the Blue Mountains behind them in the haze. He may be thinking of an old house built tall and grey with narrow windows that is the only house visible around the whole horizon, and therefore the only house in the world to his young eyes.

—Nard Jones, *Evergreen Land: A Portrait of the State of Washington,* 1947

■ TRI CITIES

The Yakima River enters the Columbia at **Richland,** the largest of what virtually everyone in Washington knows as the "Tri Cities." The Snake River joins the Columbia a little downstream, just below the cities of **Pasco** and **Kennewick,** the second and third legs of this triangle. The Tri Cities supply the southern part of

HANFORD

Early in World War II, the government needed a place to make plutonium for atomic bombs—some place remote enough from urban areas to provide for safety and secrecy, and close enough to a major water source to provide water for cooling reactors. Hanford fit the profile.

Soon workers from all over the country were streaming in to build three reactors and all the buildings, roads, and power lines needed to support them. The hamlet of Richland, where only a couple of hundred people had lived, was developed into a government town for the thousands of people who would actually run the production site. "It was kind of wild," a woman who had moved there in the early days told S. L. Sanger, author of *Hanford and the Bomb: An Oral History of World War II.* "There was nothing here. The sand was knee-deep….When I got to Pasco on the train from the East it was terrible….The station was all the time crowded with men. The men never shaved, it was hard to get laundry done. Construction workers would wear their overalls until they couldn't wear them any more and then they would buy a new outfit." Out at the construction site, thousands of those workers lived in barracks.

The reactors went up with incredible speed. Little more than two years after construction started, Hanford had produced the five kilograms of plutonium that exploded at the Trinity test site in the New Mexico desert on July 16, 1945, and the plutonium that destroyed Nagasaki. It went on to produce the plutonium for all the bombs that American bombers carried during the Berlin crisis of 1948, the Korean War and the Cold War '50s.

Then relations with the Soviet Union grew a little less chilly. Kennedy and Khrushchev agreed to stop atmospheric nuclear testing. Demand for Hanford's plutonium plummeted. Production was cut back, reactors were closed, people were laid off, and the government launched the first effort to diversify the Tri Cities economy.

Before the last reactor closed in the 1980s, politicians started talking about finding a new mission for Hanford. They found it under their noses: cleaning up more than 40 years' worth of radioactive waste at the site. Although it will eventually take billions of dollars, thousands of workers, and at least a generation, Hanford is now becoming a center of the nuclear clean-up industry.

In a curious way, Hanford's long history of secrecy has produced some environmental benefits. Large parts of Hanford's 540,000 acres have been off-limits to human beings since 1942, so natural communities within the reservation have remained uniquely undisturbed. One hundred twenty square miles of Hanford have been designated an arid lands ecology research area. Thirty thousand acres of that form the largest Research Natural Area in Washington.

This photograph of the Hanford nuclear plant was released on August 6, 1945, the day President Roosevelt made public the existence of the atomic bomb. Hiroshima was bombed the same day. (Underwood Archives, San Francisco)

the Columbia Basin Project, including the nearby Yakima Valley and Walla Walla wine country. Aside from shipping agricultural products by barge and train, they manufacture huge cranes and titanium golf club shafts. Above all, since World War II, they've been the bedroom communities, headquarters, and sources of labor and supplies for the Hanford Atomic Works. Richland High School's athletic teams are still called the Bombers. Thanks to Hanford's presence, the federal government never built a dam near the Tri Cities, preserving the last free-flowing stretch of the river above Bonneville Dam. Chinook salmon still spawn in the gravel of Vernita Bar, in what is known as the river's Hanford Reach.

■ COLUMBIA RIVER GORGE

Downstream from the Tri Cities, dry, rolling hills slide abruptly into the wide dam pools, and huge rafts of waterbirds bob in the slack water. As you approach the Columbia River Gorge, the hills plunging to the river on the opposite shore grow steeper. Outcroppings of dark basalt appear. The steep, tawny slopes become studded with the dark verticals of black rock and lone pines. And suddenly, driving through this empty, arid landscape, you come upon a cloud of industrial haze and the long metal buildings that enclose the potlines of an aluminum plant. The aluminum plant stands right by John Day Dam, close to the immense supply of electricity that is needed to produce the ubiquitous light metal. The plant's proximity to the dam is both practical and symbolic. There's only one reason why more than one-third of the nation's aluminum is produced in the Northwest, and that is the availability of power from the Columbia River dams.

A few miles beyond the aluminum plant, on a high cliff overlooking the river, you encounter **Stonehenge**—not quite the Stonehenge you see on England's Salisbury Plain but a slightly scaled-down model with all the stones in their original places, the circle unbroken. It was built as a memorial to the soldiers who died in World War I by Sam Hill, a wealthy man with a grand imagination and son-in-law of the great railroad builder, James J. Hill.

A little beyond Stonehenge, on another dry bluff above the River of the West, you reach an even grander work of Hill's imagination, the improbable mansion that is now the **Maryhill Museum.**

For a more thorough description of the Columbia River Gorge refer to the "SOUTH-CENTRAL" chapter and the section entitled "Columbia River Gorge," which takes the traveler from Vancouver, Washington, east to Maryhill.

US 97 leads north from Maryhill toward **Goldendale**, through rolling hills of wheat and stubble. The road climbs into pines, through woods broken by rock outcroppings and silence broken by the sound of truckers riding their air brakes down from Satus Pass. A **state observatory** open to the public stands on a high point near Goldendale. The town itself contains some nice Victorian houses and turn-of-the-century brick commercial blocks.

From Goldendale, you can return to the river on US 97 or follow narrow, twisting Route 142 down the valley of the Klickitat River. The road down into the canyon from the high plateau offers great views, but it's a real nail-biter. Down lower, you pass through the town of **Klickitat**—"this community supported by perpetual forest resources"—with its houses occupying the few wide spots on the canyon floor and its big Champion sawmill with stacks of finished lumber outside and a mural painted on one metal wall. The road runs through scattered pines, through thickets of oak with lichen-crusted branches, always staying close to the rapids and flat water of the river.

Along the Columbia, you pass a fruit warehouse with great stacks of wooden

The Maryhill Museum is the most isolated major museum in the United States (above). The Columbia River is considered one of the best windsurfing spots to be found anywhere (right).

boxes outside; you pass small sawmills and rock outcroppings softened by moss. The trees change from pine to fir. On the opposite shore, mountains plunge straight to the river, appear and disappear in the mist, their forested slopes broken by rock and split by ravines. A high waterfall cascades down a cliff. In winter, snow dusts the upper slopes. The road along the Washington shore provides a much more dramatic view than the freeway on the Oregon side but much slower driving. It winds around rock walls, bores through the rock in short tunnels. Eventually, just east of 848-foot **Beacon Rock,** which you can climb for views of the river, you reach Bonneville Dam, the first of the great federal dams built across the Columbia, the irreversible step toward transforming the river and much of the region with millions of tons of concrete. Below Bonneville, the river widens out naturally; there are no more barriers between here and the ocean.

■ WALLA WALLA AND WINE

Walla Walla, at the edge of the Palouse Hills, has been a wheat town for more than a century. It is also a prison town—early legislators, dividing up the spoils of state government, gave Olympia the capital, Seattle the university, Walla Walla the pen. And it is a college town—Whitman College is one of the most highly regarded liberal arts schools in the state. In the mid-nineteenth century, it prospered as a supply center for mining rushes farther east; by 1870, the mining booms had made it the largest city in Washington. But for generations, wheat has paid most of the bills.

Not that wheat is the only crop that grows around here. On the highway near town, you pass roadside stands that sell the onions known as Walla Walla sweets. And in small farm towns and along side roads, you see signs for wineries. Some of Washington's best wines are made around Walla Walla. In the old farming community of **Lowdon,** where you see lots of junk machinery standing around, the **Woodward Canyon Winery,** arguably the state's best, occupies metal shed buildings that might just as well be storing feed or fertilizer. The **Ecole no. 41 Winery** occupies the old, two-story schoolhouse, the kind you see in once-significant small towns all over, standing in their weedy schoolyards, evoking memories of wide, worn floorboards and the smell of fresh wax. It's always a relief to find one of the old buildings that's not boarded up.

Downtown Walla Walla has a wonderful collection of old brick buildings,

WASHINGTON WINES

Within Washington there are three official viticultural appellations, and all are located in the drier, warmer eastern portion of the state. The **Columbia Valley** appellation is the largest. Located within it are two smaller areas: the Yakima Valley along the Yakima River just east of the Cascades, and the Walla Walla Valley, located in the far southeastern region of the state and reaching into Oregon. The **Columbia Valley** is the largest wine- and grape-producing region in the state and extends from the Okanogan wilderness south into Oregon and east along the Snake River to Idaho. To the west the appellation follows the Cascades to the beginning of the Columbia Gorge. The grapes planted throughout Columbia Valley include cabernet sauvignon, chardonnay, and riesling.

The high concentration of wineries along Interstate 82 in the **Yakima Valley** make this region a fine place for wine tasting. Both the Columbia and Yakima valleys are known especially for their red grapes, but also produce a superb selection of white grapes.

The **Walla Walla Valley** is Washington's newest wine region and lies along US 12. The mild climate is ideal for a variety of winegrapes including cabernet sauvignon, merlot, riesling, and chardonnay.

■ WASHINGTON WINEGRAPES OF SPECIAL NOTE

Cabernet Sauvignon. This is the major red winegrape of Washington. It's a full-bodied red wine that goes well with steak, rich stews, duck, or lamb.

Chardonnay. Rich and buttery white wine with a crisp acid finish. Delicious with oysters, grilled seafood, or chicken. Nicely complements herb seasonings such as rosemary or tarragon.

Gewurztraminer. A spicy and fruity flavor. Good choice for Chinese, Southeast Asian, or other heavy-on-the-garlic cuisine.

Lemberger. Washington is the only state in the nation to grow this particular grape, especially prolific in the eastern part of the state. Its full body and fruitiness complement meats (especially wild meats such as rabbit or buffalo), rich pasta sauces, or highly-flavored cheeses.

Merlot. Washington State is known for its merlots—softer than the cabernets but full-flavored with a plummy or rich berry flavor. Excellent with a variety of cheeses and meats.

Sauvignon Blanc. Austere and clean. Excellent with seafood, cold meats, or light pasta dishes. Also, as an aperitif.

Semillon. A fruity and herbal sipping wine. Often served with hors d'oeuvres or light entrees. Frequently blended with sauvignon blanc.

White Riesling. (Also called **Johannisberg Riesling**) Washington's rieslings are honeyed white wines, with peach and apricot flavors. Varietals include a soft sipping wine, a rich dessert wine, and an increasingly trendy dry style. Appropriate with light and spicy entrees, seafood (particularly for the drier variety), and desserts.

Rob Stuart, winemaker at Station Hills
Winery in the Yakima Valley.

Much of southeastern Washington receives less than 10 inches of rainfall a year. Were it not for irrigation, most of the area would look like this.

many of which were spruced up in 1992. Late nineteenth-century, two-story brick commercial buildings, a perfect architectural evocation of the period, line the intersection of Second and Main. Main Street itself was originally built over an old Indian trail along the Walla Walla River.

The history most people associate with the Walla Walla area, though, took place a generation or two before those buildings were built: the Whitman Massacre, which happened about 12 miles west of the current city in what is now the **Whitman Mission National Historic Site.** Marcus and Narcissa Whitman built a mission here in 1836. Seven years later, Marcus led the first group of wagons to the Columbia River through the mission grounds. The site lies off in the wheat fields. Run by the National Park Service, it includes an interesting interpretive center that tries hard to portray the Indians with whom the Whitmans worked and who eventually killed them as members of a complex and legitimate culture, with a technology and a world view, not just a bunch of murderers. Outside, the old mission buildings have vanished, and are only outlined in the grass near the reconstructed irrigation ditches and mill pond, headstones, a hilltop memorial obelisk, and wheel ruts left in the 1840s by wagons following the Oregon Trail. It all evokes the Whitmans and their white contemporaries, and it is of them, not the Indians, that you will probably think.

It's a nice spot. A curve of low-lying land filled with wetland plants shows you where the Walla Walla River once ran. A great blue heron flies with slow wing-beats over the millpond and lands on the far bank. A golden eagle soars overhead, riding the wind, turns into the current, hangs still in the air, then slips sideways and flies out of sight.

The outlines of the mission buildings are less impressive; they don't have much impact until, perhaps, an interpretive sign lets you know that you're standing just about exactly on the spot at which Narcissa Whitman died. Then you may think about the lives that were lived here, about the moments of terror at the end, about the long history of well-intentioned people risking their lives in remote places to do good among people whom they don't really understand—and who don't really want them there. Look at today's headlines. Alter the names. How much has changed?

You have to take on faith the archaeological evidence that the buildings stood just here. There's no need to take the wagon tracks on faith; there they are, narrow

RIDING LIKE CENTAURS

Thursday, May 24th [1855]

*A*bout 2500 of the Nez Percé tribe have arrived. It was our first specimen of this Prairie cavalry, and it certainly realized all our conceptions of these wild warriors of the plains . . . . Going out on the plain to where the flag staff had been erected, we saw them approaching on horseback in one long line . . . . Trained from early childhood almost to live up on horseback, they sat upon their fine animals as if they were centaurs. Their horses, too, were arrayed in the most glaring finery. They were painted with such colors as formed the greatest contrast; the white being smeared with crimson in fantastic figures, and the dark colored streaked with white clay. Beads and fringes of gaudy colors were hanging from the bridles, whiles the plumes of eagle feathers interwoven with the mane and tail fluttered as the breeze swept over them . . . .

—Lawrence Kip, *The Indian Council in the Valley of the Walla-Walla,* 1855

parallel tracks worn in the grass, too widely spaced to have been made by a car. They lead off into the distance, then disappear into the grass. This part of the country has historic places but so few genuine historical artifacts: no stone ruins, no ancient churches, no Civil War battlefields, no houses where George Washington slept—but these are the real thing, a link to the nation's early history and to a genuinely epic event—a migration of peoples, like the first crossing of the Bering ice bridge. It's a lot easier to put names and personalities on these people who followed the wagon ruts west in the early nineteenth century than to understand, perhaps, what lured them from comfortable houses and cabins, from friends and churches to the dust, fatigue, danger, and, above all, uncertainty of the long trail across the continent. That was, perhaps, the truly epic quality of the West's settlement by people whose ancestors hadn't ever lived there: the acceptance of uncertainty, of the unknown—and, of course, the prodigious labor required to survive and even prosper once they arrived in the unknown land.

Nearby lie the remains of people who slipped off into that void and vanished. The Whitmans and other victims of the massacre lie beneath a large stone slab, but in a grassy spot at the base of the hill, an unknown number of pioneers who died here after the Whitman Massacre lie in an unknown number of graves. Nobody knows who they were. Did anyone know their names when they died? Did mothers, fathers, friends, lovers, ever know where they had gone? Had there been letters? Or did each of these people simply head west one day—on impulse, out of desperation, following a dream—and disappear?

■ THE PALOUSE

In 1878, Lucy Ide arrived in Dayton, east of Walla Walla, with a wagon train from Wisconsin. Ide and her relatives and friends had left home on May 1, passed through parts of Nebraska, Wyoming, Utah, Idaho, and Oregon, and reached Walla Walla on September 13. Two days later, they followed the Touchet River into Dayton, where they were greeted by the town's founder, Jesse Day. Some planned to stay in Dayton. Others planned to go farther east into the Palouse Hills. All were nearly out of money and food. "Aunt Sallie's prayer has been answered," Ide wrote in her diary for September 15—"her prayer was, that she might be permitted to live to see her new home and see her children once more settled; coming over the Blue Mountains, now and then could be seen lonely graves close by the roadside; and when she began to be sick, she prayed that she might not die on the mountains, the graves looked so lonely to her."

Astonishing though it may be that people once came out here to live—and die—in the empty hills, it is equally astonishing that within a generation or two, there were towns, farms, and wheat fields, that people were putting up elaborate buildings and shipping grain to markets in Great Britain. Drive east from Walla Walla on US 12, which winds through much of the Palouse, and you find yourself among steep hills bright green with young winter wheat. People once plowed the steep hillsides with huge teams of horses or mules. Up to 44 animals would pull a single combine over the hills. The threshed wheat would be loaded into sacks, each of which would be sewn shut by hand. It was unimaginably hard work. One old sack sewer told Alexander C. McGregor that "The first three or four days [of the harvest], the blood would just run out of your fingers where you grabbed the sacks." Another "well remember[ed] a certain day when I[,] just turning sixteen years, was one of the two sack sewers . . . . We threshed that day a few more than 1800 sacks. Their overall weight was about 120 tons. Each sewer sewed about 900 sacks, throwing about 3,600 half-hitch 'ear' loops, making well over 8,000

Wheat fields surround a Palouse Hills grainery (above). In the heart of the hills some fifty miles north of Walla Walla, the Palouse Waterfall drops dramatically several hundred feet (right).

Wheat harvesting in the 1920s (Pemco Webster and Stevens Collection, Museum of History and Industry, Seattle)

stitches, and picking up and carrying to the sack pile over 60 tons of wheat. Without doubt that was the hardest physical day's work I ever performed."

Now, when internal combustion engines do most of the physical work, tall grain silos still rise above small towns like medieval church towers in European villages. Grain elevators stand beside the railroad tracks in living towns, and abandoned elevators stand beside unused railroad spurs where communities used to be.

The town of **Dayton** prospered early, and today, people stop there to see the dozens of Victorian houses, the gingerbread two-story 1881 railroad depot (the state's oldest) now restored as a museum, and the state's oldest high school, with pink stone columns and patterned brickwork, which is still in use. They also check out the oldest courthouse in Washington, a three-story Italianate structure with an outrageous cupola, built in 1887.

Inside the courthouse, you can climb either side of a splendid double staircase to the second floor, where you find a picture-perfect small-town courtroom with high ceilings, spectators' balconies, wooden railings and shelves of old law books— plus a VCR and screen for presenting evidence in a late twentieth-century way.

The Palouse Hills fill much of southeastern Washington, where they receive roughly twice as much rainfall as the dryland wheat country farther west. As a rule

A cattle auction in Touchet (left). The small town of Waitsburg is typical of farming communities in eastern Washington (above).

of thumb, every 10 miles you move farther east, you get another inch of precipitation. Historically, the areas with greater rainfall supported denser growths of native grasses. Over the centuries, the more the rain fell, the more grass plants grew, only to die back, decompose, and turn into soil. The first farmers who came to the Palouse found black topsoil that in places was four to five feet thick. Working the hillsides with their teams of horses or mules, they raised amazing crops of wheat. Their descendants, working those same hillsides with big tractors, still raise amazing crops. Whitman County often produces more wheat than any other single county in the United States.

People seldom get rid of a farm in the Palouse, and new people can seldom afford to buy one. Rural sociologists at Washington State University and the University of Idaho found in 1981 that the Palouse "is an area of very little mobility among the farm population. Most farmers have either operated the same farm most of their life or, if they are younger, have grown up in one of the local communities and are now taking over the family farm or that of a neighbor." Even absentee landlords tended to be "older people who inherited their land or became owners through kinship ties . . . . Nearly 30 percent reported they (or their spouse) had once farmed the land."

The same families are still making a living from the same hills, but after generations of plowing, the hills have lost countless tons of topsoil. Until recently, some farms in the Palouse were probably losing 20 tons per year. This is no dustbowl, but when the topsoil is gone, farmers can either stop planting or spend large sums of money on nitrogen fertilizer. The last 20 years have seen an interest in "conservation tillage" that will save the soil. Now, in the hills of bright green wheat, occasional strips of pale stubble run horizontally along the planted slopes, separating the swaths of green. Once upon a time, the stubble would have been considered a sign of poor farming; any thrifty farmer's field would have been turned over so that nothing showed but soil. Farther west where less rain falls, farmers leave stubble on fallow fields to keep the wind from blowing soil away.

Palouse farmers have always shipped wheat to market down the Snake River. Today, the dams and locks along the Snake and Columbia allow tugs to push their barges all the way to Idaho. (Along the river, barges are pushed, not pulled, and the tugs have tall superstructures that allow captains to see over the loads.) Originally, there were rapids and falls that no boat—and certainly no boat laden with sacks of wheat—could safely pass.

Just getting wheat down to the river was a challenge: the Snake River winds through the Palouse sometimes *thousands* of feet below the farmland. Early farmers eased wagons down to wheat landings on the river bank dragging logs as brakes or using heavy ropes snubbed around immovable objects on the slopes above. Then, as Stewart Holbrook described it in *The Columbia:*

> *In* 1879, at a Snake wheat landing, shippers built a wooden pipe, four inches square, and laid it from the canyon rim to the river. At the first trial the wheat went down with such speed that it was ground into coarse flour. It also cut holes in the pipe. The chute was rebuilt with a series of upturns or baffles . . . .This was the answer to getting grain down to the stern-wheelers.

Getting the wheat down to the riverbank was, of course, only the first step. Beyond lay the rapids through which the Snake and Columbia poured until the big dams transformed both waterways into chains of lakes. Essentially, the sacks of grain had to be portaged around every rapid. Even starting from the relative convenience of Walla Walla, wheat had to be handled and re-handled many times. Holbrook wrote that:

> . . . *A* sack of Walla Walla wheat . . . was first hauled . . . to the railroad warehouse in Walla Walla City . . . then it went by [rail] to Walulla, where it was transferred to a boat and taken to Umatilla; at Umatilla Rapids it was transferred to another boat for Celilo; at Celilo it went through a warehouse and to a car of the Portage railroad and was wheeled to The Dalles, and stored again even if briefly; then it was put aboard a boat and taken to Upper Cascades, and there transferred by Portage railroad to Lower Cascades. Here it was put into the hold or on the deck of another boat for Portland. At Portland it was stored again, and at last was loaded into an ocean-going vessel.

Most contemporary visitors to the Snake River probably have more interest in its stark overpowering setting than its transport possibilities. As it enters Washington from the Oregon-Idaho borderlands, the Snake pours through 5,500-foot-deep **Hell's Canyon**, the deepest gorge on the continent. From Clarkston (or its sister city of Lewiston, Idaho), jet-boat tours roar up the canyon on one- and multi-day excursions, visiting such sites as remote Dug Bar, where Chief Joseph and his band of Nez Percé crossed the Snake on their flight to Canada.

Up above the river, the Palouse landscape invites comparison to the ocean. Driving through these rich, rolling hills of wheat, you can see far enough to get a sense of vastness, but not far enough to see anything different. The hillsides are all wheat, brilliant green when the crop is young, golden when it matures, pale straw and dust after it has been harvested. Trees, houses, whole towns are hidden in the hollows. **Rosalia,** site of the Steptoe battlefield where in the 1850s, the Indians chased off the U.S. Cavalry, stands in a hollow among the wheat fields. The town of **Colfax,** with its old brick downtown blocks, lies below rocky bluffs.

By far the largest Palouse town is **Pullman,** where Washington State University, the state land grant college, spills over a hill overlooking downtown. Pullman may be a college town—and it is just across the state line from Moscow, Idaho, where the University of Idaho is located—but it has long been a wheat town, too, and old grain elevators stand along the railroad track where you drive in.

The university has long since outgrown its origins as an agricultural college. It remains a center of research and education on raising crops and livestock—the Cougar Gold cheese produced on campus has a wide following—but most of the faculty works in other areas. The Edward R. Murrow School of Communications commemorates the pioneer radio newsman who provided much of the nation's news from World War II London not long after he graduated from WSU.

■ NORTH OF THE PALOUSE

Most of Washington's dryland wheat grows in much harsher country than the Palouse. You see rock outcroppings among the fields, sagebrush in uncultivated patches beside the road. The smooth hillsides are broken by basalt bluffs, and areas of sand and sage appear among the wheat, but this is certainly no wasteland. Fields of ripe wheat look classically golden in the sunlight, and blooming canola— "canola" being the nicer and more marketable name for "rapeseed"—crowns a hill with bright yellow. But all this land is naturally desert. A dust devil dances across a newly plowed field. Mini-dust storms rise from the turned soil. A farmer plowing on a steel-tracked tractor works in a perpetual cloud of dust.

And yet, this is fertile ground that has been producing crops for more than a century. That becomes obvious in **Ritzville,** on I-90 east of Spokane, a wheat town since the 1880s. (A lot of the early settlers were German-Russian, and as late as World War II, two of the town's eight churches were German-speaking.) Whole blocks of fine turn-of-the-century brick commercial buildings stand downtown, and a 1907 Carnegie library with a two-story neoclassical entrance is the oldest Carnegie library in the state that is still lending out books.

The wooden gallery of an old hotel building—wood with a brick veneer—gives its part of main street a kind of Wild West look. At the edge of town, past the main street, past the art deco marquee of the Ritz movie theater, past a U.S. Department of Agriculture office in which wheat rates are posted on a chalkboard in the front window, past the big grain elevators, a road rises straight into the wheat fields.

Irrigation changes the character of the landscape. As you enter the Columbia Basin Project near **Othello,** for example, the greens take on a new intensity, cattails grow in roadside ditches where irrigation runoff collects, and the air is filled with the scent of mint. (Eastern Washington grows most of the nation's spearmint and is the second leading producer of peppermint.) Out in the fields irrigated with Columbia River water, big circle irrigators create perpetual rainbows as they swing through the crops.

A cowboy in his '59 Fairlane.

Luminous Summer Evenings

West of the Cascade crest, the sky is a luminous blue, burnished pink, and orange in the far west where the sun is preparing to set. East of the divide, ominously dark clouds obscure the sky. By the time we reach the valley floor, the clouds have burst, gushing water onto a murky landscape. In the deepening gloom, we see campers frantically tugging on their tents. Lightning flashes; thunder rolls down the rocky slopes and growls among the trees. Families pile into their cars and head for town. But the storm is short-lived.

■ WINTHROP EVENING

As we approach Winthrop, the sun breaks through. It changes the clouds' somber hue to purple and gold and paints a rainbow across the valley. After dinner, we walk into town. The sky has cleared. The rain has intensified the aromas of pine and brush wafting down the hillside. They intermingle with the scent of damp soil and freshly mown grass. A warm, rustic odor drifts up from the paddock where horses frolic in the damp pasture. Birds sing with renewed vigor. A hawk's shrill call pierces the sky. Later that evening, we sit by the river in the last gleam of silvery light, listening to the water gurgle by, twist around the gnarled roots of alders, fall over boulders, purl across the pebbles. A lonely frog intermittently croaks for love, a wren chirps in its sleep, a screech owl softly hoots.

■ PAINTING AN EASTERN SUNSET

Summer sunsets are more spectacular east of the mountains than they are in the gentle misty lands of the westside. Painting a summer sky, my brush dips into delicate blues, creamy pinks, pale magentas, and sallow gold and deposits them on the paper in broad smooth washes. The eastern sky calls for more dramatic colors: sonorous reds, streaks of vibrant yellow, intense gray, dynamic white, and deep indigo. Often great cumulus clouds drift across the sky, into the darkness of approaching night.

■ SUNNYSIDE EVENING

Summer days in eastern Washington may be hot and sultry but, as the sun vanishes behind the Cascades, the air cools noticeably. Summer evenings east of the mountains take on a life of their own, a life quite separate from that of the day. This difference is unmistakable, no matter where you live or travel on the dry side. We feel it as we sit in a Sunnyside backyard, with Mexican friends, drinking beer, munching *carne asada taquitos*. It's in the air, carried on the wind, in the sleepy song of birds.

Life renews itself in the coolness of night: a lonely coyote stands by the side of the freeway, sniffing the air, taking a wistful look at the summer moon. Ignoring the cars and trucks rushing past, it squats down on its haunches and howls the same howl its ancestors hurled at the wagon trains of the pioneers who came this way more than a century ago. A great horned owl flies forth on noiseless wings to hunt amongst the thickets and hidden dells of the mountain.

■ LAKE ROOSEVELT EVENING

We have stopped in the north-central hills of the state, where grasses have been burned to a pale gold by the summer sun, to visit friends who make their home in the pine woods east of Lake Roosevelt. "No," says Rick, "It's not right to call these the boonies. You'll be surprised how close we really are to everything, even Spokane."

We move to the back porch, to talk and sip wine. But it's too perfect an evening for just sitting around. In a little while, we walk down to the shore of Lake Roosevelt and take a leisurely stroll along the rocky verge separating the water from the brush and trees. The lake lies quiet in the dusk—only the sound of water swirling past the shore and the drone of insects break the all-encompassing tranquility, and, occasionally, the plop and splash of a fish as it jumps into the air to catch a juicy bug. Bats flit and flutter, soaring, diving as they snatch up insects buzzing around our heads. Ducks squabble in the reeds and a doe and her fawn sneak down to the shore to snatch a drink. Willows—soft light, delicately fragrant, lining a stream course—fade with the light and finally dissolve into darkness. Only the rustle of their leaves remains. The night is warm—so warm we can't resist taking a quick dip in the lake, then we lie in the tall, dry grass and tell stories as a cooling night breeze soughs in the willows.

■ YAKIMA VALLEY EVENING

The Yakima Valley stretches to both sides of the freeway, and we are engulfed by a perfume of ripening apples and freshly crushed grapes permeating the air. The sun brushes the ridges as we approach the Yakima River canyon, painting the basalt cliffs with luminous colors from its spectral palette. The tints turn somber as the sun vanishes behind the mountains. Yet all of a sudden the dry, hot, dusty smell of the mountains is pushed aside by a fresh, cool fragrance rising from the river. Wisps of fog drift through the valleys and the shadows grow. By the time we reach Ellensburg, night has fallen.

■ EVENING IN THE SAN JUANS

We're in the San Juans; our boat is beached in a small cove on Sucia Island. We've fished all day: in the Spieden Island tide rips, in President's Channel, along the south shore of Patos Island—we didn't catch any fish, but we did snare some crabs. Now it's dinner time. Having planned to live off our catch—with optimism fishermen bring to their enterprise—we may end up having crab for appetizer, main course and dessert.

But in the nick of time, we are rescued from culinary monotony by a group of divers. These young men and women have worked hard all afternoon gathering pink scallops and spearing a couple of rockfish. But while they have plenty of food, they've run out of beer—a commodity with which we are still amply supplied. So, with true island spirit, we share our beer and crab, they share their fish and scallops. For dessert we walk into the woods to pick fresh berries. Later, we sit around the campfire, telling tales of land and sea and faraway places and singing the old songs.

As the shadows lengthen, we throw a few extra logs on the fire. This may be the middle of summer, but the night is cool. Beyond the fire, between us and the red sky, atop a surreally sculpted sandstone cliff, a gnarled shore pine reaches for the sky. It resembles a young dragon coiled on the rock, full of hidden powers, ready to jump up and make a mad grab for the sinking sun. I bed down in the sand, but go to sleep reluctantly.

I'd rather stay up to savor the night, to listen to the lapping of the waves on the shore, the wind playing in the grasses, the sighing of the pines. I breathe deeply to inhale the heady fragrance of sea and land, tideflats and wildflowers, which permeates the air. I am waked from my rose-colored dreams by gulls, screaming as they fight over a dead sculpin brought in by the tide.

■ ONE NIGHT EACH SUMMER

I try to stay up at least one night each summer. As the heat of the day fades, with the onset of the evening

Sunset in the Palouse.

coolness, the swallows come out, darting through the sky. The rattling call of a kingfisher disturbs the serenity of the shore. In the lake a beaver cruises towards the slough, his head barely above the water. Reaching a shallow channel, he laboriously climbs onto the gravelly strand, pushes past the blackberry vines and sinks his teeth into a succulent alder. A few feet further down, muskrats scurry about the shore, digging up freshwater mussels. Just before darkness falls, the red fox appears from the darkness and slinks up to the back door, looking for a handout.

I walk to the lake to watch the moon paint broad ribbons of silver across its surface. But not all is quiet in this bright summer night. Soon I hear the crunch and slurp of otters feasting on crayfish. I am roused from my meditations by a squawk followed by a harsh call of protest and the flapping of heavy wings as a heron, disturbed at his fishing station by the otters, rises into the sky, crosses the moon, and vanishes into darkness. Later, I watch otters chasing each other in the bright moonlight up and down the stairs and through the rhododendron bushes, and I am startled by the shrill nocturnal cries of a killdeer. I wonder if that raccoon is hunting for eggs again.

Birds break into song before the first gray of dawn steals across the lawn. Soon the light turns golden and a creamy fog rises from the lake, flowers open, gulls scream, the heat returns.

■ MOON VIEWING FESTIVAL

We bid farewell to summer by celebrating the Moon Viewing Festival with Japanese friends. To our friends, the full harvest moon signifies the mysteries of the universe and the transition from summer to autumn. We nibble on foods of the season as we wait for the moon to appear above the ridge: albacore sashimi, chum salmon caviar, and chestnuts. We sip sake on the rocks and chilled plum wine. The fragile aromas of firs and cottonwoods, grasses and dry flower stalks mingle with the bouquet of our wine. The air is still warm and the darkened lake reposes in silence as the perfectly round platinum disk rises above the water. As we toast the rising moon our host recites an ancient haiku by the Japanese poet Yosa Buson:

> The night is brief
> On the lake remains
> A piece of the moon.

—John Doerper

Mrs. McKee bags the largest salmon of the 1927 season. It weighed in at 40 pounds and 43 inches. (Underwood Archives, San Francisco)

NORTHWEST CUISINE

by John Doerper

COME TO WASHINGTON PREPARED FOR an embarrassment of gustatory riches. Expect restaurant fare to include the freshest seafood and lamb you've ever tasted, the crunchiest apples, the sweetest cherries, and the tangiest goat cheeses. Washington is a state of food, with more apples, pears, cherries, asparagus, clams, and oysters than any other state in the Union, more crab and salmon than any state but Alaska, and second in grapes only to California. Chances are, your first talk with Washington natives will be about food, commonly expressed as "the bounty." Because, truly, this is a state where delicious foods abound.

Washingtonians are great home cooks, know the way food tastes when it's at its best and freshest, and go to great pains to search it out. Cooks often grow their own fruits and vegetables or shop at farmers' markets, in season, because freshness and purity of flavor are of prime importance in the local cookery. Many chefs buy directly from fishermen, foragers, and farmers for the best and freshest fish, shellfish, mushrooms, herbs, vegetables, and fruits. Some kitchens contract with truck gardeners to raise produce specially for the restaurant. Others grow their own herbs and vegetables, most notably Jerry Traunfeld at **The Herbfarm** in the Snoqualmie Valley.

■ CLAMS, CRAB, AND SALMON

Many Washingtonians dig their own clams and catch crab and salmon if they have the time; if not, they buy them directly from the fisherman or from reliable fish markets, like **Seattle's Mutual Fish** or **University Poultry and Seafood.** Connoisseurs drive to shoreside farms for oysters or enjoy them at restaurants serving them impeccably fresh, like **Shuckers** in Seattle or the **Shoalwater** in Seaview. You may be surprised how easily you can tell the difference between Dungeness crab fresh from the water or crab that has been cooked a few days ago or was frozen. Once you've tasted both, it's difficult not to tell the difference, because it's so obvious. With oysters, you can tell their freshness almost by the hour; if they have been shucked, by the minute. (Never eat oysters that are not shucked fresh with each order. A few restaurants, annoyingly, shuck theirs in the afternoon, during the slow time, then serve them for dinner. Send those back!)

Clams and mussels are a bit hardier, but not much, when they're served steamed with wine and herbs or in savory chowders. Washington's largest clam, on the other hand, the geoduck (pronounced "gooeyduck") needs to be as fresh as an oyster, since it is too large to fit in its shell (it may reach a weight of more than three pounds) and spoils rapidly unless it is kept alive until just before it is cooked. It is at its best when served sliced as thin as magnolia petals, and cooked for just a few seconds. That's how geoduck is served at Chinese seafood restaurants like Seattle's **Sea Garden**. Prepared this way, it's even better than the raw geoduck served at sushi bars like **I Love Sushi** in Bellevue.

Having acquired new kitchen techniques from their Japanese and Chinese compatriots, Washington restaurant chefs and home cooks who come from a European or American tradition have learned to look for and expect unusual harmonies in food and wine. Take a wine and food tasting put on by Doug Charles at the **Oyster Creek Inn,** a country cafe on Skagit County's scenic Chuckanut Drive, to prove that the foods and wines of Northwest cuisine conform to rules of their own.

■ MEMORABLE TASTING

The first rule Doug Charles broke at a gathering of culinary experts and amateurs related to wine. Many connoisseurs of fine wines know that Washington makes good whites—riesling, sauvignon blanc, semillon—but also believe that the state's vineyards lie too far north to produce reds of distinction, and that "big" wines (like cabernets) are best left to California. Yet Charles served only red wine, and from one vintage. The 1983 cabernet sauvignons he presented (from a dozen Washington wineries) were not only big but possessed uncommon elegance and finesse.

Charles broke a second rule with the food he served at the tasting. A less adventuresome host would have served Charles's offerings with dry white wines: raw and smoked oysters, smoked steelhead, cold poached fillet of Chinook salmon, wild mushroom pate, and prawns steamed in pale ale. Only the assorted local cheeses of the dessert platter catered to traditional notions of food and wine matching.

The sauces, a possible flavor bridge to create an affinity between red wine and food (in the fashion of a matelote au vin rouge), were seemingly designed to conflict rather than harmonize with the wines: lavender and rose mignonette, horseradish and cumin dressing, dill buttermilk sauce, gewürztraminer with black cabernet mustard, peppermint mayonnaise, cranberry cocktail sauce . . . .

A plate of soft shell clams looks as inviting as the sunset.

But, surprisingly, it all worked. There was no clash of flavors—perhaps because Washington reds are sufficiently high in natural acids and complex in flavor to complement a wide variety of foods. What may be most significant, however, is that no one at the tasting was taken aback by this uncommon juxtaposition of food and wine.

A few of my favorite Washington vintages are: Kiona Lemberger, Kiona Riesling, Gordon Brothers Merlot, Chinook Merlot, Chinook Sauvignon Blanc, Waterbrook Reserve Chardonnay, Woodward Canyon Chardonnay, Woodward Canyon Cabernet Sauvignon, Leonetti Cabernet Sauvignon, Hogue Fumé Blanc, Apex Chardonnay, Tefft Cellars Merlot.

I cannot mention them all—there's simply too much good wine!

■ DIVINE MUSHROOMS

While the local cookery does not combine unusual elements for the sake of creating peculiar, palate-challenging contrasts, it does search for new combinations of aromas, flavors, and textures, to probe for hitherto hidden affinities and harmonies. Local herbs, berries, and mushrooms play a major role in this quest. Fresh cranberries, for example, are in favor with many chefs because their natural acidity accents fish and shellfish. The delicacy of oyster mushrooms, the robust flavors of morels and chanterelles, the distinctive textures of boletus and chicken-of-the-wood, play a major role in the cuisine.

Bruce Hiebert at **Patit Creek Restaurant** in Eastern Washington's Palouse tries ever new combinations of morels and beef (foods common to his region); at Richland's **Hanford House,** Chef Courtney Vogt blends wild mushrooms and smoked duck into a rich consommé; on the coast, boletus mushrooms grow so large that chef Cheri Walker at the **42nd Street Café** in Seaview serves them as steaks, as entrées in their own right, rather than as a mere vegetable or condiment.

■ SERVING THE FRESHEST FOODS

When eating at their favorite restaurant, the locals expect to find the best and freshest of everything from fresh salmon or oysters to handmade goat cheese. Occasionally, you may come across special treats, like the fresh sturgeon caviar or local escargot served at the **Shoalwater Restaurant** in Seaview, the very delicate oysters grown on a beach just a few blocks upshore from **Christina's** in Eastsound, the perfect, tree-ripened apricots at the **Birchfield Manor** in Yakima.

Procurement of these delicious foods is not always easy or inexpensive. The reason they are served—and stay on the menu—is because there is a demand for them, because Washingtonians are willing to reward their restaurateurs by paying a little extra for quality.

But there's a special quality even to the most simple of foods. Take chicken, for example. In Washington it reaches restaurants and markets while its tender, white meat is still absolutely fresh, with a delightfully delicate flavor. Chef J. Tim Kelly at Seattle's **Painted Table** restaurant brings out its full flavor with lemon cous cous and grilled vegetables, while Chef Peter Cady at Bellingham's **Cobblestone Café** goes with the seasons, lightly grilling chicken breasts during cold weather and simmering them in a spicy pumpkin seed, chile, and roasted tomato sauce. Like many Washington chefs, Cady always offers at least one vegetarian dish, even at Thanksgiving, where stuffed pumpkin served as a vegetarian substitute for the traditional turkey.

You can find at least one vegetarian dish on many restaurant menus, but you'll discover heartier fare as well.

■ GAME

Game is very popular in Washington. While the game served in restaurants comes from farms, almost every home cook—if he or she does not hunt—knows a hunter who is willing to share the bounty of wild duck and grouse, deer, elk, and bear. Game is quite definitely a food to be shared. Don't be surprised if a man sitting next to you in a rural pub offers you a taste of bear sausage or beaver salami. Don't turn it down. Taste it. You'll be surprised how good it is. Buffalo, America's largest game animal, is making a strong comeback, thanks to ranchers who go to the trouble of raising these wild beasts. Preparations range from the simple buffalo burgers served at the **Yakama Nation** restaurant in Toppenish, to the absolutely luscious buffalo chop with port wine sauce at Seattle's **Union Square Grill.**

■ BEERS AND WINES

Whether you eat a light luncheon of oysters and smoked salmon, or a rib-sticking buffalo dinner, be sure to accompany your meal with one of Washington's many microbrewed beers from such tiny local breweries as Maritime Pacific, Pyramid, Grants, or the Pike Place Brewery. Or with one of the state's superb wines: effervescent sparkling wine, pale semillon or sauvignon blanc, golden chardonnay, deeply red lemberger, cabernet sauvignon, or merlot. And, of course, a sweet riesling or gewürztraminer for dessert.

■ FRUITS AND BERRIES

You will taste many of the state's fruits long before you're ready for dessert: blackberries or dried cherries with lamb, raspberries or cranberries with sturgeon, apples with venison sausage, blueberries with quail—but that does not mean you cannot finish the meal with fruits as well, especially when the strawberries are topped with fresh cream, the apples or cherries come baked in a pie, and the pears are poached in red wine. Or you can indulge in simpler, though not less tasty, pleasures like a perfectly ripened pear or apple accompanied by a well-aged Washington cheddar or farmstead cheese.

Please, pour me another glass of that riesling!

FINE CUISINE IS NOTHING NEW

This observer traveled from San Francisco to Puget Sound in the late 1860s:

If there is one thing, indeed, more than another among the facts of civilization which the Pacific Coast organizes most quickly and completely, it is good eating. From the Occidental at San Francisco to the loneliest of ranches on the most wilderness of weekly stage routes, a "good square meal" is the rule; while every village of five hundred inhabitants has its restaurants and French or Italian cooks. . . . When the Puritans settled New England their first public duty was to build a church with thrifty thought for their souls. Out here their degenerate sons begin with organizing a restaurant and supplying Hostetter's stomachic bitters and a European or Asiatic cook.

—Samuel Bowles, *Our New West,* 1869

PRACTICAL INFORMATION

NOTE: Compass American Guides makes every effort to ensure the accuracy of its information; however, as conditions and prices change frequently, we recommend that readers also contact the local visitors' bureaus for the most up-to-date information—see "Visitor Information."

■ AREA CODES

Washington has three area codes. Use 509 east of the Cascades; 206 for Seattle, Tacoma, Everett, and surrounding areas; and 360 for the rest of the area west of the Cascades.

■ METRIC CONVERSIONS

1 foot = .305 meters
1 mile = 1.6 kilometers
Centigrade = Fahrenheit temperature minus 32, divided by 1.8

■ TRANSPORTATION

■ BY AIR

Most major airlines fly into both Sea-Tac International (Seattle-Tacoma) and Spokane International. Smaller carriers such as Horizon Air and San Juan Airlines serve the smaller cities throughout the state.

■ BY TRAIN

Amtrak links Seattle to most major American cities, and from Seattle, Amtrak's **Mount Rainier** has frequent service to Tacoma, Olympia, and Portland, Oregon. For schedules and information, call (800) 872-7245.

■ BY BUS

Greyhound Lines has the greatest number of scheduled bus routes in the state but runs mainly along I-5 and I-90. For more information call (800) 531-5332. Call the local chamber of commerce for the telephone numbers of independent companies who service towns and cities not along these two highways.

■ BY FERRY

Washington operates the largest ferry system in the United States. Most of the ferries carry cars, although some smaller boats that run between Seattle and Bremerton or Bainbridge and Vashon islands carry passengers only. All ferries carry bikes. At commuting hours and on summer weekends, cars line up well in advance of the scheduled departure time.

For information and schedules call Washington State Ferries at (206) 464-6400 or when in Washington State (800) 84-FERRY. Ferry routes within the state include:

• Seattle – Bremerton (Kitsap Peninsula)

• Seattle – Bainbridge Island

• Seattle – Vashon Island

• Fauntleroy (West Seattle) – Vashon – Southworth
(near Port Orchard on the Kitsap Peninsula)

• Point Defiance (Tacoma) – Tahlequah (the southern tip of Vashon Island)

• Edmonds (just north of Seattle) – Kingston
(on the Kitsap Peninsula near the Hood Canal Bridge)

• Mukilteo (near Everett) – Clinton (on the southern end of Whidbey Island)

• Anacortes (west of Mount Vernon) – San Juan Islands
(San Juan, Orcas, Lopez, and Shaw islands) – Sidney, British Columbia

• Port Townsend – Keystone (on Whidbey Island)

Alaskan Ferries depart from Bellingham. Call the Alaska Marine Hwy. at (800) 642-0066.

■ CLIMATE

CITY	FAHRENHEIT TEMPERATURE			ANNUAL PRECIPITATION	
	Jan. Avg. High/Low	July Avg. High/Low	Record High/Low	Average Rain	Average Snow
Mt. Rainier Nat'l Park	33 21	64 44	92 -22	106"	582"
Omak	30 15	90 55	114 -23	10"	36"
Port Angeles	42 34	62 51	80 11	24"	10"
Quillayute	46 34	68 49	99 5	104"	15"
Seattle-Tacoma	44 33	75 54	100 0	38"	13"
Spokane	30 20	82 55	108 -30	17"	51"
Yakima	38 20	87 53	111 -25	8"	24"

■ THE RAIN

It does rain a lot in western Washington. But east of the Cascades, it rains very seldom. And even west of the Cascades, summers tend to be dry. (That summer dryness may in fact be the reason why western Washington is covered with conifers instead of deciduous trees; deciduous trees couldn't survive the summer droughts.) Even when it rains, however, it seldom rains hard. Seattle has many more cloudy and drizzly days than New York, but it has less annual precipitation. Real downpours are rare.

■ ACCOMMODATIONS AND RESTAURANTS

America's major hotel and motel chains are well-represented in Washington. To find out what is available, where, and for what price, it's best to use the following toll-free numbers.

Best Western. (800) 528-1234.
Days Inn. (800) 329-7466.
Doubletree. (800) 222-TREE.
Hilton Hotels. (800) HILTONS.
Holiday Inn. (800) HOLIDAY.
Hyatt Hotels & Resorts. (800) 233-1234.

ITT Sheraton. (800) 325-3535.
Marriott Hotels. (800) 228-9290.
Radisson. (800) 333-3333.
Ramada Inn. (800) 2-RAMADA.
Stouffers. (800) HOTELS-1.
Westin Hotels & Resorts. (800) 228-3000.

A partial selection of hotels, resorts, bed-and-breakfasts, and country inns appears below, listed by town. For more lodging information, call Washington State Tourism at (800) 544-1800. The restaurants, cafes, and diners, also listed by town, provide a good cross section of the state's diverse eateries. Those restaurants marked with an * are especially recommended.

---

*A*ccommodation prices, per person, double occupancy:
$ - under $50; $$ - $50-$80; $$$ - over $80
*R*estaurant prices, per person, without drinks, tax, or tip:
$ - $8 or less; $$ - $8 to $15; $$$ - over $15

ABERDEEN (PACIFIC COAST)

✗ **Parma.** 116 West Heron St.; (360) 532-3166
Great pasta dishes and freshly baked bread. Amazingly good restaurant for such a small town. $$

ANACORTES (NORTH-CENTRAL)

🏠 **Majestic Hotel.** 419 Commercial Ave.; (360) 293-3355
A small hotel housed in a renovated building in the historic downtown. Victorian furnishings in the lobby, antiques in the bedrooms, and a gazebo on the fourth floor. $$$

BELLEVUE (METROPOLITAN SEATTLE)

✗ **I Love Sushi.*** 11818 NE Eighth St.; (206) 454-5706
Modern decor, no-nonsense chefs, and the most exquisitely arranged sushi in town. The Seattle location, though not as spacious, offers pleasant views of Lake Union at 1001 Fairview Ave. North; (206) 625-9604. $$$

BELLINGHAM (NORTH-CENTRAL)

🏠 **Best Western Lakeway Inn.** 714 Lakeway Dr.; (360) 671-1011
Large and lacking in character, but includes a pool, sauna, and weight room. Conveniently located downtown. Children under 12 stay free. $$
🏠 **Schnauzer Crossing.** 1807 Lakeway Dr.; (360) 733-0055 or (360) 734-2808
Elegant bed-and-breakfast right on Lake Whatcom. $$$
✗ **The Archer Ale House.*** 1212 Tenth St.; (360) 647-7002
The main attractions here are the classic European brews and Northwest microbrews, but pub fare—Welsh pasties, hot wings, enormous slices of pizza— is also on hand. $

✕ **Cobblestone Café.** *See John Doerper's 12 Favorite Restaurants on page 302.*

✕ **Colophon Cafe.** 1208 11th St., Fairhaven; (360) 647-0092
The fine Village Bookstore in historic Fairhaven houses this little cafe where the soups and sandwiches are quite tasty. **$**

✕ **Il Fiasco.** 1309 Commercial St.; (360) 676-9136
Il Fiasco—which means "the flask"—serves northern Italian food with both Italian and Northwestern wines. **$$$**

✕ **Pacific Cafe.*** 100 N. Commercial St.; (360) 647-0800
Next door to the ornate old Mount Baker Theater, the Pacific Cafe serves seafood and pasta with an Asian touch. The decor is somewhat Asian, too. **$$**

BOW (NORTH-CENTRAL)

✕ **Oyster Bar.** 240 Chuckanut Dr.; (360) 766-6185
An elegant restaurant with stunning views of Samish Bay. **$$**

✕ **Oyster Creek Inn.** *See John Doerper's 12 Favorite Restaurants on page 304.*

CHINOOK (PACIFIC COAST)

✕ **The Sanctuary.** US 101 and Hazel; (360) 777-8380
A comfy place in a converted church. Best steaks on the coast. Fishermen eat here. Open Thurs–Sun. **$$ - $$$**

DAYTON (SOUTHEAST)

▲ **The Purple House.** 415 E. Clay; (509) 382-3159
Decorated to the hilt but comfortable and hospitable, this bed-and-breakfast occupies a restored nineteenth-century house in Dayton's Victorian residential neighborhood. **$$ - $$$**

✕ **Patit Creek.** *See John Doerper's 12 Favorite Restaurants on page 304.*

FORKS (OLYMPIC PENINSULA)

▲ **Kalaloch Lodge.** US 101, Forks-Kalaloch; (360) 962-3411
The old lodge and the rustic cabins on a bluff above the Pacific have made this place a lot of people's favorite. Newer accommodations are also available. **$$ - $$$**

GLACIER (NORTH-CENTRAL)

✕ **Milano's Market and Deli.** 9990 Mount Baker Hwy.; (360) 599-2863
A fun deli and sandwich place with good pasta and reasonably priced wine, on the way to and from Mount Baker. A great stopover whether you're planning to ski, hike, or loaf. **$**

GLENOMA (SOUTH-CENTRAL)

St. Helens Manorhouse. On State Hwy. 12; (360) 498-5243
Less than one hour from I-5, this unique bed-and-breakfast is a converted farmhouse, filled with antiques and good books. A pleasant base for trips to Mount Rainier or Mount St. Helens. **$$**

GOLDENDALE (SOUTHEAST)

Highland Creeks Resort. 2120 Scenic Hwy. 97; (509) 773-4026
You may occasionally hear trucks laboring up Hwy. 97 toward Satus Pass and Yakima, but you can sit under the trees in a hot tub overlooking a creek, then go inside and sit in front of the fireplace to stay warm. **$$ - $$$**

GRAYLAND (PACIFIC COAST)

The Dunes. 783 Dunes Rd. (off State Hwy. 105 at the sign of the giant razor clam); (360) 267-1441
Literally in the dunes. Best razor clam fritters on the coast. **$$ - $$$**

KIRKLAND (METROPOLITAN SEATTLE)

Woodmark Hotel at Carillon Point. 1200 Carillon Point; (206) 822-3700
On the shores of Lake Washington, this elegant hotel charms business and pleasure travelers with stunning views and cozy rooms. A favorite feature is complimentary late night snacks. **$$$**

LAKE QUINAULT (OLYMPIC PENINSULA)

Lake Quinault Lodge. 340 S. Shore Rd.; (360) 288-2900
The old lodge, built in 1926, sits right on the shore of Lake Quinault, on the western side of the Olympic Peninsula. Guests can take boats out on the lake, walk or run on nearby nature trails, or drive relatively short distances to serious hikes in the Olympics. **$$$**

LEAVENWORTH (NORTH-CENTRAL)

Abendblume Pension. 12570 Ranger Rd.; (800) 669-7634 or (509) 548-4059
An intimate, five-room pension styled after an Austrian country inn.

Run of the River. 9308 E. Leavenworth Rd.; (800) 288-6491 or (509) 548-7171
Hand-crafted by local artisans, the log furniture throughout the inn lends a rustic charm, while the available mountain bikes and hot tubs are more modern appeals.

LONG BEACH PENINSULA (SOUTH-CENTRAL)

Sandpiper Beach Resort. State Hwy. 109 (1.5 mi. south of Pacific Beach); (360) 276-4580
A modern resort near the beach. Suites, cottages—no TV nor telephones. $$

Shelburne Inn. 4415 Pacific Way, Seaview; (360) 642-2442
The 1896 building is on the National Register of Historic Places. The interior is bright and stuffed with antiques. The highway right out front can be loud. $$$

Sou'wester. Beach Access Rd., Seaview; (360) 642-2542
The old lodge was built in 1892 by Sen. Henry Winslow Corbett, a Portland plutocrat, and later converted into a quirky, delightful bed-and-breakfast by a South African couple. This is a refuge for artists, poets, musicians, and people looking for good conversation and an extremely informal atmosphere. $ - $$

The Ark. 273 Sandridge Rd., Nahcotta; (360) 665-4133
Right next to an oyster dock on Willapa Bay, the Ark has earned a reputation that goes far beyond southwestern Washington. Dinner here is the main event of many people's visits to this part of the state. Seafood is the big attraction but not the only one. $$$

Forty-Second Street Cafe. *See John Doerper's 12 Favorite Restaurants on page 302.*

The Lightship Restaurant and Columbia Bar. 409 10th St. SW (in Nendel's Inn),Long Beach; (360) 642-3252Yes, it's in a motel, but it has a view of the beach—much harder to come by on the Washington coast than you might guess—and the food is very good, especially the fish 'n' chips. $$ - $$$

The Shoalwater Restaurant. *See John Doerper's 12 Favorite Restaurants on page 305.*

NORTH BEND (NORTH-CENTRAL)

Mar-T Cafe. 137 W. North Bend Way; (360) 888-1221
Reasonably good cafe food on the way to the mountains—and it was the cafe in the television series "Twin Peaks." $

OLYMPIA (SOUTH-CENTRAL)

Harbinger Inn. 1136 East Bay Dr.; (360) 754-0389
This renovated 1910 mansion is now a bed-and-breakfast overlooking Puget Sound and the Capitol. $$

Westwater Inn. 2300 Evergreen Park Dr.; (360) 943-4000
A large, modern motel with views of downtown Olympia and Budd Inlet. The dining rooms are popular with politicos for lunch. $$

La Petite Maison.* 2005 Ascension Street; (360) 943-8812

This old farmhouse in downtown Olympia is more formal than most Olympia restaurants—and better, too. It serves French cuisine built around local seafood and meats. **$$ - $$$**

✕ **The Spar.** 114 E. Fourth Ave.; (360) 357-6444
The Spar is an institution. The old workingman's-cafe interior, the wonderful old logging photographs on the walls, the milkshakes, and the traditional American food draw a diverse clientele. **$**

✕ **Urban Onion.** 116 Legion Way; (360) 943-9242
Located downstairs in the old Olympian Hotel, once the center of Olympia political and social life, the Urban Onion serves good soups and sandwiches, as well as more ambitious dishes. **$ - $$**

ORCAS ISLAND (SAN JUAN ISLANDS)

⬥ **Doe Bay Village Resort.** Star Route 86, Olga; (360) 376-2291
"Funky" is the adjective used most often to describe the Doe Bay Resort. A former artists' colony, it offers some living spaces with kitchens and some without private showers or baths. Both guests and visitors can use the hot tubs. **$ - $$**

⬥ **Rosario Spa and Resort.** Horseshoe Hwy., Eastsound; (800) 562-8820 or (360) 376-2222
The main lodge was built in 1905 by Seattle shipbuilder Robert Moran after he was told he had only six months to live. The doctors were wrong. Moran lived another 30 years. Now, his opulent copper-roofed dream house forms the heart of the best-known lodge in the San Juans. Upkeep can be inconsistent, so check out rooms before moving in. **$$$**

⬥ **Spring Bay Inn.** DNR Trailhead Rd., Olga; (360) 376-5531
Sunny bed-and-breakfast where the friendly owners offer kayaking lessons by day and cozy fires by night. **$$$**

✕ **Christina's.** *See John Doerper's 12 Favorite Restaurants on page 302.*

PARADISE (SOUTH-CENTRAL)

⬥ **Paradise Inn.** State Hwy. 706; (360) 569-2413.
This is exactly what a big mountain lodge should look like. The large lobby belies the small rooms. The food isn't much but the location is spectacular: a mile up the southern slope of Rainier. The mountain is right there, as are paths through flower meadows, hiking trails, and the main climbing route to the top. **$$ - $$$**

PORT ANGELES (OLYMPIC PENINSULA)

✗ **C'est Si Bon.** 2300 US 101 East; (360) 452-8888
A French couple runs this French restaurant four miles east of Port Angeles. Seattle diners who have stumbled into it more or less by mistake, remember it fondly. Fine views of the Olympics, a good wine list, and a menu that includes local seafood and chocolate mousse. $$$

⌂ **Lake Crescent Lodge.** 416 Lake Crescent Rd.; (360) 928-3211
This old lodge stands on the shore of deep, scenic Lake Crescent, west of Port Angeles and just north of Olympic National Park. People come for the scenery and the proximity to the mountains and beach. $

PORT TOWNSEND (OLYMPIC PENINSULA)

⌂ **James House.** 1238 Washington St.; (360) 385-1238
Virtually everyone's favorite Port Townsend bed-and-breakfast. Stuffed with antiques, the house is listed in the National Register of Historic Places. All the rooms have character and some have views. The house stands in the Victorian residential neighborhood up on the bluff. $$ - $$$

⌂ **Palace Hotel.** 1004 Water St.; (360) 385-0773
Housed in an 1889 brick building that was once a bordello. Near the heart of Port Townsend's historic downtown. $$

✗ **Fountain Cafe.** 920 Washington St.; (360) 385-1364
Nothing fancy, but the Fountain's seafood, pasta, and other cafe dinners served on linen tablecloths have given it a reputation as one of Port Townsend's best. Waiting lines are common, so it's best to make reservations. $$

✗ **Salal Cafe.*** 634 Water St.; (360) 385-6532
Run by a cooperative, the Salal offers large and tasty breakfasts. The lunch menu of sandwiches, pasta, and seafood is also consistently well-prepared. $

RICHLAND (SOUTHEAST)

⌂ **Red Lion Hanford House.** 802 George Washington Way; (509) 946-7611
Right on the river, and the best place to stay in the Tri Cities. A lovely jogging path beside the river runs for nearly three miles. $$

✗ **Emerald of Siam.*** 1314 Jadwin Ave; (509) 946-9328
What's a good Thai restaurant doing in a Richland shopping center? Just count your blessings. $

ROSLYN (NORTH-CENTRAL)

✗ **Roslyn Cafe.** 28 Pennsylvania Ave.; (509) 649-2763
This roomy cafe occupies an old brick building in the former coal-mining town of
Roslyn, just east of Snoqualmie Pass. Roslyn has become famous as the real-life
location for the fictional town of Cicely, Alaska on the television show "Northern
Exposure." The crowd at the cafe includes locals, travelers heading to or from Seattle,
and tourists who have come to watch film crews shooting scenes downtown. $

SAN JUAN ISLAND (NORTH-CENTRAL)

⌂ **Hillside House Bed and Breakfast.** 365 Carter Ave., Friday Harbor.; (360) 378-4730
A charming bed-and-breakfast overlooking Friday Harbor and Mount Baker.
Particularly impressive to avid birders are mounted binoculars on the outdoor deck
and a two-story aviary on the premises. $$ - $$$

⌂ **Roche Harbor Resort.** 4950 Tarte Memorial Dr., Friday Harbor; (360) 378-2155
Rooms in the restored 1886 hotel that forms the heart of the Roche Harbor Resort
aren't much, but newer quarters are available, and this place is an institution. $$ - $$$

SEATTLE

⌂ **Alexis Hotel.** 1007 First Ave.; (800) 426-7033 or (206) 624-4844
Small, understated, chic, and expensive. Near the Seattle Art Museum and the Pike
Place Market. $$$

⌂ **Four Seasons Olympic Hotel.** 411 University St.; (206) 621-1700
This was the classiest place in town when it opened in the 1920s, and after a 1982
renovation, it is again. When the President visits Seattle, he stays here. $$$

⌂ **Inn at the Market.** 86 Pine St.; (206) 443-3600
This is a pleasant place, and many of the comfortable rooms have views over Elliott
Bay, but the main attraction is the location: right in the Pike Place Market. $$ - $$$

⌂ **The Landes House.** 712 11th Ave. East; (206) 329-8781
Bed-and-breakfast across from Volunteer Park and once the private home of Seattle's
first female mayor. $$

⌂ **Mayflower Park Hotel.** 405 Olive Way (Fourth Ave.); (800) 426-5100 or
(206) 623-8700
A soothing, handsomely appointed hotel with European furnishings and Oriental
rugs. Excellent service. $$$

⌂ **Meany Tower Hotel.** 4507 Brooklyn Ave.; (206) 634-2000
A pleasant, old-fashioned hotel, only a few blocks from the University of Washington
campus. $$

Pensione Nichols. 1923 First Ave.; (206) 441-7125
With views of Elliott Bay, this bed-and-breakfast offers the warmth of a cozy inn and the chic of a French salon. Only steps away from Pike Place Market. $$

Sheraton Hotel. 1400 Sixth Ave.; (800) 325-3535 or (206) 621-9000
A big hotel right near the Washington State Convention & Trade Center, the Sheraton takes in a lot of meetings and a lot of groups. The lobby features glass works by the ubiquitous local artist Dale Chihuly. $$$

Sorrento Hotel. 900 Madison St.; (206) 622-6400
Built in 1909 for the Alaska-Yukon-Pacific Exposition and restored in 1981, the Sorrento—with its Italian-villa-style exterior and fountain—is an oasis in the largely medical environs of First Hill, a few blocks above downtown. The warm, mahogany-paneled lobby is particularly inviting at Christmas. $$$

WestCoast Camlin Hotel. 1619 Ninth Ave; (800) 426-0670 or (206) 682-0100
Built in 1926 and remodeled in 1987, the Camlin has an elegant small lobby and plain but spacious rooms. One of the better bargains in downtown hotels. $$

Westin Hotel. 1900 Fifth Ave.; (800) 228-3000 or (206) 728-1000
The Westin's cylindrical twin towers give every room a view and plenty of light—or as much light as Seattle offers at any given time of the year. $$$

✗ **Cafe Flora.*** 2901 E. Madison St.; (206) 325-9100
Flora serves vegetarian food that looks good and tastes good and would be worth going out of your way to eat even if it weren't good for you. $$$

✗ **Campagne.*** Inn at the Market, 86 Pine St.; (206) 728-2800
An elegant French country restaurant right at the Pike Place Market, with a view out over Elliott Bay. Service is often slow. $$$

✗ **Canlis.** * 2576 Aurora Ave. North; (206) 283-3313
A fine-dining fixture in Seattle where steaks and oysters are the main draw.

✗ **Casa-U-Betcha.** 2212 First Ave.; (206) 441-1026
A bright and lively restaurant with a hodge-podge of influences. Blends of South American, Caribbean, Spanish, and Mexican cuisine are all found here. $$

✗ **Dahlia Lounge.**** 1904 Fourth Ave.; (206) 682-4142
Tom Douglas, the chef who owns the Dahlia Lounge, is one of the gurus of Northwest cuisine. He uses local ingredients, a lot of Asian touches, and a lot of combinations you would never have thought of. The food is terrific. The informal room has extremely high ceilings and a small balcony. $$ - $$$

✗ **Elliott's Oyster House.*** Pier 56, Alaskan Way; (206) 623-4340
The place for oyster aficionados. Inventive seafood entrees and an airy, attractive dining room are other lures of this well-regarded restaurant.

✗ **El Puerco Lloron.*** 1501 Western Ave. (on the Pike Place Market Hillclimb);
(206) 624-0541
People come for the kitschy Mexican-cafe decor and for some of the best
Mexican food in Seattle. $

✗ **5-Spot.** 1502 Queen Anne Ave. North; (206) 285-SPOT
The 5-Spot features American regional cooking. You'd be comfortable taking your kids
or your grandmother. $$$

✗ **Fullers.** *See John Doerper's 12 Favorite Restaurants on page 303.*

✗ **Georgian Room.** *See John Doerper's 12 Favorite Restaurants on page 303.*

✗ **The Painted Table.*** 92 Madison St. (in the Alexis Hotel); (206) 624-3646
Local artists display their works on the walls of this stylish restaurant while the
Northwest artists in the kitchen turn out sophisticated regional fare. $$$

✗ **Ray's Boathouse.*** 6049 Seaview Ave. NW; (206) 789-3770
Ray's isn't fancy, but no place in Seattle offers a better waterfront location, better
seafood, or a better wine list. Be prepared to make reservations. The upstairs cafe is
easier to get into and cheaper. $$$

✗ **Rover's.** *See John Doerper's 12 Favorite Restaurants on page 304.*

✗ **Saigon Gourmet.** 502 S. King St.; (206) 624-2611
One of the International District's best offerings is this informal, yet superb
Vietnamese cafe. $

✗ **Saleh al Lago.** *See John Doerper's 12 favorite restaurants on page 302.*

✗ **Salty's on Alki.** 1936 Harbor Ave. SW, West Seattle; (206) 937-1600
Hard to believe this polished restaurant was once an old sea dogs' diner. Nicely
prepared seafood and sweeping views of the city's skyline in a festive, if somewhat
noisy, setting. $$ - $$$

✗ **Santa Fe Cafe.*** Two locations: 2255 NE 65th St.; (206) 524-7736
5910 Phinney Ave. N.; (206) 783-9755
Southwestern cuisine—blue corn tortillas, plenty of chiles—in two relatively upscale
settings. $$$

✗ **Sea Garden Restaurant.*** 509 Seventh Ave South; (206) 623-2100
Highly acclaimed Chinese cuisine, prepared with only the freshest fish and vegetables.

✗ **Shuckers.*** 411 University Ave.; (206) 621-1924
Just as one would expect from a restaurant tucked inside the Four Seasons Hotel,
Shuckers is refined and gracious. Fabulous oysters. $$$

✗ **Trattoria Mitchelli.** 84 Yesler Way; (206) 623-3885
An informal place with Italian food (and good thin-crust pizza) in an old brick
building off Pioneer Square. Open late and often crowded. $$$

✗ **Union Square Grill.** * 621 Union St.; (206) 224-4321
Dark wood, prime rib, and a gentlemens' club feel to the place. $$
✗ **Wild Ginger.** * 1400 Western Ave.; (206) 623-4450
The menu is eclectically Asian, with dishes from China, Thailand, Vietnam, Indonesia, and elsewhere. Wild Ginger doesn't pretend to be an Asian restaurant; it's a very good restaurant that serves delightful Asian food. $$

SEQUIM (OLYMPIC PENINSULA)

⌂ **Granny Sandy's Orchard Bed-and-Breakfast.** 405 W. Spruce; (360) 683-5748 or (800) 841-3347
Guests praise the gourmet breakfasts here—crêpes with fresh nectarines, for example—and the close proximity (30 miles) to Olympic National Park. $$$

SNOQUALMIE/ FALL CITY (NORTH-CENTRAL)

⌂ **Salish Lodge.** 37807 Snoqualmie-Fall City Rd; (800) 826-6124 or (206) 888-2556
A luxurious lodge from a bygone era—a large stone fireplace, maple bookshelves, overstuffed chairs, and a beamed ceiling. $$$
✗ **The Herbfarm.** *See John Doerper's 12 Favorite Restaurants on page 303.*
✗ **Salish Lodge Restaurant.** (206) 888-2556
The main dining room, overlooking the falls, is strictly a linen tablecloth affair, serving nicely prepared Northwest seafood and game. The upstairs **Attic Lounge** serves lighter meals and offers an equally impressive view. $$$

SPOKANE (NORTHEAST)

⌂ **Cavanaugh's Inn at the Park.** 303 W. North River Dr. (Division and Washington streets); (800) THE-INNS or (509) 326-8000
One of Spokane's poshest hotels. Indoor and outdoor pool, and two restaurants on the premises. $$$
⌂ **West Coast Ridpath Hotel.** W. 515 Sprague Ave.; (509) 838-2711
A comfortable place with reasonable downtown rates and a good location. $$
✗ **The Downtown Onion.** W. 302 Riverside; (509) 747-3852
The attractions are the room with a pressed-tin ceiling, and good burgers and beers. $
✗ **Patsy Clark's.** 2208 W. Second St.; (509) 838-8300
A luxuriously decorated mansion built by a mining millionaire around the turn of the century and today an opulent restaurant with somewhat ordinary prime rib fare.

TACOMA (SOUTH-CENTRAL)

⌂ **Sheraton Tacoma Hotel.** 1320 Broadway Plaza; (206) 572-3200

A big downtown hotel with fine views of Mount Rainier and Commencement Bay. Tacoma's downtown has a limited number of attractions, but they're all, more or less, at your door. Be cautious when walking the neighborhood at night. $$$

✗ **Antique Sandwich Company.** 5102 N. Pearl St.; (206) 752-4069.
Just up the street from Point Defiance Park, this neighborhood sandwich shop serves three meals a day among comfortable, eclectic furnishings and a rather counter-cultural atmosphere. $

✗ **Fujiya.** 1125 Court C (between Broadway and Market); (206) 627-5319
This very good Japanese restaurant occupies a pleasant second-floor space near the Sheraton and the heart of downtown. $$

✗ **Harbor Lights.** 2761 Ruston Way; (206) 752-8600
Fresh seafood on the tables, stuffed seafood on the walls, and a view over Commencement Bay have made Harbor Lights a standard for decades. $$

✗ **Katie Downs.** 3211 Ruston Way; (206) 756-0771
One of many restaurants along the Ruston Way waterfront, Katie Downs serves good pizza and an array of Northwestern microbrews at the water's edge. This is not a place to come for quiet or solitude. $

✗ **Pacific Rim.** 100 S. Ninth St.; (206) 627-1009
One of Tacoma's finest restaurants with an eclectic menu from many Pacific Rim countries. $$$

✗ **Stanley and Seaforts Steak, Chop and Fish House.** 115 E. 34th St.; (206) 473-7300
The location, a bluff above the Tacoma Dome, provides a sweeping view over Commencement Bay toward the Olympic Mountains. People come for good seafood and steaks, in addition to the view. $$

VANCOUVER (SOUTH-CENTRAL)

✗ **Pinot Ganache.** 1004 Washington St.; (360) 695-7786
A fun, bright place with fresh flowers, an international menu, and great desserts. $$

WAUCONDA (NORTHEAST)

✗ **Wauconda Café.** 2432 State Hwy. 20; (509) 486-4010
This small general store-cum-gas station-cum-restaurant is rife with rustic atmosphere. The hearty hamburgers, sandwiches, and homemade soups are very tasty. A must-stop for locals and visitors alike. Besides, there's no other place for miles and miles east or west. $

WALLA WALLA (SOUTHEAST)

✗ **Merchants Ltd.*** 21 E. Main St.; (509) 525-0900
Yes, you can find a good cup of coffee outside western Washington; you can also find

ACCOMMODATIONS IN WHEAT COUNTRY

I thought the deepest misery of tavern life had been sounded at Walla Walla and Palouse City; but, bless you! I was inexperienced. The "gentlemanly clerk" of the Cheney Hotel was a homicide, not only under conviction, but actually undergoing a year's sentence, and he went up to the jail to sleep every night, carrying the key to his cell in his pocket.

—Ernest Ingersoll, "Wheat Fields of the Columbia," *Harper's* magazine, September 1884

good soups, baked goods, and other edibles in this pleasantly cluttered deli and restaurant in an old commercial space. **$$**

WHIDBEY ISLAND (NORTH-CENTRAL)

The Anchorage Inn. 807 N. Main St., Coupeville; (360) 678-5581
Victorian-style bed-and-breakfast situated in the center of town, near the waterfront. Private baths in all the rooms and expertly prepared breakfasts. **$$ - $$$**

Captain Whidbey Inn. 2072 Captain Whidbey Inn Rd. at Madrona Lane, Coupeville; (800) 366-4097 or (360) 678-4097
An inviting inn built of madrona logs with water views from one side, and forest views from the other. Rooms and cottages. **$$$**

WINTHROP (NORTHEAST)

⌂ **Duck Brand Cantina, Bakery, and Hotel.** 248 Riverside Ave.; (509) 996-2192
What's a duck brand? A brand shaped like a duck, not a brand used on a duck—an early settler used it. This is a plain, comfortable hotel and restaurant on the main street. Some rooms have views. **$ - $$**

YAKIMA (SOUTHEAST)

✗ **Birchfield Manor.** *See John Doerper's 12 Favorite Restaurants on page 302.*

ZILLAH (SOUTHEAST)

✗ **El Ranchito.** 1319 E. First Ave. (off I-82); (509) 829-5880
Good Mexican food near a small hop- and wine-growing center in the Yakima Valley. To call this big cafeteria informal would be an understatement. A tortilla bakery is attached to the restaurant. **$**

JOHN DOERPER'S 12 FAVORITE RESTAURANTS

John Doerper is the publisher of Pacific Epicure.

Birchfield Manor. *2018 Birchfield Rd. Yakima; (509) 452-1960*
Swiss-trained chef Wil Masset has turned a Yakima Valley farmhouse into an oasis of elegant dining and repose. The food, prepared with fresh local ingredients, in season, is worth a special trip. (You might want to reserve one of the Manor's five guest rooms and stay the night.) Be sure to try the fresh asparagus in spring, the local lamb, and whatever seafood is on the menu. Oh yes, and the fruits of summer. You ll be talking about the perfectly ripened apricots, peaches, apples, and pears forever. The cellar has one of the best collections of Yakima Valley wines in the state. $$$

Christina's. *North Beach Rd. and Horseshoe Hwy. Eastsound; (360) 376-4904*
Eastsound is the largest village on Orcas Island, the largest island in the San Juan Archipelago. Which means it's fairly small, even cozy. Thats what you can also say about Christina's, a homey restaurant on the waterfront. But the food is anything but rustic. Christina's is the place for oysters from nearby Crescent Beach, local rockfish and salmon, and the freshest of vegetables grown by Orcas Island gardeners. The ambience is casual; the food is elegant. Yes, it's worth a ferry ride. $$-$$$

Cobblestone Café. *1308B 11th St., Bellingham; (360) 650-0545*
Peter Cady was an established chef Back East and taught at a renowned cooking school when he and his wife Marlene decided they needed a quieter lifestyle and bought an old soup kitchen in Bellingham's historic Fairhaven district. Classically trained, Cady turns out dishes that are surprisingly light. The menu changes constantly, but always includes chicken, seafood, and a vegetarian dish. The fresh local fish, cooked to just the right degree and lightly sauced and herbed, is world class. The wine list is short but well selected and includes some Washington State rarities. In warm weather you can dine outside, in the cobblestone yard, under a spreading horse chestnut tree. $$

Forty-Second Street Café. *Pacific Hwy. 103 and 42nd Pl., Seaview*
(Long Beach Peninsula); (360) 642-2323
Cheri Walker and her husband Blaine spent the last decade putting the Shoalwater Restaurant up the street on the national culinary map. In the fall of 1994 they broke away and bought a place of their own, a small chicken-and-dumplings-cafe known for its homespun fare. The Walkers aren't planning any radical changes, but

with Cheri in the kitchen you know the fried chicken is going to be very special. We've already heard rave reports about her pot roast. Yes, pot roast! Food for the gods. $$-$$$

Fullers. *Seattle Sheraton Hotel, 1400 Sixth Ave., Seattle; (206) 477-5544*

During the last decade, the kitchen of this very elegant restaurant has seen a number of star chefs pass through, but it's never been better than now, under the guidance of Monique Barbeau. That's because Barbeau understands the foods of the Northwest and the seasonings they require. The menu changes all the time, but I have never been disappointed. This is a great place to linger over appetizers and to study the restaurant's splendid collection of Pilchuck glass art. $$$

Georgian Room. *411 University St.; Seattle; (206) 621-1700*

This grand dining room in the Four Seasons Olympic Hotel had a history of serving stodgy food until Kerry Sear took over. The food presentations are so beautiful, it's hard to tell whether you're dealing with Sear the chef or Sear the artist (he is very good at both professions), but you stop wondering with the first bite: this is beautiful food that tastes good. The vegetarian dishes in particular are worth trying. Even the most ordinary vegetable changes into a sybaritic treat under Sear's masterly touch. $$$

The Herbfarm. *32804 Issaquah-Fall City Rd., Fall City; (206) 784-2222*

This small country restaurant serves only a couple of prix-fixe luncheons and dinners each week, and it can be devilishly difficult to get a reservation. Chef Jerry Traunfeld relies heavily on herbs and vegetables from the restaurant's kitchen gardens, and he buys everything else from local producers. Herbs flavor every imaginable dish with sometimes odd combinations and mixed success (herb-flavored champagne does not work for me, I'd rather drink tonic water). When the dishes work, they're spectacular, especially the fish and shellfish preparations. Desserts can have strange herb flavors (lavender, to mention just one). All in all a truly great restaurant run by an inspired chef. $$$

Oyster Creek Inn. *190 Chuckanut Dr., Bow; (360) 766-6179*

The waters off Chuckanut Mountain grow great oysters, and this is the place to taste them (unless you want to take the drive from the restaurant's parking lot down the hill to Samish Bay Oyster Farm). But to me, the Oyster Creek Inn means more than good food. It's the place I drive to when I want to relax. Tucked into a green bend of the road, away from the distracting saltwater views, it is a perfect haven. The menu stays the same from lunch through dinner, which means you can drop in any time between noon and 9:00 P.M. and nibble food, sip wine, or quaff a microbrew. The pace is very relaxed; the service highly professional. Best of all, when you want to be left alone, they leave you alone. Of course there is a drawback to lingering for a long time: the food is so good you'll be eating too much. The wine list has some older Washington reds at very reasonable prices. $$$

Patit Creek Restaurant. *725 East Main, Dayton; (509) 382-2625*

There's an old saying that cooks are made, but roasters are born, meaning that it's rare to find a cook who knows how to properly cook meat. Chef Bruce Hiebert does. His steak in green peppercorn sauce is a gourmet's dream and warrants the lengthy drive to Dayton, a small Palouse farming community in the empty southwestern corner of the state. So are his lamb and pork dishes. Hiebert uses fresh local fruits and vegetables in season to enhance the meats. This is a very small but comfortably casual restaurant. The small but well-chosen wine lists includes wines from the local Walla Walla appellation. The pies and other desserts baked by Heather Hiebert are in themselves worth a trip to Dayton. $$-$$$

Rover's. *2808 East Madison St., Seattle, (206) 325-7442*

Tucked away in a small house, this restaurant may be difficult to find the first time around, but it's well worth the search. Owner/chef Thierry Rautureau has a delightfully light touch with seafood and vegetables. He sauces the dishes with a gentle hand in such a way that the flavor of the food is enhanced, no matter how delicate it may be. Rover's is the one restaurant where I never order off the menu but let Rautureau prepare whatever he knows is best, and have him match wines to the various courses as well. This is dining at its absolute best. $$$

Saleh al Lago. *6804 East Green Lake Way North, Seattle; (206) 524-4044*

This small, comfortably, appointed place near Green Lake is Seattle's best Italian restaurant. Owner/chef Saleh Joudeh loves food and he has been able to share that love with his diners, mostly regulars who insist that Saleh's beautiful food is as good for the soul as for the body. His roasted eggplant is sheer ambrosia, his light hand transforms any seafood he touches, and this is the place to come to if you like veal. Like the meat, fish, and fowl, the vegetables are always cooked to perfection. The crème caramel is by far the best in town. The service is gracious and attentive. $$$

The Shoalwater Restaurant. *Shelburne Inn, Pacific Hwy. 103 and 45th St., Seaview (Long Beach Peninsula); (360) 642-4142*

The Shoalwater has long been the best restaurant on the Long Beach peninsula

Francis Shafer runs the kitchen and owner Toni Kischner oversees the dining room. Toni's wife, Ann, bakes the restaurant's hearty breads and exquisite pastries. Across the entryway from the restaurant is the **Heron and Beaver Pub** (under the same management), the snuggest place on the coast, with hearty pub fare and enough microbrews on tap to keep you nicely warm even during an icy Northeaster. **$$-$$$**

■ MUSEUMS AND HISTORICAL PARKS

■ BELLINGHAM (NORTH-CENTRAL)
Whatcom Museum of History and Art. 121 Prospect St.; (360) 676-6981. Collection includes Native American artifacts, exhibits on pioneering and logging, and Northwest contemporary art.

■ GOLDENDALE (SOUTHEAST)
Maryhill Museum of Art. 35 Maryhill Museum Dr. (off State Hwy. 14); (509) 773-3733. Eclectic collection assembled by Sam Hill in a building that was originally designed as Hill's private mansion on a site overlooking the Columbia River.

■ KELSO (SOUTH-CENTRAL)
Cowlitz County Historical Museum. 405 Allen St. (between Fourth and Fifth); (360) 577-3119. A remarkable museum dedicated to the region's history. Artifacts and full-scale exhibits portray Native Americans, Hudson's Bay Company, and the early logging and shipping industries.

■ LONG BEACH PENINSULA (PACIFIC COAST)
Lewis and Clark Interpretive Center. Fort Canby State Park, 2½ miles west of Ilwaco; (360) 642-3029. Photo murals and excellent informational displays about the Lewis and Clark expedition, which reached the ocean here at the southern tip of the peninsula.

■ LOPEZ ISLAND (SAN JUAN ISLANDS)
Lopez Historical Museum. Weeks Road and Washburn Place, Lopez Village. (360) 468-3447. A small but noteworthy museum dedicated to the island's history.

■ MOSES LAKE (SOUTHEAST)
Adam East Museum. In the Civic Center at 122 W. Third St.; (509) 766-9395. A large collection of Native American artifacts from the Columbia Basin. Fossils and pioneer relics are also on display.

■ N E A H B A Y (O L Y M P I C P E N I N S U L A)
Makah Cultural and Research Center. State Hwy. 112, across from the Coast Guard base; (360) 645-2711. In 1970 archeologists from Washington State University unearthed thousands of Makah artifacts buried by a mudslide over 500 years ago. The artifacts and reconstructions of early Indian homes are displayed at this remarkable museum.

■ O L Y M P I A (S O U T H - C E N T R A L)
Washington State Capitol Museum. 211 W. 21st Ave. at Capitol Way; (360) 753-2580. Local history and natural history in what was once a banker's private mansion.

■ P U L L M A N (S O U T H E A S T)
Fine Arts Center. Washington State University, the corner of Stadium Way and Wilson Rd.; (509) 335-6607. The emphasis here is on contemporary works including photography, paintings, sculptures, design, and crafts.

■ R E P U B L I C (N O R T H E A S T)
Stonerose Interpretive Center. 15 N. Kean St.; (509) 775-2295. Displays thousands of insect, fish, and plant fossils from the Eocene period. The center also leads fossil-hunting expeditions to nearby sites.

■ R I C H L A N D (S O U T H E A S T)
Hanford Museum of Science and History. 825 Jadwin Ave.; (509) 376-6374. Exhibits on environmental clean-up, nuclear energy, the Hanford nuclear center, and Hanford's town history. Also includes interactive displays and videos.

■ S A N J U A N I S L A N D (N O R T H - C E N T R A L)
San Juan Island National Historical Park. From downtown Friday Harbor take Spring St. west to Mullis Rd. Turn left on Argyle, which will turn into Cattle Point Rd. and lead you to the visitors' center; (360) 378-2240. Offering miles of scenic trails, a quiet beach, and picnic spots above the rocky shoreline, the park also features several preserved army buildings. From the American Camp visitors' center off Cattle Point Rd., ask for directions by car or by foot to the English Camp on the opposite side of the island.
The Whale Museum. 62 First St. North, Friday Harbor; (360) 378-4710. The name says it all: paintings, carvings, photographs, and wall displays of all types of whales and porpoises.

■ S E A T T L E
Frye Art Museum. 704 Terry Ave. (near Cherry); (206) 622-9250. Nineteenth- and twentieth-century European and American paintings; some traveling exhibits.

Henry Art Gallery. 15th Ave. NE and NE 41st St.; (206) 543-2280. Nineteenth- and twentieth-century textiles and paintings.

Klondike Gold Rush National Historical Park. 117 S. Main St. (near First Ave.); (206) 553-7220. Photo murals and slide shows about the Klondike Gold Rush.

Museum of Flight. Twenty minutes from downtown Seattle, off I-5 exit 158, 9404 E. Marginal Way South; (206) 764-5720. A wide variety of aircraft housed in the original Boeing factory and a dramatic steel-and-glass gallery.

Museum of History and Industry. Mott Lake Area, off Lake Washington Blvd. at 2700 24th Ave. East; (206) 324-1126. Old resource-based industries, new high-tech industries, and turn-of-the-century Seattle.

Nordic Heritage Center. 3014 NW 67th St. (near 32nd Ave. NW); (206) 789-5707. Nordic immigration to the Northwest and traditional industries in which Nordic immigrants worked.

Pacific Science Center. 200 Second Ave. in Seattle Center; (206) 443-2001. Over a hundred hands-on exhibits in the main center, but the building also houses the **Children's Museum,** which runs a terrific art program pairing children with professional artists, and the IMAX **Theater** for ultimate film-viewing on a wide screen.

Seattle Art Museum. 100 University (between First and Second avenues); (206) 654-3100. Permanent collections of Northwest Coast, African, and modern American art downtown; Asian collection in Volunteer Park; traveling exhibits.

Thomas Burke Museum. 15th Ave. NE and NE 45th St.; (206) 543-5590. Natural history museum on the University of Washington campus; Northwest Indian displays plus birds, mammals, minerals, etc.

Wing Luke Asian Museum. 407 Seventh Ave; (206) 623-5124. Asian-American experiences in King County.

■ S P O K A N E (N O R T H E A S T)

Cheney Cowles Museum. W. 2316 First Ave.; (509) 456-3931. An outstanding portrayal of Native American and pioneer history.

Museum of Native American Cultures. 200 E. Cataldo Ave.; (509) 326-4550. An extensive collection of weapons, beadwork, basketry, and pottery.

Fort Spokane. About an hour drive from Spokane, 24 miles north of Davenport on State Hwy. 25; (509) 633-3836. Original buildings of an old military post where the Spokane River meets the Columbia.

■ T A C O M A (S O U T H - C E N T R A L)

Fort Nisqually Historic Site. 5400 N. Pearl St.; (206) 591-5339. Original buildings from the Hudson's Bay Company outpost—one of the many attractions found at Point Defiance Park.

State Historical Society. Point Defiance Park, 315 N. Stadium Way; (206) 593-2830.
Regional history, including maps and other original documents and artifacts.
Tacoma Art Museum. 1123 Pacific Ave.; (206) 272-4258. A small permanent collection
of European and American art plus interesting temporary shows.

■ **V A N C O U V E R   (S O U T H - C E N T R A L)**
Fort Vancouver National Historic Site. E. Evergreen Blvd. and E. Fifth St.;
(360) 696-7655. Restored and reconstructed buildings and living-history
demonstrations on the site of Fort Vancouver, which was the Hudson's Bay Company's
nerve center in the Northwest and subsequently a U.S. military post for many years.

■ **W A L L A   W A L L A   (S O U T H E A S T)**
Fort Walla Walla Museum. 755 Myra Rd. (between Dalles Military Rd. and Rose Ave.);
(509) 525-7703. Original and replica buildings with historical exhibits that include
antique agricultural machinery.
Whitman Mission National Historic Site. Seven miles west of Walla Walla on US 12;
(509) 522-6360. A fine museum focusing on the lives of Marcus and Narcissa
Whitman and their mission, with a self-guided trail of the site. Living history
demonstrations include candle-making, cornhusk-weaving, and butter-churning.

■ **Y A K I M A   A N D   E N V I R O N S   (S O U T H E A S T)**
Fort Simcoe Interpretive Center. Fort Simcoe State Park, 20 miles W. of Toppenish off
State Hwy 97; (509) 874-2372. History and restored buildings of American fort
established in 1856.
Yakama Nation Cultural Center. 280 Buster Rd. off State Hwy 97; (509) 865-2800.
One of the best Native American museums in the Northwest.
Yakima Valley Museum. 2105 Tieton Dr., (509) 248-0747. Highlights Yakima Valley's
natural and agricultural history. Other exhibits dedicated to the Yakama Indian Nation
and Yakima resident Supreme Court Justice William O. Douglas.

■ FESTIVALS AND EVENTS

■ J A N U A R Y
Chelan: Fire and Ice Winterfest. Chili cook-off, snow sculpting, snowmobiling,
ice fishing, and cross-country skiing. (800) 4-CHELAN or (509) 682-2381.
San Juan Island: Bald eagle count.
Seattle: Chinese New Year celebration. Hosted by the International District.
January or February. (206) 323-2700.

Spokane: Northwest Bach Festival. Performances by the Bach Festival Orchestra. (509) 326-4942.

■ F E B R U A R Y
Aberdeen: Rain or Shine Dixieland Jazz Festival. (360) 532-1924.
Bainbridge Island: Chilly Hilly Bike Ride. (360) 522-BIKE.
Marblemount: Upper Skagit Bald Eagle Festival. Celebration of eagle migration. Festivals are held in Concrete and Rockport. (360) 853-7009.
Seattle: Fat Tuesday. Parade, pub run, Spam carving contest. (206) 622-2563.
Wenatchee: Valentine's Sweetheart Social and Liberty Theatre Pipe Organ Event. A vintage silent movie accompanied by pipe organ and dancing. (509) 664-5989.

■ M A R C H
Spokane: Lilac Festival. (509) 747-3230.
Westport: Gray whale migration.

■ A P R I L
Hoquiam: Shorebirds arrive at Grays Harbor.
Mount Vernon: Skagit Valley Tulip Festival. (800) 4-TULIPS or (360) 428-8547.
Tacoma: Daffodil Festival Grand Floral Parade. Events also held in Puyallup. (206) 627-6176.
Wenatchee: Washington State Apple Blossom Festival. Parades, arts and crafts, musical performances, and carnival. (509) 662-3616.

■ M A Y
Bellingham: Ski-to-Sea Festival. Street fair and relay race from Mount Baker to saltwater. Memorial Day weekend. (360) 671-3990.
Ellensburg: International Western Art Show and Auction. (509) 962-2934.
Port Townsend: Rhododendron Festival. The most popular event in Port Townsend. (360) 385-1456.
Poulsbo: Viking Fest. Street fair on the waterfront and parade in honor of the town's Norwegian heritage. Also call the Chamber of Commerce for information on the Skandia Midsommarfest in June and the Yule Log Festival in November. (360) 779-4848.
Seattle: International Film Festival. (206) 324-9996. May to June.
Seattle: Northwest Folklife Festival. Immensely popular music festival. Crafts,

clothing, and incense vendors. Memorial Day weekend. (206) 684-7300.
Walla Walla: Balloon Stampede. Week-long festivities including hot air balloons, skydivers, barbecues, arts and crafts. (509) 525-0850.

■ J U N E
Ocean Park: Garlic Festival. (360) 665-4448.
Port Townsend: Fiddle Tunes Festival. (800) 733-3608 or (360) 385-3102.
Seattle: Seattle-to-Portland Bicycle Ride. (206) 522-BIKE.
Seattle: Seattle Chamber Music Festival. (206) 328-1425.
Seattle: Seattle International Music Festival. Chamber music. (206) 233-0993.
Toppenish: Mural in a Day. Mural painting in Pioneer Park. (509) 865-3262.

■ J U L Y
Coulee Dam: American Indian Pow Wow. Held at the Colville Reservation. Fourth of July weekend. (509) 634-4712.
Darrington: Darrington Bluegrass Festival. (360) 436-1177.
Friday Harbor: San Juan Island Dixieland Jazz Festival. (360) 378-5509.
Seattle: Seafair. Parades, hydro races, crowds. (206) 728-0123.
Vancouver: Fort Vancouver Fourth of July Fireworks. (360) 693-5481.
Walla Walla: Mountain Men Rendezvous and Indian Salmon Bake. (509) 525-0850.
Walla Walla: Sweet Onion Festival. (509) 525-0850.
Whidbey Island: Loganberry Festival. Whidbey's Greenbank Berry Farm, Greenbank; (360) 678-3005.

■ A U G U S T
Long Beach: Washington State International Kite Festival. (800) 451-2542.
Monroe: Evergreen State Fair. (360) 794-7832.
Neah Bay: Makah Days. Traditional dancing and singing, salmon bakes, and canoe races. (360) 645-2711.
Omak: Omak Stampede and Suicide Run. The largest rodeo in northeastern Washington. (800) 933-6625 or (509) 826-1002.
Whidbey Island: Island County Fair. Langley; (360) 221-4677.

■ S E P T E M B E R
Ellensburg: Rodeo. Labor Day weekend. (509) 925-3137.

Leavenworth: Autumn Leaf Festival. Parade, outdoor art show. (509) 548-7914.
Port Townsend: Wooden Boat Festival. Races, rides, craft shows. (360) 385-3628.
Puyallup: Western Washington State Fair. (206) 845-1771.
Seattle: Bumbershoot. Music and arts festival. Labor Day Weekend. (206) 684-7337.
Walla Walla: County Fair and Frontier Days. Labor Day weekend. (509) 527-FAIR.

■ OCTOBER
Ilwaco: Cranberry Festival. Food booths, musical entertainment, and tours through the cranberry bogs. (800) 451-2542.
Issaquah: Issaquah Salmon Days. Parade, arts and crafts, children's fair. (206) 392-0661.
Whidbey Island: Squash Festival. Coupeville; (360) 678-5434.

■ NOVEMBER
Pullman/Seattle: Apple Cup. Football game between University of Washington and Washington State University. (206) 543-2200.
Yakima Valley: Thanksgiving in Wine Country. Over 20 wineries serve samplings of their wine, paired with the right food.

■ DECEMBER
Bellingham: Lighted Boat Parade. Children's activities and music. (360) 671-3990.
Granger: Berry Patch. A winter hayride—complete with hot cocoa and cookies— to chop down your own Christmas tree. (509) 854-1413.
Leavenworth: Christmas Lighting Ceremony. First Saturday in December. (509) 548-7914.
Marblemount: Eagles return to the Skagit River.
Seattle: The Nutcracker. The traditional ballet, but here performed with elaborate sets by Maurice Sendak. (206) 292-ARTS.
Sequim: Victorian Tea and Home Tour. Self-guided tours of homes throughout the Sequim and Dungeness valleys. Begins at the Old Dungeness Schoolhouse. (360) 683-8110.
Tacoma: Zoolights. Holiday light display at the Point Defiance Zoo & Aquarium. (206) 591-5337.

Walla Walla: Christmas Lighting Tour. A holiday music celebration and walking tour. (509) 525-0850.

White Swan: New Year's Pow Wow. Traditional Indian food, dancing, and games beginning December 30 and lasting until New Year's Day. (509) 865-5121.

■ NATIONAL PARKS AND FORESTS

Columbia Gorge National Scenic Area. Waucoma Ctr., Suite 200, 902 Wasco Ave., Hood River, OR; (503) 386-2333.

Colville National Forest. Federal Building, 695 S. Main St., Colville; (509) 684-3711.

Coulee Dam National Recreation Area. 1008 Crest Dr., Coulee Dam, (509) 633-9441.

Gifford Pinchot National Forest. 6926 E. Fourth Plain Blvd., Vancouver (WA); (206) 696-7500.

Mount Baker–Snoqualmie National Forest. 21905 64th Ave. West, Mountlake Terrace; (206) 775-9702.

Mount Rainier National Park. Tahoma Woods, Star Route, Ashford; (206) 569-2211.

Okanogan National Forest. 1240 Second Ave. South, Okanogan; (509) 826-3275.

North Cascades National Park. 210 State Hwy. 20, Sedro Woolley; (360) 856-5700.

Olympic National Forest. 1835 Black Lake Blvd., Olympia; (360) 956-2300.

Olympic National Park. 600 E. Park Ave., Port Angeles; (360) 452-4501.

Wenatchee National Forest. 301 Yakima St., Wenatchee; (509) 662-4335.

■ SKIING

Crystal Mountain Resort. About 76 miles southeast of Seattle, Crystal is known for its close-up views of Mount Rainier, as well as for excellent downhill skiing. The longest vertical drop in the state. (206) 663-2265.

49 Degrees North. Chewelah. You've probably never heard of it, but this downhill area north of Spokane has the fourth largest vertical drop (1,900 feet) in the state. An uncrowded family spot, with free day care on weekdays. (509) 935-6649.

Hurricane Ridge. In Olympic National Park, reached via a road from Port Angeles that's kept open all winter long. With its miles of wilderness trails and open meadow, Hurricane Ridge is used primarily by cross-country skiers but also offers a little downhill skiing. (360) 457-5559.

Methow Valley. Perhaps the most popular place in Washington for cross-country skiing. Accommodations in nearby Winthrop, Mazama, and Twisp. (800) 422-3048.

Mission Ridge. Just 12 miles from Wenatchee, this smaller operation offers some of the best sun and dry snow. (509) 663-7631.

Mount Baker. This relatively remote area 56 miles east of Bellingham has become a mecca for snowboarders, as well as downhill skiers. (206) 734-6771.

Mount Spokane. Located in Washington's largest state park, Mount Spokane is just 27 miles from downtown Spokane. Nearly 2,100 vertical feet and the least expensive lift tickets in the Northwest. (509) 238-6281.

The Pass. The collective term for four ski areas: Alpental, Snoqualmie Summit, Ski Acres, and Hyak. An hour east of Seattle on I-90, Snoqualmie Pass offers three different downhill areas and one cross-country area, all under the same management. After the sun sets, this becomes the largest night-skiing operation in the world. (206) 232-8182.

Ski Bluewood. In the Blue Mountains southeast of Dayton and Walla Walla, this off-the-beaten-track area offers both downhill and cross-country skiing. Special snowboard park and half-pipe. (509) 382-4725.

Stevens Pass. Right off US 2 in the mountains east of Everett, an easy drive west from the faux Bavarian village of Leavenworth. Extensive lighting for night skiing. Five miles away is Stevens Pass Nordic Center. (509) 973-2441.

White Pass. On State Hwy. 410 east of Mount Rainier National Park, closer to Yakima than to Seattle or Tacoma. White Pass gained a lot of publicity when Phil and Steve Mahre, who grew up skiing on its slopes, won the gold and silver medals in the giant slalom at the 1984 Winter Olympics. (509) 453-8731.

■ OUT-OF-STATE SKI AREAS

Some of the best skiing in the Washington area isn't actually in Washington State, and locals often cross the border to ski. Some major ski areas close to Washington include Oregon's **Mount Bachelor Ski Area**, just west of Bend, and **Mount Hood,** just east of Portland; Idaho's **Schweitzer Mountain Resort;** and British Columbia's **Whistler-Blackcomb,** north of Vancouver.

■ OUTDOOR EXPEDITIONS AND OUTFITTERS

■ COLUMBIA RIVER GORGE

Gorge Tours. Van tours and helicopter tours of the Columbia River Gorge; (509) 427-7800.

Renegade River Rafting. (509) 427-7238. Runs river rafting expeditions down the Columbia River.

■ FIDALGO AND WHIDBEY ISLANDS (NORTH-CENTRAL)

Beachcomber Charters. 221 Cornet Bay Rd., Deception Pass; (360) 675-7900. Skippered sailboat charters.

The Pedaler. 5603 ½ S. Bayview Rd., Langley; (360) 321-5040. Bike rentals.

Ship Harbor Inn Bicycle Rental. 5316 Ferry Terminal Rd., Anacortes; (360) 293-5177.

■ LAKE CHELAN (NORTHEAST)

Ship-n-Shore Boat Rental. 1230 Woodin Ave; Chelan; (509) 682-5125. Boat, jet ski, and snowmobile rentals.

Rush's Fishing Guide Service. 118 Park St., Chelan; (509) 682-2802. Guided fishing excursions.

■ LEAVENWORTH/WENATCHEE (NORTH-CENTRAL)

Allrivers Adventures. Cashmere; (800) 74-FLOAT. Half-day, full-day, and overnight whitewater rafting expeditions on eight different rivers including the Wenatchee, Methow, and Klickitat. Also offers more mild, scenic trips along the upper Wenatchee and Yakima rivers.

Enchanted Mountain Tours. 18555 Hazel Lane, Leavenworth; (509) 763-2975. Dog sled tours.

Gustavs. 617 US Hwy. 2, Leavenworth; (509) 548-4509. Cross-country ski rentals.

Leavenworth Outfitters. 21312 Hwy. 207, Leavenworth; (800) 347-7934. Ski and other sports equipment rentals.

Leavenworth Ski and Sports Center. 12700 State Hwy. 2, Leavenworth; (509) 548-7864. Climbing gear, bike, ski, and toboggan rentals.

■ **L E W I S T O N / C L A R K S T O N (S O U T H E A S T)**
Mac's Cycle. 700 Bridge St., Clarkston; (509) 758-5343. Snowmobile and jet ski rentals.

Snake Dancer Excursions. P.O. Box 635 Lewiston, ID; (800) 234-1941 or (208) 743-0890. Jet boat trips through Hell's Canyon.

■ **L O N G B E A C H P E N I N S U L A (P A C I F I C C O A S T)**
Pacific Salmon Charters. Ilwaco; (360) 642-3466. Year-round fishing charters.

Stormin' Norman's Kites. 205 S. Pacific Ave., Long Beach; (360) 642-3482. Kite flying.

■ **M O U N T R A I N I E R (S O U T H - C E N T R A L)**
Rainier Mountaineering, Inc. Tacoma; (206) 627-6242 or Paradise; (360) 569-2227. Leads expeditions up Mount Rainier and rents equipment.

■ **M O U N T S T . H E L E N S (S O U T H - C E N T R A L)**
Mount St. Helens Adventure Tours. Castle Rock; (360) 274-6542. Offers van tours, shuttles to trailheads, and overnight camping trips in the blast zone: hiking, biking, boating, and fishing followed by a hearty dinner including Washington wines, microbrews, and homemade pies.

■ **N O R T H E R N C A S C A D E S (N O R T H - C E N T R A L)**
American Alpine Institute. 1513 12th St., Bellingham; (360) 671-1505. Rents gear for rock-climbing, mountain climbing, and ice-climbing and leads expeditions in the North Cascades. Instruction also available.

Chewack River Ranch Riding Stables. (509) 996-2497. Six miles east of Winthrop on Chewack Rd. Horseback riding on a working ranch.

North Cascade Outfitters. Winthrop; (509) 997-1015. Leads horsepacking trips.

Rendevouz Outfitters. Winthrop; (509) 996-3299. Rents ski huts and guides cross-country skiers.

■ SAN JUAN ISLANDS (NORTH-CENTRAL)

Emerald Seas Diving Center. 2A Spring St., Friday Harbor; (360) 378-2772. Rents diving gear and conducts chartered dives.

Harmony Sailing Charters. (360) 468-3310. Skippered sailing charters.

San Juan Island Bicycles. 380 Argyle St., Friday Harbor; (360) 378-4941.

San Juan Kayak Expeditions. Friday Harbor; (360) 378-4436. Rentals and expeditions.

Seaquest. San Juan Island; (360) 378-5767. Day trips and longer kayaking expeditions.

Wind 'n' Sails. Friday Harbor; (800) 752-4121. Rents sailboats and conducts sailing charters.

■ SEATTLE

Urban Surf. 2100 N. Northlake Way. (206) 545-9463. Sailboard, in-line skates, kayak, and bike rentals.

Cascade Adventures. 1202 E. Pike St., Suite 1142; (206) 323-5485. Whitewater rafting trips and Bald Eagle safaris in the winter.

Northwest Outdoor Center. 2100 Westlake Ave. North; (206) 281-9694. Rents one-person and two-person kayaks for expeditions around Lake Union, Lake Washington, and Elliott Bay. Instruction provided.

Pacific Water Sports. 16055 Pacific Highway S., near Sea-Tac Airport; (206) 246-9385. Rents canoes and kayaks for trips up the Duwamish River.

REI. 1525 11th Ave.; (206) 323-8333. One of the largest outdoor outfitters in the country. Rent or buy equipment for mountaineering, backpacking, camping, cross-country skiing, and other outdoor sports.

Emerald City Charters. Departs from Pier 56; (206) 624-3931. Sailboat excursions into Puget Sound.

■ SEQUIM AND PORT ANGELES (OLYMPIC PENINSULA)

Olympic Raft and Guide Service. Elwha Resort, eight miles west of Port Angeles; (360) 452-1443. Conducts two-hour trips down the Elwha River.

Fairholm General Store. US 101, on the western end of Lake Crescent, 26 miles west of Port Angeles; (360) 928-3020. Boat launching, boat rentals, fishing tackle and supplies.

Olympic Van Tours & Shuttles. Port Angeles; (360) 452-3858. Tours into Olympic National Park, trailhead shuttles, and transportation from Seattle.

■ S N O Q U A L M I E (N O R T H - C E N T R A L)
Ski Acres Mountain Bike and Hunting Center. Snoqualmie Pass; (206) 434-6646. Mountain bike rentals, shuttles, and instructions.
WA Outfitters and Guides Association. 3020 Issaquah Pine Lake Rd.; Issaquah; (206) 392-0111.

■ T A C O M A (S O U T H - C E N T R A L)
Boathouse Marina. Point Defiance Park; (206) 591-5325. Fishing tackle and boat rentals.

■ Y A K I M A V A L L E Y (S O U T H E A S T)
River Raft Rentals, Inc. 9801 State Hwy. 10, Ellensburg; (509) 964-2145. Rafts and inflatable kayak rentals and float trips up the Yakima River.

■ ZOOS AND WILDLIFE PRESERVES

Breazelae Interpretive Center and Padilla Bay National Estuarine Reserve. 1043 Bayview-Edison Rd., Mount Vernon; (360) 428-1558. Exhibits, aquarium, and nature trails highlight the marine life and coastal birds of the Pacific Northwest.

Grays Harbor National Wildlife Refuge. State Hwy. 109, just south of US 101; (360) 532-6237. Hundreds of thousands of shorebirds congregate here. Spring and early summer are prime times for birders here.

Julia Butler Hansen National Wildlife Refuge for the Columbian White-Tailed Deer. Cathlamet; (206) 795-3915. Visitors to this refuge will find not only the small endangered deer, but also waterfowl on the Pacific Flyway, bald eagles, great blue herson, swans, and herds of elk. Twenty-five miles west of Longview and one and a half miles west of Cathlamet off State Hwy. 4.

Nisqually National Wildlife Refuge. Off I-5, exit 114, Nisqually Delta. Home to over 300 species of wildlife, including red-tailed hawks, blue herons, bald eagles, duck, and geese. Six-mile hiking trail.

Northwest Trek. 11610 Trek Dr. East, Eatonville; (800) 433-TREK. Tram ride through a 600-acre refuge for bighorn sheep, elk, bison, caribou, mountain goats, and moose. Five miles of foot trails are also available.

Port Defiance Zoo and Aquarium. 5400 N. Pearl, Point Defiance Park, Tacoma; (206) 591-5335. Celebrated as one of the nation's best zoos showcasing a host of Northwest species including beluga whales, polar bears, seals, and sea lions.

Seattle Aquarium. Pier 59, Waterfront Park, Seattle; (206) 386-4320. A lively aquarium where visitors observe diving sea otters and seals, interact with marine life in the Discovery Lab, and learn about the ecology of Puget Sound from tide pool replicas.

Washington Zoological Park. 19525 SE 54th St., Issaquah; (from I-90 east take Newport Way exit); (206) 391-5508. An unusual teaching zoo specializing in rare and endangered species.

Willapa National Wildlife Refuge. Ilwaco; (360) 484-3482. The refuge occupies a large swath of southern Long Beach Peninsula, encompassing a rich diversity of habitat: salt marshes, coastal forest, coniferous forest, slough, and pasturelands. Over 250 species of birds are found here as are deer, elk, and bear.

Wolf Haven International. 3111 Offut Lake Road, Tenino; (800) 448-9653 or (360) 264-4695. Guided tours of this wolf sanctuary are offered daily (weekends only during winter months). Summers at Wolf Haven feature "howl-ins" most Friday evenings where participants roast marshmallows, join in Indian songs, and howl with the wolves.

Woodland Park Zoological Gardens. 5500 Phinney Ave. North, Seattle; (206) 684-4800. Giraffes, elephants, lions, and zebras are found roaming throughout the splendidly landscaped grounds. The tropical rain forest and Asian elephant forest are among the many clever exhibits.

■ VISITOR INFORMATION

Bellingham/Whatcom County Convention & Visitors Bureau. 904 Potter St., Bellingham 98227; (800) 487-2032.

Bremerton/Kitsap County Visitor & Convention Bureau. 120 Washington Ave., Suite 101; Bremerton 98337; (360) 479-3588.

East King County Convention & Visitors Bureau. 520 112th Ave. NE, Suite 101; Bellevue 98004; (800) 252-1926.

Edmonds Chamber of Commerce & Visitors Bureau. 120 Fifth Ave. North, P.O. Box 146, Edmonds 98020; (206) 776-6711.

Everett/Snohomish County Convention & Visitors Bureau. 1710 W. Marine View Dr., Everett 98206; (206) 252-5181.

Lake Chelan Chamber of Commerce. P.O. Box 216, Chelan 98816; (800) 4-CHELAN.

North Olympic Peninsula Visitor & Convention Bureau. 338 W. First St., Suite 104, P.O. Box 670, Port Angeles 98362; (800) 942-4042.

Ocean Shores/Grays Harbor County Visitor & Convention Bureau. 120 West Chance a la Mer, P.O. Box 1447, Ocean Shores 98569; (800) 874-6737.

Pullman Chamber of Commerce. N. 415 Grand Ave., Pullman 99163; (800) ENJOY IT.

San Juan Islands Visitor Information Service. P.O. Box 65, Lopez Island 98261; (360) 468-3663.

Seattle/King County Convention & Visitors Bureau. 800 Convention Pl. (corner of Eighth and Pike), Seattle 98101; (206) 461-5840.

Spokane Convention & Visitors Bureau. W. 926 Sprague Ave., Suite 180, Spokane 99204-0552; (800) 248-3230.

Tacoma/Pierce County Visitor & Convention Bureau. 906 Broadway, P.O. Box 1754, Tacoma 98401-1754; (800) 272-2662.

Tri Cities Visitor & Convention Bureau. 6951 W. Grandridge Blvd. (Kennewick), P.O. Box 2241; Tri Cities 99302-2241; (800) 666-1929.

Vancouver/Clark County Visitors & Convention Bureau. 404 E. 15th St., Suite 11, Vancouver 98663-3451; (800) 377-7084.

Wenatchee Area Visitor & Convention Bureau. 2 S. Chelan Ave., P.O. Box 850, Wenatchee 98807-0850; (800) 57-APPLE.

Yakima Valley Visitors & Convention Bureau. 10 N. Eighth St., Yakima 98901-2521; (800) 221-0751.

Pacific Bed & Breakfast Agency. 701 NW 60th St., Seattle 98107; (206) 784-0539.

RECOMMENDED READING

■ HISTORY

Alexander, Carmela, and Ruth Kirk. *Exploring Washington's Past: A Road Guide to History.* Seattle: University of Washington Press, 1990. An interesting historical guide designed for those traveling the state by car.

Bergon, Frank, ed. *The Journals of Lewis and Clark.* New York: Penguin, 1989. The journals of the classic early nineteenth-century journey of exploration.

Brewster, David and David M. Buerge, eds. *Washingtonians: A Biographical Portrait of the State.* Seattle: Sasquatch Books, 1989. Short profiles of historical figures.

Brown, John A. and Robert H. Ruby. *Indians of the Pacific Northwest.* A detailed portrait of the culture and history of the tribes from this region.

Clark, Norman H. *Mill Town: A Social History of Everett, Washington, from its Earliest Beginnings on the Shores of Puget Sound to the Tragic and Infamous Event Known as the Everett Massacre.* Seattle: University of Washington Press, 1970. An excellent history of a classic Washington mill town.

Doig, Ivan. *Winter Brothers: A Season at the Edge of America.* New York: Harcourt Brace Jovanovich, 1980. Meditations on the mid-nineteenth-century experiences of James Swan, and Doig's contemporary experience of the same places.

Edwards, G. Thomas, and Carlos Schwantes, eds. *Experiences in a Promised Land: Essays in Pacific Northwest History.* Seattle: University of Washington Press, 1986. Essays on a variety of historical topics.

Egan, Timothy. *The Good Rain: Across Time and Terrain in the Pacific Northwest.* New York: Knopf, 1990. A personal exploration of the regional essence.

Frederick, Richard and Jeanne Engerman. *Asahel Curtis: Photographs of the Great Northwest.* Tacoma: Washington State Historical Society, 1983. A series of pictorial essays featuring the photographs of Pacific Northwest photographer and mountaineer Asahel Curtis. An exceptional insight into regional history and development.

Gates, Charles Marvin, ed. *Readings in Pacific Northwest History: Washington 1790-1895.* Seattle: University Bookstore, 1941. An anthology of memoirs from a variety of Washington's founding fathers.

Holbrook, Stewart H. *The Columbia.* New York: Holt, Rinehart and Winston, 1974. The river itself and the inland Northwest.

Hunn, Eugene S., and James Selam. *Nch'i-wana, "'The Big River."* Mid-Columbia Indians and their Land.* Seattle: University of Washington Press, 1990. Ethnography and history of inland peoples who lived and fished along the Columbia.

Kirk, Ruth, with Richard D. Daugherty. *Exploring Washington Archaeology.* Seattle: University of Washington Press, 1978. Major pre-1980 archaeological sites in the state.

Morgan, Murray. *Puget's Sound: A Narrative of Early Tacoma and the Southern Sound.* Seattle: University of Washington Press, 1979. Emphasis on nineteenth-century explorers and development; some wonderful descriptions.

Morgan, Murray. *Skid Road: An Informal Portrait of Seattle.* Sausalito: Comstock Editions, 1978. Nineteenth- and early twentieth-century Seattle plus teamster leader Dave Beck.

Sale, Roger. *Seattle, Past to Present.* Seattle: University of Washington Press, 1978. A history of the city with emphasis on progressive politics and urban design.

Swan, James G. *The Northwest Coast, or, Three Years' Residence in Washington Territory.* Seattle: University of Washington Press, 1972. Swan's classic account of life on the Washington coast in the 1850s.

■ NATURAL HISTORY

Alt, David D., and Donald W. Hyndman. *Roadside Geology of Washington.* Missoula, Montana: Mountain Press, 1984. A quick look for non-specialists at the state's geology.

Brown, Bruce. *Mountain in the Clouds: A Search for the Wild Salmon.* New York: Simon & Schuster, 1982. The look, feel, and history of major salmon rivers on the Olympic Peninsula.

Chasan, Daniel Jack. *Mountains to Sound: The Creation of a Greenway Across the Cascades.* Seattle: Mountains to Sound Greenway Trust, Sasquatch Books, 1993. The character, history, and rationale for preserving the corridor from Seattle east through the Cascades.

Chasan, Daniel Jack. *The Water Link: A History of Puget Sound as a Resource.* Seattle: Washington Sea Grant Program, distributed by University of Washington Press, 1981. An economic and environmental history of Puget Sound.

Kruckeberg, Arthur R. *The Natural History of Puget Sound Country.* Seattle: University of Washington Press, 1991. The basics of the natural world in much of western Washington.

Manning, Harvey. *Washington Wilderness: The Unfinished Work.* Seattle: The Mountaineers, 1984. Descriptions of and arguments for saving many de facto wilderness areas, some of which have subsequently been made de jure wilderness areas by federal legislation; excellent photographs by Pat O'Hara.

Pyle, Robert Michael. *Wintergreen: Rambles in a Ravaged Land.* New York: Scribner, 1986. A naturalist's fond but outraged portrait of southwestern Washington.

Whitney, Stephen. *A Field Guide to the Cascades & Olympics.* Seattle: Mountaineers, 1983. The basic flora and fauna of the state's two main mountain ranges.

Writers' Program. *Washington: A Guide to the Evergreen State.* Portland: Binfords & Mort, 1941. Terrific snapshots of Washington places more than half a century ago.

■ FICTION AND POETRY

Robbins, Tom. *Another Roadside Attraction.* New York: Ballantine Books, 1971. Pop-philosopher Tom Robbins offers provocatively twisted, beautiful, and insightful descriptions of his home state.

Sund, Robert. *Bunch Grass*. Seattle: University of Washington Press, 1969.
Poems about wheat country.

Sund, Robert. *Ish River*. San Francisco: North Point Press, 1983. Poems
about the wet side of Washington.

■ NON-FICTION

McCarthy, Mary. *How I Grew*. Orlando: Harcourt Brace Jovanovich, 1987.
A wry, sophisticated, and entertaining autobiography of a young woman
growing up during the 1920s in Seattle's social circle.

MacDonald, Betty. *The Egg and I*. Philadelphia: Lippincott, 1945. Ma and
Pa Kettle were based on this cleverly written story of a Seattle socialite
adapting to farm life in the rugged Olympic Mountains.

■ TRAVEL

Bed & Breakfasts, Country Inns, and Other Weekend Pleasures: The West Coast.
New York: Fodor's Travel Publications, 1992. Detailed descriptions of
inns and a good-sized batch of interesting sites and restaurants in the
nearby regions.

The Berkeley Guides: Pacific Northwest & Alaska. New York: Fodor's Travel
Publications, 1995. A fun, comprehensive guide to the Northwest with
a slant towards the active, budget traveler.

Fodor's Seattle & Vancouver. New York: Fodor's Travel Publications, 1995.
Copious practical advice for visiting Seattle, Puget Sound, and Vancouver.

Irving, Stephanie. *Seattle Best Places*. Seattle: Sasquatch Books, 1994. A jam-
packed guide to Seattle's restaurants, hotels, and sights.

I N D E X

COMPASS AMERICAN GUIDES

Critics, Booksellers, and Travelers All Agree You're Lost Without a Compass

"This splendid series provides exactly the sort of historical and cultural detail about North American destinations that curious minded travelers need... they offer good maps, beautiful color photography and — far more importantly — a strong historical and cultural perspective."
— *Washington Post*

"Use them not only to plan your trip, but to savor the memories once you're back home."
— *Mademoiselle*

"Highly evocative... the chapter on food forced me to stop reading and go eat."
—*New York Times*

"Compass Guides capture the true spirit of a place from its early settler days to modern times."
— *America Online*

Arizona (2nd Edition)
1-878-86732-6
$16.95 ($21.50 Can)

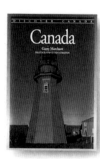

Canada (1st Edition)
1-878-86712-1
$14.95 ($19.95 Can)

Chicago (1st Edition)
1-878-86728-8
$16.95 ($21.50 Can)

Maine (1st Edition)
1-878-86751-2
$16.95 ($22.95 Can)

Manhattan (1st Edition)
1-878-86737-7
$17.95 ($25.00 Can)

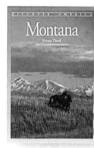

Montana (2nd Edition)
1-878-86743-1
$17.95 ($25.00 Can)

South Carolina (1st Edition)
1-878-86766-0
$16.95 ($23.50 Can)

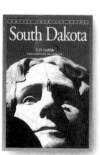

South Dakota (1st Edition)
1-878-86726-1
$16.95 ($22.95 Can)

Texas (1st Edition)
1-878-86764-4
$17.95 ($25.00 Can)

Colorado (2nd Edition)
1-878-86735-0
$16.95 ($21.50 Can)

Hawaii (2nd Edition)
1-878-86769-5
$17.95 ($25.00 Can)

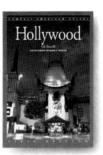

Hollywood (2nd Edition)
1-878-86771-7
$16.95 ($23.50 Can)

Las Vegas (3rd Edition)
1-878-86736-9
$16.95 ($22.50 Can)

New Mexico (1st Edition)
1-878-86706-7
$15.95 ($19.95 Can)

New Orleans (1st Edition)
1-878-86739-3
$16.95 ($21.50 Can)

Oregon (1st Edition)
1-878-86733-4
$16.95 ($21.50 Can)

San Francisco (3rd Edition)
1-878-86770-9
$16.95 ($23.50 Can)

Utah (2nd Edition)
1-878-86731-8
$16.95 ($22.95 Can)

Virginia (1st Edition)
1-878-86741-5
$16.95 ($22.95 Can)

Wisconsin (1st Edition)
1-878-86744-X
$16.95 ($22.95 Can)

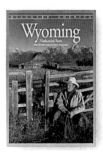

Wyoming (2nd Edition)
1-878-86750-4
$17.95 ($25.00 Can)

■ ABOUT THE CONTRIBUTORS

Daniel Jack Chasan is the author of *The Water Link,* an economic and environmental history of Puget Sound, and other books about Northwestern history and resources. He has also written about the region for *Smithsonian, Audubon, Modern Maturity, National Fisherman, Pacific Northwest, The Seattle Weekly,* and other publications. He lives on Vashon Island where he has served on the community planning committee, the groundwater advisory committee and the school board, and has coached high school soccer.

Matthew Chasan has worked as a bicycle messenger and bagel maker in Seattle, a carpenter on Lopez Island and a reporter on Vashon Island, and has hiked and climbed in the Olympics and Cascades.

John Doerper is the author of *Eating Well, A Guide to Foods of the Pacific Northwest, The Eating Well Cookbook, Shellfish Cookery,* and *Absolutely Delicious Recipes from the West Coast.* He has worked as the Food Editor for both *Washington, The Evergreen State Magazine* and *Pacific Northwest Magazine* and is the publisher and editor of *Pacific Epicure: A Quarterly Journal of Gastronomic Literature, Philosophy, & Travel.*

■ ABOUT THE PHOTOGRAPHER

Bruce Hands is a Seattle photographer who has had his work published in numerous magazines including *Countryside, Outdoor Photographer, Modern Maturity,* and *Bon Appétit.* He has also provided photography for many books including the "Beautiful Cookbooks" series, and *Casting Illusions.* He has earned several awards of distinction in professional international competitions, and his photography has been displayed at Kodak's Professional Photographers' Showcase in Disneyland's EPCOT Center.